THEORY
AND
PRACTICE OF
COUNSELING
AND
PSYCHOTHERAPY

THEORY
AND
PRACTICE OF
COUNSELING
AND
PSYCHOTHERAPY

GERALD COREY
California State University, Fullerton

BROOKS/COLE PUBLISHING COMPANY
MONTEREY, CALIFORNIA
A Division of Wadsworth Publishing Company, Inc.

Printed in the United States of America

10   9   8   7   6   5   4   3

Library of Congress Cataloging in Publication Data

Corey, Gerald F
    Theory and practice of counseling and psychotherapy.

    Includes index.
    1. Counseling.   2. Psychotherapy.   I. Title.
BF637.C6C574   158   76-21836
ISBN 0-8185-0191-X

Manuscript Editor: *Karen Craig*
Production Editor: *Valerie Daigen*
Interior and Cover Design: *John Edeen*
Illustrations: *Jamie S. Brooks*

TO—my daughter Cindy, who said
"The part of your book I like
best is where you write about
us!" and my daughter Heidi,
who said "Daddy gonna write
another book?"

—my wife, Marianne, who said
"I'll be glad when that damn
book is finished!" and

—my mother, Josephine Corey,
who said "When are you going
to slow down and take it easy?"

PREFACE

This book is intended primarily for counseling courses for both under-graduate and graduate students in psychology, counselor education, and the human-services and mental-health professions. I saw a need for a single book, designed for the first course in counseling, that would survey the major concepts and practices of the contemporary therapeutic systems and, in addition, address itself to some basic issues in counseling practice, in-cluding ethical issues and the issue of the counselor as a person. Formulated from my experience as a practicing counseling psychologist and as a univer-sity professor, the book is a result of revisions of my notes and articles de-veloped for the courses I teach, including "Theories and Techniques of Counseling," "Advanced Theory and Practice of Individual and Group Counseling," and "Seminar in Counseling and Psychotherapy." I have tried to communicate in a way that will enable the beginning student to under-stand theoretical concepts and their relationship to counseling practice. The broad goal of the book is to help the student learn how to select wisely from all the theories those aspects that can be incorporated into his or her own developing and, I hope, personalized style of counseling.

In general, I have found that students appreciate an overview of the divergent contemporary forms of counseling and therapy. Because students tend to do wide supplementary reading as they study each therapy system, I have included a reading list after each chapter to guide students to sources that treat various aspects of the material with greater depth and detail than is possible in this survey book. My students have strongly suggested also that the first course in counseling has more meaning to them when it em-phasizes the personal dimensions of them as counselors. Rather than pre-sent counseling systems and basic issues in a way that is detached from the reader, I made every effort to present the material in a personal and practical manner and to encourage personal reflection and introspection on the part of the learner so that using this book can be a personal as well as academic growth experience. I emphasize practical aspects in cases of integration of concepts, techniques, and basic issues and give consideration throughout to how students relate to the material and to their questions concerning the applications of each theory. A *Manual for Theory and Practice of Counseling and Psychotherapy* is available to assist the student in gaining maximum benefit from this book. The manual includes questions, suggested activities, self-inventories, structured exercises, summary charts, chapter reviews, annotated reading suggestions, study guides, and illustrations and examples of cases with open-ended alternatives for counseling practice.

I want to express my appreciation to those who helped me in various ways as I was developing this book. My wife, Marianne Schneider Corey, who recently obtained her license as a Marriage, Family, and Child Counselor, and with whom I work in professional practice and regularly co-lead couples groups and personal-growth groups, has been one of my best critics—and one of the severest. Her evaluation of the complete manuscript helped me address myself to my readers.

My friends and colleagues read the manuscript in its developmental stages and offered valuable suggestions, many of which I have incorporated into the revisions. These persons include Barbara D'Angelo from the Counseling Center and the Human Services Program at California State University, Fullerton, and William Lyon, Director of the Master's Program in Counseling and Clinical Psychology at Chapman College. Both Patrick Callanan and Michael Russell have challenged my thinking on therapeutic issues and have helped me refine my views. Two other colleagues from Cal State, Fullerton, read selected chapters: Treva Sudhalter from the Counseling Center reviewed Transactional Analysis, and Geoff White of Psychology reviewed the chapter on behavior therapy.

Others who reviewed the manuscript and offered helpful comments are Edmund E. Allen of the University of South Florida; William H. Blau of the Day Treatment Center, Norwalk, California; Frederick Borgen of Iowa State University; J. Perry Carter of Richland College; Anthony D'Augelli of Pennsylvania State University; James Dugger of Metropolitan State College; Albert Ellis of the Institute for the Advanced Study of Rational Psychotherapy; Joen Fagan of Georgia State University; Gerald Goodman of the University of California at Los Angeles; Paul J. Kessler III of Delaware Technical and Community College; David G. Martin of the University of Manitoba; and Robert Miller of Sacramento, California.

I am particularly appreciative of the support I received from my editors at Brooks/Cole, Claire Verduin and Terry Hendrix. Their suggestions and encouragement made writing this book a more exciting project. To Karen Craig I am grateful for a splendid job of editing the final manuscript.

Also, some of my best critics of the manuscript were students who had completed my Theories and Techniques of Counseling course at California State University at Fullerton: Merri Chalenor, Randy Corliss, and James Morelock. Karen Palmer, a friend and former student, carefully read the manuscript in its developmental stages and then again in its final form. I greatly appreciate her suggestions concerning reader interest, continuity, and other aspects of the material. In addition to offering very creative suggestions for the manuscript, Merri Chalenor also undertook the task of typing it. Eris Hirdler assisted in typing the manuscript.

Gerald F. Corey

CONTENTS

CHAPTER FOUR

THE CLIENT-CENTERED APPROACH   55

CHAPTER FIVE

GESTALT THERAPY   72

CHAPTER SIX

TRANSACTIONAL ANALYSIS   95

CHAPTER SEVEN

BEHAVIOR THERAPY   117

THEORY
AND
PRACTICE OF
COUNSELING
AND
PSYCHOTHERAPY

CHAPTER ONE

INTRODUCTION

AND

OVERVIEW

Introduction

This book surveys a variety of approaches to counseling and psychotherapy. Instead of emphasizing the theoretical foundations of these models, it presents the concepts basic to each of the therapeutic approaches and discusses topics such as the therapeutic process (including goals), the client-therapist relationship, and specific techniques and procedures applicable to individual and group practice. This book is not, therefore, primarily a text on theories of counseling, nor is it merely a "how to" book that focuses on techniques and methodology. Instead, it aims at developing a balanced view of the major concepts of various therapies and the practical applications and implementation of techniques in the therapeutic process.

My hope is that the student will remain open and seriously consider the unique contributions as well as the limitations of each therapeutic system presented in this book. In the present stage of theory development, no single theoretical model fully accounts for all the unique dimensions of the various therapies. Although attempts have been made to integrate and unify many of the diverse approaches, those practitioners who align themselves with a specialized theoretical viewpoint still tend to assume that their approach contains the entire truth. For instance, a psychoanalytic practitioner may view behavior therapy as technique oriented and superficial and as a quick and economical therapy that fails to produce long-term changes in clients. Some behavior therapists are convinced that psychoanalysis is based on unfounded premises and simply does not work. Some existential-humanistic psychologists criticize both psychoanalytic therapy and behavior therapy on the grounds that they are mechanistic, reductionistic, and deterministic approaches that are very limited in dealing with genuine human struggles to create a purposeful existence. It is not uncommon to find advocates of either conventional or newer therapies who refuse to find validity in any approach other than their own.

The viewpoint assumed in this book is that beginning students of counseling, by familiarizing themselves with the current major approaches to therapeutic practice, can acquire a basis for a style of counseling tailored to their own personalities. Thus I recommend an eclecticism as a framework for the professional education of counselors. The danger in presenting one model that all students are expected to advocate to the exclusion of other fruitful approaches is that it can lead the beginning counselor to unduly limit his or her effectiveness with different clients. Valuable dimensions of human behavior can be overlooked if the counselor is restricted to a single counseling theory.

On the other hand, an undisciplined and unsystematic eclectic approach can be an excuse for failing to develop a sound rationale for systematically adhering to certain concepts and to the techniques that are extensions of the concepts. It is easy to pick and choose fragments from the various therapies that merely support one's biases and preconceived ideas. I hope that a study of the various models presented in this book will show that some form of integration among many of the approaches is possible.

I have a strong conviction that the values and personhood of counselors are the groundwork for creating a philosophy and practice of counseling. Thus it seems essential to me that counselors explore in depth their own values, attitudes, and beliefs and that they work toward increasing their own awareness. Throughout the book, I encourage the reader to find ways of personally relating to each of the therapies. Unless these therapeutic approaches are studied and applied to ourselves, I fear that a superficial understanding is the best that can be hoped for. I assume that most beginning counselors have an implicit notion of what counseling is and how they might proceed to help others, even though their views may be fuzzy. I believe that if we discover some way of personally relating to each of the therapies and look for specific concepts and methodologies, we can begin to construct a meaningful frame of reference for understanding and working with clients.

My own philosophical orientation is strongly influenced by the existential-humanistic force in psychology. The existential view addresses itself to significant issues for the population I work with and it seems most congruent with my own values and personhood. Because techniques and specific procedures are not indicated in this approach, I find that I continue to invent new techniques that grow out of my work with groups. I also borrow techniques from others and then adapt them to my counseling style. Gestalt-therapy techniques, combined with psychodrama and role-playing techniques, have been very useful to me in my practice. Many specific techniques in my approach are derived also from behavior therapy: assertive training, behavior rehearsal, modeling, and a variety of coaching and role-playing techniques. My own counseling philosophy and style continue to take new shape through my experience and therapeutic practice.

As I developed the material for this book, I became increasingly aware that there are useful dimensions of each therapy approach and that accepting the validity of one model does not necessarily imply a rejection of seemingly divergent models. For instance, I am firmly convinced that a practitioner might be oriented toward humanistic psychology and have as a conceptual and philosophical base the existential view of the person. At the same time, the humanistic therapist might use many techniques drawn from behavior therapy and from some of the other cognitively oriented therapies that focus on behavior and action. Thus in my own framework I do not assume that these therapies are incompatible.

In my individual and group therapy practices, I respect the psychoanalytic view of the importance of early psychosexual and psychosocial development. I believe that one's past plays an enormous role in shaping one's current personality and behavior. Although I reject the deterministic stance that claims that humans are the products of their early conditioning and thus the victims of their past, I believe that an exploration of the past is essential, particularly to the degree that the past is related to present emotional-behavioral difficulties.

Of the therapies oriented more toward the cognitive-behavior-action aspects, I value the emphasis on specificity of goals and on encouraging clients to formulate concrete goals that they choose for their own therapy sessions. I find that contracts developed by clients are extremely useful, and I frequently either suggest specific "homework assignments" or ask my clients to formulate their own. I find that the use of those techniques has resulted in expanding the effects of an individual or group session to the client's outside life. Although I accept the validity of insight and increasing awareness on the client's part, I consider it essential that clients actually put into practice in their lives what they are learning in therapy.

A major assumption I make is that my clients are capable of accepting increasing freedom to choose how they will be in the future. Although I accept that we are surely shaped by our sociocultural environment and that much of our behavior is a product of learning and conditioning, I assume that, with increased awareness of the forces that have molded us, we are able to transcend these deterministic influences. It seems to me that most of the contemporary models of counseling and therapy operate on the basic assumption that clients are able to accept personal responsibility and that their failure to do so has largely resulted in their present emotional and behavioral difficulties.

My philosophy of psychotherapy does not include the assumption that therapy is exclusively for the "sick" and aimed at "curing" psychological ailments. I find that the medical model severely restricts therapeutic practice. Counseling and therapy are increasingly regarded as a vehicle for self-exploration to assist "normal" people in more fully realizing their human potentials. My clientele is mainly a relatively healthy population composed of people who seek therapy as a personal growth experience or as a means to assist them in resolving situational crises.

The existential-humanistic approach and client-centered therapy both emphasize the client-therapist relationship as the major factor that leads to constructive personal change in clients. I have come to believe in the importance of the therapeutic relationship with more certainty as a result of my experience as a psychologist. Thus I contend that the character or personhood of the therapist is what leads to significant change. Although I think it important that a psychotherapist or counselor have a comprehensive knowledge of personality dynamics and learning theory and theoretical understanding of therapeutic intervention skills, I do not think that this knowledge is enough. If a practitioner possesses wide knowledge, both theoretical and practical, yet lacks human qualities of compassion, caring, good faith, honesty, realness, and sensitivity, then he or she is merely a technician. In my judgment, those who function exclusively as technicians do not make a significant difference in the lives of their clients.

I see the process of psychotherapy as a dialogue and engagement between two persons. Therapists must be willing to remain open to their own growth and be willing to struggle in their lives, or else they lose their therapeutic potency. Why should clients seek therapists who are "finished products" and who do not do in their own lives what they expect their clients to do in theirs? In short, I think therapists teach clients by their modeling, and, perhaps by being willing to share their own humanity, they enrich their clients' lives. Although I emphasize that the human qualities of a therapist are of primary importance, I do not think it is sufficient to be merely a good person with good intentions. To be effective, the therapist also requires life experiences, supervised experiences in counseling, and a knowledge of counseling theory and techniques.

Overview

Table 1-1 presents an overview of the eight therapeutic approaches that are explored in Chapters 2–9.

I have selected eight models of counseling and psychotherapy that fit into three general categories. First is the psychodynamic approach, based largely on insight, unconscious motivation, and reconstruction of the personality and is the approach of *psychoanalytic therapy*. Second are the experiential and relationship-oriented therapies based on humanistic psychology, which include the *existential therapies, client-centered therapy,* and *Gestalt therapy*. Third are the behavior-oriented, the rational-cognitive, and the "action" therapies, which include *Transactional Analysis,* the *behavior therapies, rational-emotive therapy,* and *reality therapy*. For the purpose of consistency, these chapters share a common format that includes discussions of key concepts, therapeutic processes, and applications of therapeutic techniques and procedures, a summary and my evaluation, and questions for the reader's evaluation.

Table 1-1   Overview of Contemporary
Counseling and Therapy Models

Psychoanalytic Therapy	Key figure: Freud. Other figures: Jung, Adler, Sullivan, Rank, Fromm, Horney, Erikson. Historically, the first system of psychotherapy. Psychoanalysis is a personality theory, a philosophical system, and a method of psychotherapy.
Existential-Humanistic Therapy	Key figures: May, Maslow, Frankl, Jourard. The "third force" in psychology developed as a reaction against psychoanalysis and behaviorism, which the humanistic psychologist asserts do not do justice to the study of humans.
Client-Centered Therapy	Founder: Carl Rogers. Originally a nondirective approach developed during the 1940s as a reaction against the psychoanalytic approach. Based on a subjective view of human experiencing, it places more faith in and gives more responsibility to the client in dealing with problems.
Gestalt Therapy	Founder: Fritz Perls. Largely an experiential therapy stressing awareness and integration, which grew as a reaction against analytic therapy. Integrates body and mind functioning.
Transactional Analysis (TA)	Founder: Eric Berne. A contemporary model that leans toward cognitive and behavioral aspects. Designed to help people evaluate decisions they have made in light of the appropriateness at present.
Behavior Therapy	Key figures: Wolpe, Eysenck, Lazarus, Salter. Application of the principles of learning to the resolution of specific behavioral disorders. Results are subject to continual experimentation. This technique is continuously in the process of refinement.
Rational-Emotive Therapy (RET)	Founder: Albert Ellis. A highly didactic, cognitive, action-oriented model of therapy that stresses the role of thinking and belief systems as the root of personal problems.
Reality Therapy	Founder: William Glasser. A reaction against conventional therapy. Short-term, with focus on the present. Stresses a person's strengths. Basically, a way clients can learn more realistic behavior and thus achieve success.

Following the survey of the major counseling approaches, Chapter 10 presents a case illustration that is designed to clarify the various ways each theory might approach the same client and to demonstrate a basis for integration of the therapies by highlighting their similarities and their differences.

In teaching counseling courses, and in supervising counseling interns, I have found that certain basic issues related to therapeutic practice tend to permeate all the counseling and therapy approaches. Chapter 11 deals with those underlying issues common to all therapies. Chapter 12 emphasizes ethical issues in counseling practice, including the role of the practitioner's value system and the impact of his or her personality on the client. Because I believe that no book on counselor education is complete without a discussion of the personhood of the counselor, Chapter 13, the final chapter, explores how the counselor as a person is perhaps the most important variable in therapeutic effectiveness—surely more important than theoretical orientation or knowledge of techniques.

A list of suggested readings follows each chapter, so that the student can pursue a deeper knowledge of areas of special interest. I encourage supplementary reading, for the limitations of this book necessitated focusing on only the highlights of each approach.

Suggestions for Using the Book

I have some specific recommendations on how to get the fullest value as you read. Because students often ask to see how the various approaches actually work with clients, I strongly encourage you to begin by reading Chapter 10, the case illustration of one client, Stan, to obtain an overview of how each of the therapies might view Stan and how they might proceed during the course of the sessions. I suggest reading this chapter at two points: before you read the preceeding eight theory chapters and then again after you have studied each of the modalities.

Next, and also before you study each theory in depth in Chapters 2–9, I suggest that you read Chapters 11, 12, and 13, for these three chapters deal with the basic issues that underlie all the approaches to counseling and psychotherapy and with the central issue of the counselor's personhood as a key variable in creating successful outcomes in counseling. These chapters have been placed at the end of the book because it is hoped that they will have even more meaning, particularly in assisting you in the task of attempting some integration and synthesis of the approaches, if you give them a careful second reading after you have studied each of the models.

A Few Comments on Terminology

Throughout the book I have chosen to use the term *client* to refer to the person receiving psychological assistance. I prefer *client* over *patient* because the latter term has historically been associated with the medical model, and the concept of patient implies sickness or mental illness. Furthermore, the word *patient* signifies a *passive* orientation, whereby the doctor performs functions for the individual. In this book, it is repeatedly mentioned that the client needs to be an active and involved party in the therapeutic process.

I use the term *counseling* to refer to the process whereby clients are afforded the opportunity to explore personal concerns; this exploration leads to an increase of awareness and of choice possibilities. The counseling process frequently is short term, focuses on problems, and assists the person to remove the blocks to growth. This process helps the individual to discover his or her resources for more effective living. *Psychotherapy* frequently focuses on unconscious processes and is much more concerned with personality-structure changes than is counseling. Rather than merely aiming at the resolution of particular life crises, psychotherapy is geared toward an intensive self-understanding of the dynamics that account for these life crises. In this book, I frequently use these terms together, and sometimes even interchangeably. It should be noted, however, that there are some differences between counseling and therapy.

Finally, I use the terms *therapist* and *counselor* in similar contexts. I imply that a therapist performs psychotherapy, and the counselor performs counseling. The choice of the term, whether one is called a therapist or a counselor, has to do with the setting in which one practices, the type of services performed, and the level of training received by the helping person.

CHAPTER TWO

THE
PSYCHOANALYTIC
APPROACH

Introduction

One of the main currents in the history of psychology is Sigmund Freud's psychoanalytic theory. This theoretical system is a model of personality development, a philosophy of human nature, and a method of psychotherapy. Psychoanalysis is historically the first of the three major schools of psychology, the second being behaviorism, the third or "third force" being existential-humanistic psychology. It is important to recognize that Freud was the creator of a psychodynamic approach to psychology, for he gave psychology a new look and discovered new horizons. For instance, he called attention to motivation of behavior. Freud stimulated a great deal of controversy, exploration, and research and poured the foundation on which many later systems rest.

The major historical contributions of psychoanalytic theory and practice include the following: (1) An individual's mental life can be understood, and the insights into human nature can be applied to alleviate some human suffering. (2) Human behavior is often governed by unconscious factors. (3) Early childhood development has a profound effect on adult functioning. (4) This theory has provided a meaningful framework for understanding the ways in which an individual attempts to cope with anxiety by postulating mechanisms to avoid becoming engulfed in anxiety. (5) The psychoanalytic approach offers ways of tapping the unconscious through the analysis of dreams, resistances, and transferences.

Key Concepts

Structure of Personality

According to the psychoanalytic view, the structure of personality con-sists of three systems: the id, the ego, and the superego. These are names for psychological processes and should not be thought of as manikins that sepa-rately operate the personality; personality functions as a whole rather than as three discrete segments. The id is the biological component, the ego is the psychological component, and the superego is the social component.

The Id

The id is the original system of personality; a person is all id at birth. The id is the primary source of psychic energy and the seat of instincts. It lacks organization, and it is blind, demanding, and insistent. Like a caul-dron of seething excitement, the id cannot tolerate tension, and it functions to discharge tension immediately and return to a homeostatic condition. Ruled by the pleasure principle, which is aimed at reducing tension, avoid-ing pain, and gaining pleasure, the id is illogical, amoral, and driven by one consideration: to satisfy instinctual needs in accordance with the pleasure principle. The id never matures but remains the spoiled brat of personality. It does not think but only wishes or acts. The id is unconscious.

The Ego

The ego has contact with the external world of reality. The ego is the executive of personality that governs, controls, and regulates. As the "traffic cop" for the id, superego, and external world, its principal job is to mediate between the instincts and the surrounding environment. The ego controls consciousness and exercises censorship. Ruled by the reality principle, the ego does realistic and logical thinking and formulates plans of action for satisfying needs. What is the relation of the ego to the id? The ego is the seat of intelligence and rationality that checks and controls the blind impulses of the id. Whereas the id knows only subjective reality, the ego distinguishes between mental images and things in the external world.

The Superego

The superego is the moral, or judicial, branch of personality. The superego is a person's moral code, the main concern being whether action is good or bad, right or wrong. It represents the ideal, rather than the real, and strives not for pleasure but for perfection. It represents the traditional values and ideals of society as they are handed down from parents to children. It functions to inhibit the id impulses, to persuade the ego to substitute moralistic goals for realistic ones, and to strive for perfection. The superego, then, as the internalization of the standards of parents and society, is related to psychological rewards and punishments. The rewards are feelings of pride and self-love; the punishments are feelings of guilt and inferiority.

View of Human Nature

The Freudian view of human nature is essentially pessimistic, deterministic, mechanistic, and reductionistic. According to Freud, human beings are determined by irrational forces, unconscious motivations, biological and instinctual needs and drives, and psychosexual events during the first five years of life.

Humans are viewed as energy systems. According to the orthodox Freudian view, the dynamics of personality consist of the ways in which psychic energy is distributed to the id, ego, and superego. Since the amount of energy is limited, one system gains control over the available energy at the expense of the other two systems. Behavior is determined by this psychic energy.

Freud also emphasized the role of instincts. All instincts are innate and biological. Freud stressed the sexual instincts and the aggressive impulses. He saw all human behavior as determined by the desire to gain pleasure and avoid pain. Humans have both life instincts and death instincts. According to Freud, the goal of all life is death; life is but a roundabout way to death.

Consciousness and Unconsciousness

Perhaps Freud's greatest contributions are the concepts of the unconscious and the levels of consciousness, which are the keys to understanding behavior and the problems of personality. The unconscious cannot be studied directly; it is inferred from behavior. Clinical evidence for postulating the concept of the unconscious includes the following: (1) dreams, which are symbolic representations of unconscious needs, wishes, and conflicts; (2) slips of the tongue and forgetting, for example, a familiar name; (3) posthypnotic suggestions; (4) material derived from free-association techniques; and (5) material derived from projective techniques.

For Freud, consciousness is a thin slice of the total mind. Like the greater part of the iceberg that lies below the surface of the water, the larger part of the mind exists below the surface of awareness. The unconscious, which is out of awareness, stores up all experiences, memories, and repressed material. Needs and motivations that are inaccessible—that is, out of awareness—are also outside the sphere of control. Freud believed that most psychological functioning exists in the out-of-awareness realm. The aim of psychoanalytic therapy, therefore, is to make the unconscious motives conscious, for only when one becomes conscious of motivations can one exercise choice. Understanding the role of the unconscious is central to grasping the essence of the psychoanalytic model of behavior. The unconscious, even though out of awareness, does influence behavior. Unconscious processes are the roots of all forms of neurotic symptoms and behaviors. From this perspective, a "cure" is based on uncovering the meaning of symptoms, the causes of behavior, and the repressed materials that interfere with healthy functioning.

Anxiety

Also essential to understanding the psychoanalytic view of human nature is grasping the concept of anxiety. Anxiety is a state of tension that motivates us to do something. Its function is to warn of impending danger—that is, to signal to the ego that unless appropriate measures are taken the danger may increase until the ego is overthrown. When the ego cannot control anxiety by rational and direct methods, it then relies on unrealistic ones—namely, ego-defense-oriented behavior (see below).

There are three kinds of anxiety: reality, neurotic, and moral. Reality anxiety is the fear of danger from the external world, and the level of anxiety is proportionate to the degree of real threat. Neurotic anxiety is the fear that the instincts will get out of hand and cause one to do something for which one will be punished. Moral anxiety is the fear of one's own conscience. A person with a well-developed conscience tends to feel guilty when he or she does something contrary to his or her moral code.

Ego-Defense Mechanisms

As counselors work with resistances and defenses, an understanding of the nature and functioning of the common ego defenses is essential. Ego-defense mechanisms help the individual cope with anxiety and defend the wounded ego. They are not necessarily pathological, and they can have adjustive value if they do not become a style of life to avoid facing reality. The defenses one uses depend on one's level of development and the degree of anxiety. Defense mechanisms have two characteristics in common: they either deny or distort reality, and they operate on an unconscious level. Freud's theory is a tension-reduction model or a homeostatic system. Following are brief descriptions of some common ego defenses:

> *Denial:* defending against anxiety by "closing one's eyes" to the existence of threatening reality. The person refuses to really accept some aspect of reality that provokes anxiety. Anxiety over the death of a loved one is often manifested by denying the fact of death. In tragic events such as wars or other disasters, people often tend to blind themselves to realities that would be too painful to accept.

> *Projection:* attributing to another those traits that are unacceptable to one's own ego. One sees in others the things one doesn't like and cannot accept about oneself. Thus, a person may condemn others for their

"sinful ways" and deny possessing such evil urges. To avoid the pain involved in recognizing in oneself impulses deemed evil, one divorces oneself from this reality.

Fixation: getting "stuck" on one of the earlier stages of development because taking the next step is fraught with anxiety. The overdependent child exemplifies defense by fixation; anxiety prevents the child from learning to become independent.

Regression: retreating to an earlier phase of development where the demands are not so great. For example, a child who is frightened in school may indulge in infantile behavior such as weeping, thumbsucking, hiding, and hanging onto a teacher. Or when a new baby arrives at home, a child might revert to less mature forms of behavior.

Rationalization: manufacturing "good" reasons to explain away a bruised ego; self-deception so that the reality of some disappointment does not hurt so much. Thus when people do not get positions they have applied for in their work, they often find all sorts of reasons why they are really glad they didn't get the positions. Or the boy whose girlfriend has left him may soothe his wounded ego by persuading himself that she wasn't much anyhow and that he was just about to dump her.

Sublimation: using a higher, or more socially acceptable, outlet for basic impulses. For example, aggressive impulses can be channeled into socially approved competitive athletic activities so that the person finds a way of expressing aggressive feelings and, as an added bonus, often is rewarded for doing well in athletic events.

Displacement: directing energy toward another object or person when the original object or person is inaccessible. The angry boy who would like to kick his parents kicks a safer target—his little sister or, if she's not available, the cat.

Repression: forgetting content that is traumatic or anxiety provoking; pushing unacceptable reality into the unconscious or never becoming conscious of painful material. Repression, which is one of the most important Freudian concepts, is the basis of many other ego defenses and of neurotic disorders.

Reaction formation: behaving in a way that is directly opposite to unconscious wishes; when deeper feelings are threatening, one uses the cover-up of opposite behavior to deny these feelings. For example, a mother who feels that she is rejecting her child may, because of her guilt, go to the opposite extreme of overprotecting and "overloving" her child. Persons who are excessively nice and sugary sweet might be concealing repressed hostility and negative feelings.

Development of Personality

Importance of Early Development

A significant contribution of the psychoanalytic model is the delineation of the stages of psychosocial and psychosexual development of the person from birth through adulthood. It provides the counselor with the conceptual tools for understanding trends in development, key developmental tasks characteristic of the various stages of growth, normal and abnormal personal and social functioning, critical needs and their satisfaction or frustration, origins of faulty personality development that lead to later adjustment problems, and healthy and unhealthy uses of ego-defense mechanisms.

In my opinion, an understanding of the psychoanalytic view of development is essential if a counselor is to work in depth with clients. I have found that the most typical problems that people bring to either individual or group counseling situations are the following: (1) the inability to trust oneself and others, the fear of loving and forming close relationships, and low self-esteem; (2) the inability to recognize and express feelings of hostility, anger, rage, and hate, the denial of one's own power as a person, and the lack of feelings of autonomy; (3) inability to fully accept one's own sexuality and sexual feelings, difficulty in accepting oneself as a man or woman, and fear of sexuality. According to the Freudian psychoanalytic view, these three areas of personal and social development (love and trust, dealing with negative feelings, and developing a positive acceptance of sexuality) are all grounded in the first five years of life. This developmental period is the foundation on which later personality development is built.

The First Year of Life: The Oral Stage

Freud postulated the theory of infantile sexuality. Society's failure, up until then, to recognize the phenomenon of infantile sexuality can be explained by cultural taboos and every individual's repression of infantile and childhood experiences in this area.

From birth to the end of the first year the infant experiences the oral stage. Sucking the mother's breasts satisfies the need for hunger and pleasure. As the mouth and lips are sensitive erogenous zones during this period, the infant experiences erotic pleasure from sucking.

Greediness and acquisitiveness may develop as a result of not getting enough food or love during the early years of life. Material things that the child seeks to acquire become substitutes for what the child really wants— namely, food and love from the mother. Later personality problems that stem from the oral stage are the development of a view of the world based on mistrust, fear of reaching out to others, rejection of affection, fear of loving and trusting, low self-esteem, isolation and withdrawal, and inability to form or maintain intense relationships.

The major developmental task of the oral stage is acquiring a sense of trust—trust in others, in the world, and in self. Love is the best safeguard against fear, insecurity, and inadequacy; children who are loved by others have little difficulty in accepting themselves. If children feel unwanted, unaccepted, and unloved, then self-acceptance becomes difficult. Rejected children learn to mistrust the world; they view it as a threatening place. The effect of infantile rejection is a tendency in later childhood to be fearful, insecure, attention seeking, jealous, aggressive, hostile, and lonely.

Ages One to Three: The Anal Stage

Just as the oral stage demands that the person experience a healthy sense of dependency, trust in the world, and acceptance of love, so the anal stage marks another step in the development of the person. The tasks to be mastered during this stage are learning independence, personal power, and autonomy and learning how to recognize and deal with negative feelings.

Beginning in the second year and extending to the third year, the anal zone comes to be of major significance in the formation of personality. Now children continually face parental demands, they experience frustrations when they handle objects and explore their environments, and they are expected to master control of their bowels. When toilet training begins during the second year, children have their first experience with discipline. The method of toilet training and the parents' feelings, attitudes, and reactions toward the child can have far-reaching effects on the formation of personality traits. Many of the attitudes children learn about their own body functions are the direct results of the attitudes of their parents. Later personality problems such as compulsivity have roots in the ways parents rear their children during this stage.

During the anal period of development, the child will surely experience so-called negative feelings such as hostility, destructiveness, anger, rage, hatred, and so on. It is important that children learn that these are acceptable feelings. Many clients in therapy have not yet learned to accept their anger and hatred toward those they love. Since they were either directly or indirectly taught that these feelings were bad and that parental acceptance would be withheld if they expressed feelings such as rage or hatred, the child repressed them. As the process of disowning feelings begins, so does the person's inability to accept many of his or her real feelings.

It is also important at this stage that children begin to acquire a sense of their own power, independence, and autonomy. If parents do too much for their children, they really teach them that they are incapable of self-functioning. The message transmitted is "Here, let me do thus-and-so for you because you are too weak or helpless to do these things for yourself." During this time children need to experiment, to make mistakes and feel they are still okay for making mistakes, and to recognize some of their own power as separate and distinct individuals. So many clients are in counseling precisely because they have lost touch with their potential for power, and they are struggling to define who they are and what they are capable of doing.

Ages Three to Five: The Phallic Stage

We have seen that between the ages of one and three the child discards infantile ways and actively proceeds to carve a distinctive niche in the world. This is the period when capacities for walking, talking, thinking, and controlling the sphincters develop rapidly. As increased motor and perceptual abilities begin to develop, so also do interpersonal skills. The child's progression from a period of passive/receptive mastery to a period of active mastery sets the stage for the next psychosexual developmental period—the phallic stage. During this period sexual activity becomes more intense, and now the focus of attention is on the genitals—the boy's penis and the girl's clitoris.

Masturbation, accompanied by sexual fantasies, is a normal accompaniment of early childhood. In the phallic period, its frequency increases. Children become curious about their bodies; they desire to explore their own bodies and to discover differences between the sexes. Childhood experimentation is common, and because many attitudes toward sexuality originate in the phallic period, the acceptance of sexuality and the management of sexual impulses are vital at this time. This is a period of conscience development, a time when children learn moral standards. One critical danger is the parental indoctrination of rigid and unrealistic moral standards, which can lead to the overcontrol of the superego. If parents teach their children that all of their impulses are evil, children soon learn to feel guilty about their natural impulses and may carry these feelings of guilt into their adult lives and be blocked from enjoying intimacy with others. This kind of parental indoctrination results in an infantile conscience—that is, children are afraid to question or to think for themselves but blindly accept the indoctrination without question; they can hardly be considered moral, but merely frightened. Other effects include rigidity, severe conflicts, guilt, remorse, low self-esteem, and self-condemnation.

During this period children need to learn to accept their sexual feelings as natural and to develop a healthy respect for their bodies. They need adequate models for sex-role identification. At this time children are forming attitudes about physical pleasure, about what is "right" and "wrong," what is "masculine," and what is "feminine." They are getting a perspective of the way women and men relate to each other. They are deciding how they feel about themselves in their roles as boys and girls.

The phallic period has significant implications for the therapist who works with adults. Many clients have never fully resolved their feelings about their own sexuality. They might have very confused feelings regarding sex-role identification, and they may be struggling to accept their sexual feelings and behavior. In my judgment, it is important that therapists give just recognition to early experiences when they are working with adult clients. I am not suggesting that therapists accept a deterministic view that people are condemned to frigidity or impotence if they have not successfully mastered the developmental tasks of the phallic period. What I do see as important, however, is that clients become aware of their childhood experiences in this area, perhaps even relive and reexperience them in fantasy. As they relive events and feel again many of their buried feelings, they become increasingly aware that they are capable of inventing new endings to dramas they experienced as children. Thus they come to realize that, although their present attitudes and behavior are surely shaped by the past, they are not doomed to remain victims of the past.

Adaptations of Psychoanalysis:
The Neo-Freudians

The neo-Freudians took issue with Freud's limited and deterministic concept of human nature. Jung, Adler, and Rank were key early defectors from Freud's orthodox position. They were followed by Horney, Fromm, and Sullivan, who objected to Freud's biological orientation and deterministic stance and emphasized the social cultural and interpersonal dimensions of human behavior. Instead of narrowly focusing on the person as a biological machine, they stressed the social variables in shaping personality. Whereas their views constitute a reaction against the instinctivist position of Freudian psychoanalysis, the neo-Freudians acknowledged their debt to Freud and built on the concept of human nature from the foundation Freud built.

Carl Jung: Key Concepts Condensed

View of Human Nature. Jung emphasized the role of purpose in human development. People live by aims as well as causes. His is an optimistic and creative view of humans, stressing the goal of self-actualization. The present is determined not only by the past but also by the future.

The Personal Unconscious. This consists of experiences that were once conscious but have been repressed or forgotten. Painful ideas and thoughts not yet ripe for consciousness are suppressed or ignored.

The Collective Unconscious. This is the storehouse of buried memories inherited from the ancestral past. It is the "racial" inheritance of significant memories (archetypes) passed from generation to generation. The archetypes are discovered through the symbolic interpretation of dreams. The collective unconscious contains the wisdom of the ages and serves as a guide for human development.

The Persona. One's persona is the mask worn in response to social situations and the demands of social convention. It is the role assigned by society, the part society expects one to play. Persona is the public self, the side one displays to the world, the social facade.

The Animus and the Anima. Humans have both feminine and masculine characteristics. The feminine side of men is *anima*, by which men can understand women. The masculine side of women is *animus*, by which women can understand men.

Two Attitudes: Extraversion and Introversion. The extraverted attitude orients the person toward the external and objective world. The introverted attitude orients the person toward the internal and subjective world.

Four Basic Psychological Functions. Although everyone uses all four in varying degrees, each person epitomizes one function:

> 1. *thinking type:* logical; meets situations in a cool, objective, and rational manner;

2. *feeling type:* emphasizes subjective aspects and values; places less emphasis on thinking;
3. *sensation type:* able to perceive everything given directly by the senses;
4. *intuitive type:* intensely alive to all possibilities in a situation; goes beyond facts, feelings, and ideas and is able to get all the essence of reality.

Key Books. Contributions to Analytic Psychology (1928); *Psychological Types* (1933); *Modern Man in Search of a Soul* (1933).

Alfred Adler: Key Concepts Condensed

View of Human Nature. Humans are motivated primarily by social urges. Men and women are social beings, and in relationship with others each person develops a unique style of life. Adler stresses the social determinants of personality, not the sexual determinants. Consciousness, not the unconscious, is the center of personality. Humans are the masters, not the victims, of their fate.

Basic Inferiority and Compensation. Humans are pushed by the need to overcome inherent inferiority and pulled by the striving for superiority. Perfection, not pleasure, is the goal in life. Adler stresses that all of us have inferiority feelings. The child (with size and helplessness) feels a sense of inferiority. The individual attempts to overcome this helplessness by compensating—that is, by developing a life-style whereby success is possible.

Striving for Superiority. A person copes with basic inferiority by seeking power. By striving for superiority a person seeks to change weakness into strength or to excel in one area of concentration to compensate for defects in other areas.

Style of Life. This concept explains the uniqueness of each individual. All people have a life-style, but no two people develop exactly the same style. In striving for the goal of superiority, some people develop their intellect; others, artistic talent; others, athletic talents; and so on. A person's life-style is formed early in childhood as a compensation for a particular inferiority.

Childhood Experiences. Adler emphasized the kinds of early influences that predispose the child to a faulty style of life. The family constellation can intensify the child's inferiority feelings. The oldest child, who is given much attention until the second is born, may become so discouraged by the fall from power that he or she may develop hostility toward others and insecurity of self. The second child may walk in the shadow of the older sibling whom he or she seeks to overtake. The youngest child tends to be spoiled and may shrink from competition with others. The only child tends to be spoiled by parents and may devote the rest of his or her life to attempting to regain the favored position.

Key Book. The Practice and Theory of Individual Psychology (1927).

Otto Rank: Key Concepts Condensed

Separation Anxiety. Rank emphasized fear of separation as a major dynamic force. The initial separation from the mother results in anxiety, or the birth trauma, at which point a reserve of anxiety is created that influences a person all through life. All separations can be threatening and often lead to feelings of abandonment. The goal is to return to the contentment and security experienced in the womb.

Struggle for Individuality. Life is characterized by a struggle for individuality, which is sometimes hindered by parents whose own needs are unmet.

Concept of the Will. The will is a positive, guiding aspect of the self that both creatively uses and controls basic impulses. Parental prohibitions lead the child to mistrust his or her own will. As a result of these prohibitions, the person in adulthood has a will both with aspects that are approved by parents and society and with aspects that are disapproved of. Resistance to authority, which Rank terms "counterwill," can develop.

Three Character Types. Rank identified three character types:

1. *average person:* has surrendered own will and accepted the will of the group; socially accepted reality becomes his or her truth; has fewer conflicts and also fewer chances to become creative;
2. *neurotic person:* does not conform to the will of the group, yet does not feel free to assert own will; struggles with internal and external conflicts;
3. *creative person:* sets own ideals and standards; fully accepts self and guides behavior by internal standards; expresses self to others by creative productions.

Key Book. The Trauma of Birth (1929).

Karen Horney: Key Concepts Condensed

Basic Orientation. Horney is identified with the social/psychological theories, which constitute a reaction against Freud's mechanistic and biological orientation. Horney believed that psychoanalysis needed to grow beyond the limitations of a psychology based on instincts.

Basic Theme. Horney's primary concept is basic anxiety, which is the child's feeling of being isolated and helpless in a world that is potentially hostile. Anything that disturbs the child's basic security in relation to the intimate family relationships produces basic anxiety.

Ten Neurotic Needs. As a result of disturbed human relationships, a person who feels unable to get love may seek to obtain power over others, exploit people, compensate for feelings of helplessness, or withdraw into self-pity. The following ten needs are developed as a way of dealing with the basic anxiety that results from a disturbed parent/child relationship:

1. the neurotic need for affection and approval;
2. the neurotic need for a partner who will take over one's life;

3. the neurotic need to restrict one's life within narrow borders;
4. the neurotic need for power;
5. the neurotic need to exploit others;
6. the neurotic need for prestige;
7. the neurotic need for personal admiration;
8. the neurotic need for personal achievement;
9. the neurotic need for self-sufficiency and independence;
10. the neurotic need for protection and unassailability.

What makes these needs neurotic are their compulsive quality, insatiability, and unrealistic nature.

Three Character Types. Horney identified three character types:

1. *compliant type:* moves toward people out of desperate need for love and approval and behaves in a highly dependent way;
2. *detached type:* moves away from people by an exaggerated need for independence; keeps emotional distance between self and others for closeness causes anxiety;
3. *aggressive type:* moves against people; has an insatiable need for power and a need to control others; sees life as a struggle for survival.

Key Books. Neurotic Personality of Our Time (1937); *New Ways in Psychoanalysis* (1939); *Our Inner Conflicts* (1945); *Neurosis and Human Growth* (1950).

Erich Fromm: Key Concepts Condensed

Basic Orientation. Fromm is identified with the social/psychological theories. Fromm focuses on describing the ways in which the structure and dynamics of a particular society shape its members so that their social character fits the value of that society.

Basic Theme. Because human beings have been separated from nature and from others, they experience isolation and alienation. People can either unite themselves with others by learning how to love, or they can find some security by conforming their will to an authoritarian society.

The Human Condition. Human beings are unique in that they possess self-awareness, reason, imagination, and the capacities to love and to experience loneliness and uprootedness. People have five needs that arise from the human condition:

1. *the need for relatedness:* actively and productively loving others, thus implying knowledge, understanding, care, respect, and responsibility;
2. *the need for transcendence:* rising above animal nature by becoming a creative being;
3. *the need for rootedness:* wanting to feel a sense of connectedness with the world, nature, and others;
4. *the need for identity:* striving for a sense of personal identity and uniqueness in order to make sense out of the world;
5. *the need for a frame of orientation:* a stable way of making sense out of the world.

Five Character Types. Fromm identified five character types having the following orientations:

1. *the receptive orientation:* depending on others for support;
2. *the exploitive orientation:* taking things from others and manipulating others;
3. *the hoarding orientation:* finding security by keeping what one has;
4. *the marketing orientation:* regarding people as objects or mere commodities to be bought and sold;
5. *the productive orientation:* implying the full development of human potentialities as expressed by creativity and loving.

Key Books. Escape From Freedom (1941); *Man for Himself* (1947); *The Sane Society* (1955); *The Art of Loving* (1956); *The Heart of Man* (1964); *The Revolution of Hope* (1968).

Harry Stack Sullivan: Key Concepts Condensed

Interpersonal Theory. Sullivan's viewpoint is identified with the social/psychological theories. He emphasizes the role of personal relations and the study of humans in relationship with significant others. Thus the unit of study is the interpersonal situation, not the individual alone. Personality manifests itself in the individual's behavior in relation to others.

The Self System. This is the result of threats to one's security. Underlying all other impulses is the power motive, which operates throughout life to overcome a basic sense of helplessness. One's self system develops as a reaction against the anxiety produced by interpersonal relations.

Unique Contribution. Sullivan stresses the role of cognitive processes in personality development. Three modes of experience are involved in ego-formation:

1. *protaxic mode:* characterizes the first year of life; no distinctions of time and place; a necessary precondition to the other two modes;
2. *parataxic mode:* characterized by an undifferentiated wholeness of experience that is broken down into parts without any logical connection; occurs during early childhood; the child accepts without evaluation whatever happens and reacts to others on an unrealistic basis;
3. *syntaxic mode:* characterized by lack of distortion; consists of consensually validated symbol activity of a verbal nature through which the child evaluates his or her own thoughts and feelings against those of others and gradually learns relationship patterns in his or her society; self-attitudes are shaped by the reactions of significant others to the child.

Stages of Development. Sullivan contends that personality is not determined at an early age and that it may change at any time as new interpersonal relations develop; humans are malleable. He stresses that personality is shaped through definite stages of development that include infancy, childhood, the juvenile era, preadolescence, early adolescence, late adolescence, and maturity. The social determinants of personality development are crucial.

Key Book. The Interpersonal Theory of Psychiatry (1953).

Erik Erikson: Key Concepts Condensed

Ego Identity. Erikson, a key writer on ego psychology, conceives ego identity as a polarity of what "one feels one is and what others take one to be." One who achieves ego identity feels a sense of belonging. Also, as one's past has meaning in terms of the future, there is a continuity in development, reflected by stages of growth; each stage is related to the other stages.

The First Five Years of Life. Erikson (1964) delineated eight stages of development, each having a *crucial need* to be met and a crisis to be resolved. The first three stages occur during infancy and early childhood.

1. What corresponds to the oral stage is the task of developing a sense of trust in self and world. Infants develop trust when they feel loved. During this time the crisis is "trust versus mistrust."
2. Corresponding to the anal stage is the period of early childhood, which Erikson terms the "stage of autonomy." The core struggle is "autonomy versus shame." The child needs to learn independence, mastery of the environment, and a sense of adequacy. This period is like a "first adolescence" for it is a time of rebellion during which children test their power. It is crucial that children get support, are allowed to experiment, and are allowed to depend on others in a healthy manner.
3. What corresponds to the phallic stage is the "stage of initiative." During this period the key conflict is "initiative versus guilt." Crucial tasks are learning basic competencies, sex-role identification, moral standards, and control of impulses.

After the first five years of life, the following five stages are delineated:

4. "industry versus inferiority" during the latency period,
5. "identity versus role confusion" during adolescence,
6. "intimacy versus isolation" during young adulthood,
7. "generativity versus stagnation" during adulthood, and
8. "ego integrity versus despair" during later maturity.

Key Book. Childhood and Society (1964).

The Therapeutic Process

Therapeutic Goals

The goal of analytic therapy is to reform the individual's character structure by making the unconscious conscious in the client. The therapeutic process focuses on reliving childhood experiences. Past experiences are reconstructed, discussed, analyzed, and interpreted with the aim of personality reconstruction. Analytic therapy emphasizes the affective dimension of making the unconscious known. Insight and intellectual understanding are important, but the feelings and memories associated with this self-understanding are crucial.

The Therapist's Function and Role

A characteristic of psychoanalysis is that the therapist, or analyst, remains anonymous and engages in very little sharing of his or her own feelings and experiences, so that the client projects onto the analyst. The client's projections, which are material for therapy, are interpreted and analyzed.

The analyst is concerned mainly with assisting the client in achieving self-awareness, honesty, and more effective personal relationships, in dealing with anxiety in a realistic way, and in gaining control over impulsive and irrational behavior. The analyst must first establish a working relationship with the patient and then do a lot of listening and interpreting. The analyst pays particular attention to the resistances of the patient. While the client does most of the talking, the analyst listens and learns when to make appropriate interpretations, the function of which is to accelerate the process of uncovering unconscious material. The analyst listens for gaps and inconsistencies in the client's story, infers the meaning of the client's reported dreams and free-associating, carefully observes the client during the therapy session, and remains sensitive to clues concerning the client's feelings toward the analyst. Organizing these therapeutic processes within the context of understanding personality structure and psychodynamics enables the analyst to formulate the real nature of the client's problems. One of the central functions of the analyst is to teach the client the meaning of these processes so that the client is able to achieve insight into his or her problems, increase his or her awareness of ways to change, and thus gain more rational control over his or her life.

The Client's Experience in Therapy

The client must be willing to commit himself or herself to an intensive and long-term therapy process. Typically, a client comes to therapy several times weekly for a period of three to five years. The sessions usually last an hour. After some sessions face-to-face with the analyst, the client then lies on the couch for free-association activity; that is, the client says whatever comes to mind. This process of free-association is known as the "fundamental rule." While lying on the couch, the client reports his or her feelings, experiences, associations, memories, and fantasies. Lying on the couch maximizes conditions for the client's deep reflections and reduces the stimuli that might interfere with the client's coming into touch with his or her internal conflicts and productions.

The client enters into an agreement with the analyst regarding paying fees, attending sessions at a certain time, and making a commitment to an intensive process. The client agrees to talk, since the client's verbal productions are the essence of psychoanalytic therapy. The client is typically asked not to make any radical changes in his or her life-style during the period of analysis.

During therapy the client progresses through certain stages: developing a growing relationship with the analyst, experiencing treatment crises, gaining insight into his or her past and unconscious, developing resistances to learning more about himself or herself, developing a transference relationship with the analyst, deepening the therapy, "working through" the resistances and uncovered material, and termination of therapy.

The Relationship between Therapist and Client

The client's relationship with the analyst is conceptualized in the transference process, which is the core of the psychoanalytic approach. Transference allows the client to attribute to the therapist "unfinished business" from the client's past relationships with significant people. The treatment process involves the client's reconstruction and reliving of the past. As therapy progresses, childhood feelings and conflicts begin to surface from the depths of the unconscious. The client regresses emotionally. Some of the client's feelings arise from conflicts such as trust versus mistrust, love versus hate, dependence versus independence, and autonomy versus shame and guilt. Transference takes place when the client resurrects from his or her early past intense conflicts relating to love, sexuality, hostility, anxiety, and resentment, brings them into the present, reexperiences them, and attaches them to the analyst. The client might see the analyst as an authority figure who punishes, demands, and controls. For example, the client might transfer unresolved feelings toward a stern and unloving father to the analyst, who, in the eyes of the client, becomes stern and unloving. Hostile feelings are the product of negative transference, but the client might also develop a positive transference toward the analyst and, for example, fall in love with the analyst, wish to be adopted by the analyst, or in many other ways seek the love, acceptance, and approval of an all-powerful therapist. In short, the analyst becomes a current substitute for significant others in the client's life.

If therapy is to effect a cure, the transference relationship must be "worked through." The working-through process involves the client's exploring the parallels between his or her past and present experience. The client has many opportunities to see the variety of ways in which his or her core conflicts and core defenses are manifested in his or her daily life. Since a major dimension of the working-through process is the transference relationship, which takes time to build in intensity and additional time to understand and dissolve, working-through requires a lengthy period in the total therapeutic process.

If the analyst develops distorted views deriving from his or her own conflicts, *countertransference* occurs. This can consist of feelings of dislike or excessive attachment and involvement. Countertransference can interfere with analytic progress, for the analyst's own reactions and problems can stand in the way of dealing with the client's problems. The analyst must be aware of his or her feelings toward the client and guard against their disruptive effects. The analyst is expected to be relatively objective as he or she receives the anger, love, adulation, criticism, and other intense feelings of the client. However, since the analyst is human and thus subject to unconscious influences and unresolved problems, countertransference is seen as an inevitable part of the therapeutic relationship. Most psychoanalytic training programs require that the candidate-analyst undergo his or her own intensive analysis as a client. It is assumed that the analyst has developed to the degree that his or her own major conflicts have been resolved and thus is able to keep his or her own needs and problems separate from the therapy situation. If the analyst is unable to resolve the inevitable countertransference, then it is recommended that the analyst return for more personal analysis.

As a result of the therapeutic relationship, particularly in working through the transference situation, the client acquires insight into his or her unconscious psychodynamics. Awarenesses of and insights into repressed material are the bases of the analytic growth process. The client is able to understand the association between his or her past experiences and his or her present life. The psychoanalytic approach assumes that this self-awareness can automatically lead to change in the client's condition.

Application: Therapeutic Techniques and Procedures

The techniques in psychoanalytic therapy are geared to increasing awareness, gaining intellectual insights into the client's behavior, and understanding the meanings of symptoms. The therapeutic progression is from the client's talk to catharsis to insight to working through unconscious material toward the goals of intellectual and emotional understanding and reeducation, which, it is hoped, lead to personality change. The five basic techniques of psychoanalytic therapy are (1) free association, (2) interpretation, (3) dream analysis, (4) analysis of resistance, and (5) analysis of transference.

Free Association

The central technique in psychoanalytic therapy is free association. The analyst instructs the client to clear his or her mind of day-to-day thoughts and preoccupations and, as much as possible, to say whatever comes to mind, regardless of how painful, silly, trivial, illogical, or irrelevant it may be. In essence, the client flows with any feelings or thoughts by reporting them immediately without censorship. The client typically lies on the couch while the analyst sits behind him or her so as not to distract the client during the free flow of associations.

Free association is a method of recalling past experiences and of discharging the emotions associated with past traumatic situations. This is known as *catharsis*. While catharsis might offer temporary relief of a client's painful experiences, it does not by itself play a major role in the contemporary analytic treatment process; catharsis allows the patient to ventilate some pent-up feelings, and it thus paves the way for acquiring insight. As a way of helping the client gain more objective self-knowledge and self-evaluation, the analyst interprets key meanings of the free association. During the free-association process, the analyst's task is to identify the repressed material that is locked in the unconscious. The sequence of associations guides the analyst in understanding the connections the client makes among events. The client's blockings or disruptions in associations serve as cues to anxiety-arousing material. The analyst interprets the material to the client, guiding him or her toward increased insight into the underlying dynamics that he or she had been unaware of.

Interpretation

Interpretation is a basic procedure used in analyzing free associations, dreams, resistances and transferences. The procedure consists of the analyst's pointing out, explaining, and even teaching the client the meanings of behavior that is manifested by dreams, free association, resistances, and the therapeutic relationship itself. The functions of interpretations are to allow the ego to assimilate new material and to speed up the process of uncovering further unconscious material. The analyst's interpretations lead to insight and an unblocking of unconscious material on the client's part.

It is important that interpretations be well timed, since the client will reject inappropriately timed interpretations. A general rule is that interpretation should be presented at a point where the phenomenon to be interpreted is close to the client's conscious awareness. In other words, the analyst should interpret material that the client has not yet seen for himself or herself, but is capable of tolerating and incorporating as his or her own. Another general rule is that interpretation should always start from the surface and go only as deep as the client is able to go while experiencing the situation emotionally. A third general rule is that it is best to point out a resistance or defense before interpreting the emotion or conflict that lies beneath the resistance or defense.

Dream Analysis

Dream analysis is an important procedure for uncovering unconscious material and giving the patient an insight into some areas of unresolved problems. During sleep, defenses are lowered and repressed feelings are surfaced. Freud saw dreams as the "royal road to the unconscious," for in dreams the unconscious wishes, needs, and fears are expressed. Some motivations are so unacceptable to the person that they are expressed in disguised or symbolic form rather than being revealed openly and directly.

Dreams have two levels of content: the *latent content* and the *manifest content*. The *latent content* consists of the disguised, hidden, symbolic, and unconscious motives. Because they are so painful and threatening, the unconscious sexual and aggressive impulses that comprise the latent content are transformed into the more acceptable *manifest content,* which is the dream as it appears to the dreamer. The process by which the latent content of a dream is transformed into the less threatening manifest content is called *dream work.* The analyst's task is to uncover disguised meanings by studying the symbols in the manifest content of the dream. During the analytic hour the analyst might ask the client to free-associate to some aspect of the manifest content of a dream for the purpose of uncovering the latent meanings.

Analysis and Interpretation of Resistance

Resistance, a fundamental concept to the practice of psychoanalysis, is anything that works against the progress of therapy and prevents the client from producing unconscious material. During free association or association to dreams, the patient may evidence an unwillingness to relate certain thoughts, feelings, and experiences. Freud viewed resistance as an unconscious dynamic that attempted to defend the person against intolerable anxiety, which would arise if the person were to become aware of his or her repressed impulses and feelings.

As a defense against anxiety, resistance operates specifically in psychoanalytic therapy by preventing the patient and analyst from succeeding in their joint efforts to gain insight into the dynamics of the client's unconscious. Since resistance prevents threatening material from entering awareness, the analyst must point it out, and the client must confront it if he or she hopes to deal with conflicts realistically. The analyst's interpretation of the resistance is aimed at helping the client become aware of the reasons for the resistance so that he or she can deal with them. As a general rule, the analyst calls to the client's attention and interprets the most obvious resistances in order to lessen the possibility of the client's rejecting the interpretation and to increase the chance that the client will begin to look at his or her resistive behavior.

Resistances are not just something to be overcome. Because they are representative of the client's usual defensive approaches in daily life, they must be recognized as devices that defend against anxiety, but that interfere with the client's ability to experience a more gratifying life.

Analysis and Interpretation of Transference

As does resistance, transference lies at the core of psychoanalytic therapy. Transference manifests itself in the therapeutic process at the point where the patient's past "unfinished business" with significant others causes him or her to distort the present and to react to the analyst as he or she did to his or her mother or father. Now, in the relationship with the analyst, the client reexperiences the feelings of rejection and hostility once felt toward his or her parents. Most analytic therapists contend that a client must eventually develop this "transference neurosis" because the client's neurosis originated during the first five years of life, and now the client inappropriately carries it into adulthood as a framework for living. The analyst encourages the transference neurosis by his or her neutrality, objectivity, anonymity, and relative passivity.

The analysis of transference is a central technique in psychoanalysis for it allows the client to relive his or her past in therapy. It enables the client to achieve insight into the nature of his or her fixations and deprivations, and it provides an understanding of the influence of the past as it relates to present functioning. Interpretation of the transference relationship also enables the client to work through old conflicts that keep him or her presently fixated and that retard his or her emotional growth. In essence, the psychopathological effects of an undesirable early relationship are counteracted by working through a similar emotional conflict in the therapeutic relationship with the analyst.

Summary and Evaluation

This chapter has briefly described psychoanalytic therapy. I stress that, although many psychologists and psychiatrists might be analytically oriented, they might demonstrate a radical departure in methodology from what I described. Analytically oriented therapists could well employ methods of dream interpretation, free association, analysis of resistances and transference and also work with past relationships, yet at the same time incorporate the contributions of other schools, particularly those of the neo-Freudians, who stress the social/cultural factors of personality development.

What are the implications of the psychoanalytic approach (as a view of human nature, as a model for understanding behavior, and as a method of therapy) for counselors? How applicable is this approach to school counseling? How useful is it in community counseling clinics and in other kinds of public and private human-services agencies? In general, considering factors such as time, expense, and availability of trained analysts, I think the practical applications of the *method* are very limited. Further, the goals of analytic therapy—that is, probing the unconscious and working toward radical personality transformations—are inappropriate for typical counseling settings. But, although the method might be limited, I believe that therapeutic counselors can deepen their understanding of clients' current struggles by appreciating the many significant contributions of Freud and the neo-Freudians. Psychoanalysis provides the counselor with a conceptual framework for looking at behavior and for understanding the origins and functions of present symptomatology. It can also be extremely useful in understanding the functions of the ego defenses as reactions to anxiety. If the counselor ignores the early history of the client, the counselor is truly limiting his or her vision of the causes of the client's present suffering and the nature of the client's present life-style. This does not mean that the counselor must be preoccupied with the past, dig it up, and dwell on it exclusively; but to deemphasize early experiences as determinants of current conflicts is to restrict the counselor's capacity to help the client grow. There is no plea here for blaming the past for the fact that a client is now, for example, unable to love. If the client is fearful of forming close relationships with people, however, the counselor must understand the roots of this handicap. In addition, counseling will involve working through some of the barriers of the past that are now preventing the client from loving.

Some specific applications of the psychoanalytic point of view include the following: (1) understanding resistances that take the form of cancellation of appointments, fleeing from therapy prematurely, and refusing to look at oneself; (2) understanding the role of early relationships that lead to weak spots and faulty personality development and recognizing that unfinished business can be worked through, so that the client can put a new ending to some of the events that have crippled him or her emotionally; (3) understanding the value and role of transference that occurs in many counseling relationships; and (4) understanding how overuse of ego defenses can keep a person from functioning effectively and recognizing the ways these ego defenses operate both in the counseling relationship itself and in the client's daily life.

In concluding, I want to comment on how often I see Freud's work diminished by both professionals and students who refuse to consider seriously Freud's findings and discard all of Freud's work as unverifiable by experimental methods, hence not valid. It is true that most of the psychoanalytic concepts do not stand the rigorous test of the experimental method, but is experimentation the only approach to truth? Much of Freudian psychology is verifiable by clinical methods, including case histories and observations. I am not encouraging you to accept uncritically the psychoanalytic model; instead, I am encouraging you to read further in this area, to keep yourself open, and to appreciate the significance of Freud in his time. His contributions were monumental, and many proponents of the newer schools of psychology have stood on the giant's shoulders as they built their own theories. Freud himself did not claim to have all the answers, and he revised much of his theory several times. One can accept certain aspects of his approach and incorporate much of the understanding and many of the methods of his view without being an orthodox Freudian.

Questions for Evaluation

Consider the following questions as you form your own appraisal of the contributions and limitations of the psychoanalytic approach.

1. Freud's model is based on a deterministic concept of human nature: the person is determined by psychic energy, unconscious motives, and childhood experiences. Do you agree with this concept? What are its implications for counseling practice?

2. The psychoanalytic approach underscores the importance of early psychosexual development. Do you see evidence that one's current problems are rooted in the significant events of one's first five years of life? When you apply this concept specifically to yourself, what connections between your childhood experiences and your present personality are you aware of?

3. Do you think that a system of counseling and psychotherapy is complete if it does not account for such concepts as the unconscious, ego-defense mechanisms, and the critical influences of one's past on one's current personality?

4. In your work as a counselor, many psychoanalytic techniques such as free association, dream interpretation, probing the unconscious, and interpretation and analysis of resistance and transference may not be appropriate, or they may be beyond your level of training. However, what are some concepts of the psychoanalytic approach that can provide you with a useful framework in deepening your understanding of human behavior? How do you see psychoanalytic views as being potentially related to your work as a counselor?

5. As you study the other therapies described in this book, compare them with the psychoanalytic approach. To what degree are other approaches based on psychoanalytic concepts, or formed as a reaction against proposed limitations of psychoanalysis?

6. What were some of your stereotypes or misconceptions of psychoanalysis before you read about this theory? Is it possible that some of your misconceptions might prevent you from seeing some valid concepts that are related to your work as a counselor?

7. How might the concept of the unconscious be important for you to understand, even though in your work as a counselor you might not deal directly with your clients' unconscious motives and conflicts?

8. The psychoanalytic concept of anxiety is that anxiety is largely the result of keeping unconscious conflicts buried and that the ego defenses develop to help the person curb anxiety. What implications does this concept have for your work with people? Do you think defenses are necessary? What are the possible values of defense mechanisms? What do you think might occur if you were able to successfully strip away a client's defenses?

9. What is your evaluation of the psychoanalytic view of personality development? Consider the stages of early development, particularly with respect to how fully a person's basic needs were met at each stage. Do you think it is necessary or important to explore with clients areas of conflict and unmet needs of the early years? Do you believe a person can resolve his or her adult problems that stem from childhood experiences without exploring past events? How much emphasis would you place on a person's past?

10. Can you apply any aspects of the psychoanalytic theory to your own personal growth? Does this approach help you in any way to deepen your self-understanding? If so, how and in what ways?

References and Suggested Readings

Books highly recommended as supplementary reading are marked with an asterisk.

Adler, A. *The practice and theory of individual psychology.* New York: Harcourt, 1927.

*Baruch, D. *One little boy.* New York: Dell (Delta), 1964.

Bettelheim, B. *Love is not enough.* New York: P. F. Collier, 1950.

Blum, G. *Psychoanalytic theories of personality.* New York: McGraw-Hill, 1953.

Blum, G. *Psychodynamics: The science of unconscious mental forces.* Monterey, Cal.: Brooks/Cole, 1966.

Brand, M. *Savage sleep.* New York: Bantam Books, 1968.

Cameron, N. *Personality development and psychopathology: A dynamic approach.* Boston: Houghton Mifflin, 1963.

Erikson, E. H. *Childhood and society* (2nd ed.). New York: Norton, 1964.

Fine, R. Psychoanalysis. In R. Corsini (Ed.), *Current psychotherapies.* Itasca, Ill.: Peacock, 1973.

Freud, S. *An outline of psychoanalysis.* New York: Norton, 1949.

Freud, S. *The interpretation of dreams.* London: Hogarth Press, 1953.

Fromm, E. *Escape from freedom.* New York: Rinehart, 1941.

Fromm, E. *Man for himself.* New York: Rinehart, 1947.

Fromm, E. *The sane society.* New York: Rinehart, 1955.

Fromm, E. *The art of loving.* New York: Harper & Row, 1956.

Fromm, E. *The heart of man.* New York: Harper & Row, 1964.

Fromm, E. *The revolution of hope.* New York: Harper & Row, 1968.

Green, H. *I never promised you a rose garden.* New York: New American Library (Signet), 1964.

*Hall, C. *A primer of Freudian psychology.* New York: New American Library (Mentor), 1954.

Hall, C., & Lindzey, G. *Theories of personality* (2nd ed.). New York: Wiley, 1970.

Horney, K. *Neurotic personality of our time.* New York: Norton, 1937.

Horney, K. *New ways in psychoanalysis.* New York: Norton, 1939.

Horney, K. *Our inner conflicts.* New York: Norton, 1945.

Horney, K. *Neurosis and human growth.* New York: Norton, 1950.

Jung, C. G. *Contributions to analytic psychology.* New York: Harcourt, 1928.

Jung, C. G. *Psychological types.* New York: Harcourt, 1933. (a)

Jung, C. G. *Modern man in search of a soul.* New York: Harcourt, 1933. (b)

*Mintz, E. *Marathon groups: Reality and symbol.* New York: Appleton-Century-Crofts, 1971.

*Nye, R. *Three views of man.* Monterey, Cal.: Brooks/Cole, 1975.

Rank, O. *The trauma of birth.* New York: Harcourt, 1929.

*Schultz, D. *Theories of personality.* Monterey, Cal.: Brooks/Cole, 1976.

Shaffer, J., & Galinsky, M. D. *Models of group therapy and sensitivity training.* Englewood Cliffs, N.J.: Prentice-Hall, 1974.

Sullivan, H. S. *The interpersonal theory of psychiatry.* New York: Norton, 1953.

CHAPTER THREE

THE EXISTENTIAL-
HUMANISTIC
APPROACH

Introduction

Psychology has long been dominated by the empirical approach to the study of the individual's behavior. Many American psychologists have considered the commitment to operational definitions, testable hypotheses, and empirical data the only valid approach to securing information about human behavior. Nor in the past has there been very much evidence of a serious interest in the philosophical aspects of counseling and psychotherapy. The existential-humanistic approach, however, emphasizes the philosophical concerns of what it means to become fully human. Many existentially oriented psychologists have argued against restricting the study of human behavior to those methods used in the physical sciences. For instance, Bugental (1965), Rogers (1961), May (1953, 1958, 1961, 1967, 1969), Frankl (1959, 1963), Jourard (1968, 1971), Maslow (1968, 1970), and Arbuckle (1975) have argued for the need for psychology to develop a broader perspective that would encompass the client's subjective experiencing of his or her private world.

A basic goal of many therapeutic approaches is to enable the individual to act and to accept the awesome freedom of and responsibility for action. In particular, existential therapy is rooted in the premise that humans cannot escape from freedom and that freedom and responsibility go hand in hand. In its therapeutic applications, the existential-humanistic approach concentrates on the philosophical assumptions underlying therapy. It provides a philosophical base for individuals in their human relationships from which to specify the nature of the existential approach to counseling, the need for this unique approach, the goals of counseling, the functions of the counselor, and the implications of the approach for helping the individual confront the basic questions of human existence.

Key Concepts

View of Human Nature

Existential-humanistic psychology focuses on the human condition. Instead of being a system of techniques used to influence clients, this approach is primarily an attitude that stresses the understanding of persons. Hence it is not a school of therapy, nor is it a unified and systematic theory. There are, instead, not one but numerous approaches to existential psychotherapy based on concepts and assumptions relating to human nature. Because those concepts concerning human nature are discussed in detail below, in the section on the application of therapeutic techniques and procedures, only a brief summary is presented here. What follows are some key aspects of the existential approach that constitute the groundwork for therapeutic practice.

Self-Awareness

Human beings are capable of self-awareness, the unique and distinctive capacity that allows them to think and decide. The more awareness, the more the possibilities for freedom. The power to choose among alternatives—that is, to decide freely within the framework of limitations— is an essential aspect of being human. With freedom to choose and to act comes a responsibility. The existentialist insists that persons are responsible for their existence and their destiny; they are not the pawns of deterministic forces of conditioning.

Freedom, Responsibility, and Anxiety

The awareness of freedom and responsibility gives rise to existential anxiety, which is a basic human attribute. The knowledge that one must choose even though the outcome is not certain results in anxiety. Existential anxiety results also from the awareness of being finite and from facing the inevitable prospects of eventual death (nonbeing). The awareness of death gives the present moment significance because it becomes apparent that one has only a limited time to actualize one's human potential. Existential guilt, also a part of the human condition, is the result of failing to fully become what one is able to become.

The Quest for Meaning

Humans are unique in that they strive toward discovering a purpose in life and creating values that will give substance to living. Being human also implies facing ultimate aloneness: a person comes into the world alone and leaves alone. Although one is essentially alone, one has a need to relate to others in a meaningful way, for humans are relational beings. Failure to create meaningful relationships results in conditions such as isolation, depersonalization, alienation, estrangement, and loneliness. The human being strives for self-actualization—that is, the fulfillment of human potential. To the degree that one does not actualize oneself, one becomes "sick." Pathology is viewed as a failure to use freedom to actualize one's potentials.

The Therapeutic Process

Therapeutic Goals

Existential therapy aims at having clients experience their existence as authentic by becoming aware of their own existence and potentials and by becoming aware of how they can open up and act on their potentials. Bugental (1965, p. 45) cited authenticity as a "central concern of psychotherapy" and the "primary existential value." There are three characteristics of authentic existence: (1) being fully aware of the present moment; (2) choosing how to live in the moment; and (3) taking responsibility for the choice. The neurotic client is one who has lost the sense of being, and the goal is to help him or her recapture or discover his or her lost humanity.

Basically, the goal of existential therapy is to expand self-awareness and thus increase choice potentials—that is, to become free and to be responsible for the direction of one's life. Accepting this responsibility is no easy matter; many fear the weight of being responsible for who they are now and what they are becoming. They must make choices, for example, of whether they will cling to the known and the familiar or will risk opening themselves to a less certain and more challenging life. That there are no guarantees in life is precisely what generates anxiety. Thus existential therapy aims also at helping clients face the anxiety of choosing for themselves and accepting the reality that they are more than mere victims of deterministic forces outside themselves.

The following letter was written by one of my former clients and is presented here with her consent. Her words describe vividly her struggles with awareness, freedom, and responsibility and the anxiety she feels in making daily decisions regarding the way she wants to lead her life.

> Often now I find myself struggling deep within me with who I really am as a person and how I really feel. Emotions don't come easily to me even now. Feelings of love and hate are new to me, and often very scary.

Many times I find it hard to reconcile myself to the fact that sometimes I can miss someone I care about one moment and then wish that they would go away the next. This inconsistency in myself, this dependency-independency struggle is confusing to me at times. Sometimes I think that I would have been better off if I had remained as emotionally dead as I once was. At least then I didn't hurt so much. But I also know that I wasn't fully alive then either.

Today a man embraced me and I felt very warm and safe for a little while. I like that feeling and yet I fear it, too. It's so alien to me. I want to trust and yet I still find it difficult to do so. Perhaps it's because there's always an element of risk involved in any relationship and I still won't allow myself to accept that risk. I worry about whether I will ever be able to overcome all the old hurts and disappointments and learn to live for today.

Occasionally, when I'm feeling especially alone and lost, I try to imagine what it would be like if I had never entered counseling, if I had never acquired the self-insight that I now have. Or what it would be like if I could magically return in time to an earlier stage of my emotional growth when I felt less threatened, and be able to stay there. I saw no beauty in the world then, and I knew no success, nor did I have much peace of mind, but I felt safer then. The pressures that I live with now didn't exist. It was a simpler, less challenging time for me. And yet if I were magically given the ability to go back I know that I wouldn't. I'm not always sure where I'm going these days, but I do know where I've been, and I would never knowingly choose to return to what I once was again. I've come too far to go back now. And yet sometimes I still wonder if it's all been worth it.

The Therapist's Function and Role

The therapist's main task is to attempt to understand the client as a being and as a being-in-the-world. Technique follows rather than precedes understanding. Because of the emphasis on experiencing a particular client in the present moment, existential therapists show wide latitude in the methods they use, and their procedures might vary not only from client to client but also with the same client at different phases of therapy.

Even though there is no single existential method but instead numerous approaches, there are some common denominators in the therapist's tasks and responsibilities. Bühler and Allen (1972) agree that humanistic psychotherapy focuses on an approach to human relationships rather than on a system of techniques. According to Bühler and Allen, humanistic psychologists share an orientation that includes the following:

1. they accept the importance of the "person-to-person approach";
2. they acknowledge the role of the therapist's responsibility;
3. they recognize the mutuality of the therapeutic relationship;
4. "they share a growth orientation";
5. they urge that the therapist should become involved with the patient as a whole person;
6. they accept that "the final decisions and choices rest with the patient";

7. they see the therapist as serving as a model in that "his own life-style and his humanistic image of man can implicitly demonstrate to the patient his own potential for creative and positive action";
8. they see that the client must be given the freedom "to express his own outlook and develop his own goals and values";
9. they work toward lessening the client's dependence and increasing the client's freedom [pp. 90–91].

May (1961) views the therapist's task as one of helping clients become aware and conscious of their being-in-the-world: "This is the moment when the patient sees that he is the one who is threatened, that he is the being who stands in this world which threatens, and that he is the subject who *has* a world" (p. 81).

Frankl (1959) describes the role of the therapist as that of an "eye specialist rather than that of a painter," whose task consists of "widening and broadening the visual field of the patient so that the whole spectrum of meaning and values becomes conscious and visible to him" (p. 174).

For an example of what an existentially oriented therapist might actually do in a therapeutic session, refer again to the letter of my former client. If this client were to express her feelings to a therapist in a session, the therapist might do the following:

1. share his or her own personal reactions in relation to what the client is saying;
2. engage in some relevant and appropriate personal disclosure of experiences similar to those of the client;
3. ask the client to express her anguish over the necessity to choose in an uncertain world;
4. challenge her to look at all the ways in which she avoids making decisions and to make a judgment concerning this avoidance;
5. encourage her to examine the course of her life in the period since she began therapy by asking: "If you could magically go back to the way you remember yourself *before* therapy, would you really do this now?"
6. share with her that she is learning that what she is experiencing is precisely the unique quality of being human: that she is ultimately alone, that she must decide for herself, that she will experience anxiety over not being sure of her decisions, and that she will have to struggle to define her own meaning for living in a world that often appears meaningless.

The Client's Experience in Therapy

In existential therapy clients are able to experience subjectively their perceptions of their worlds. They must be active in the therapeutic process, for they must decide what fears, guilts, and anxieties they will explore. Merely deciding to enter psychotherapy is itself often a scary prospect, as indicated by the notes one of my clients kept to herself during the period of her therapy. Sense the anxiety that this client experiences as she chooses to leave security and embark on a search for herself:

I started private therapy today. I was terrified, but I didn't know of what. Now I do. First of all, I was terrified of Jerry himself. He has the power to change me. I'm giving him that power and I can't go back. That's what's really upsetting me. I can't go back ever. Nothing is the same. . . . I don't know myself yet, only to know that nothing is the same. I'm sad and scared of this. I've sandblasted security right out of my life and I'm really frightened of who I'll become. I'm sad that I can't go back. I've opened the door into myself and I'm terrified of what's there, of coping with a new me, of seeing and relating to people differently. I guess I have free-floating anxiety about everything but most specifically I'm afraid of myself.

In essence, clients in existential therapy are engaged in opening the doors to themselves. The experience is often frightening, or exciting, or joyful, or depressing, or a combination of all of these. As clients wedge open the closed doors, they also begin to loosen the deterministic shackles that have kept them psychologically bound. Gradually they become aware of what they have been and who they now are, and they are better able to decide what kind of future they want. Through the process of their therapy, they can explore alternatives for making their visions become real.

The Relationship between Therapist and Client

The therapeutic relationship is of central importance to the existential therapist. The emphasis is on a human-to-human encounter and a shared journey rather than on techniques that influence the client. The content of the therapy session is the current experiencing of the client, not the client's "problem." The client is an existential partner, not an object to be diagnosed and analyzed. This relationship with the other in authentic presence focuses on the here-and-now. The past or future is significant only as it bears on the immediate moment.

In writing on the therapeutic relationship, Sidney Jourard (1971) calls for a therapist who, through his or her own authentic and self-disclosing behavior, invites the client to authenticity. Jourard asks that the therapist work toward a relationship of I and Thou, one in which the therapist's spontaneous self-disclosure fosters growth and authenticity in the client. As Jourard puts it, "Manipulation begets counter-manipulation. Self-disclosure begets self-disclosure" (p. 142). He also points out that the therapeutic relationship can change the therapist as much as it does the client. "This means that those who wish to leave their being and their growth unchanged should not become therapists" (p. 150).*

Jourard is a good example of a therapist who developed a self-styled humanistic orientation. Jourard demonstrates that it is possible to be unique and authentic and employ a diversity of techniques within a humanistic

*From *The Transparent Self,* by Sidney Jourard. Copyright © 1971 by Litton Educational Publishing Inc. These and all other quotations from this source are reprinted by permission of D. Van Nostrand Co.

framework. The therapist invites clients to grow by modeling authentic be-havior. The therapist is able to be transparent when it is appropriate in the relationship, and his or her own humanness is a stimulus for the client to tap potentials for realness. Jourard (1971) describes his own evolution as a therapist in *The Transparent Self:*

> My behavior as a therapist has changed slowly, but radically, over the years. I am as good a listener as I ever was, perhaps even better. My capacity for empathy and my overall judgment are greater now than they were earlier. I reflect feelings and content as I always did, but only when I want the patient to know what I heard him say. But I find myself some-times giving advice, lecturing, laughing, becoming angry, interpreting, telling my fantasies, asking questions . . . in short, doing whatever oc-curs to me *during* the therapeutic session in response to the other person. This change could mean either that I am growing as a person and as a therapist or else that, through lack of close supervision, I am losing in "discipline." Yet, I do discuss my work with colleagues, and I am not isolated [p. 146].

Jourard maintains that, if the therapist hides himself or herself in the therapeutic session, then he or she engages in the same inauthentic be-havior that generated symptoms in the client. According to Jourard, the way to help the client discover his or her true self and become less of a stranger to himself or herself is for the therapist to spontaneously disclose his or her own authentic experience at an appropriate time during a session. This does not mean that therapists should stop using techniques, making diagnoses, or using judgments. It does mean that they should frequently speak out loud or else tell the client that they do not want to express what they are thinking or feeling.

Application: Therapeutic Techniques and Procedures

Unlike most other therapeutic approaches, the existential-humanistic model does not have well-defined techniques. The therapeutic procedures can be borrowed from several other approaches. Methods derived from the Gestalt approach and from Transactional Analysis are particularly appro-priate, and some of the principles and procedures of psychoanalysis can be integrated into the existential-humanistic approach. James Bugental's *The Search for Authenticity* (1965) is a complete work devoted to the concepts and procedures of existential psychotherapy based on an analytic model. Bugen-tal demonstrates that the core psychoanalytic concepts of resistance and transference can be applied to an existential philosophy and therapeutic practice. He uses an analytic framework to explain the phase of therapeutic work based on existential concepts such as awareness, emancipation and freedom, existential anxiety, and existential neurosis.

Rollo May (1953, 1958, 1961), an American psychoanalyst largely cred-ited for developing existential psychotherapy in the United States, also has integrated psychoanalytic methodology and concepts into existential psychotherapy.

Existential questions that have a central place in therapy are: To what degree am I aware of who I am? What am I becoming? How can I choose to re-create my present identity? To what degree am I accepting the freedom to choose my own way? How do I cope with anxiety that is a product of my own awareness of my choices? How much am I living from within my own center? What am I doing to discover a sense of purpose in my life? Am I living life, or am I merely content to exist? What am I doing to carve an identity of the kind of person I might want to become? In the following section I present propositions that underlie the practice of existential-humanistic therapy. These propositions, developed from a survey of the works of key writers in existential psychology, including Frankl (1959, 1963), May (1953, 1958, 1961), Maslow (1968), Jourard (1971), and Bugental (1965) represent some of the most important themes that specify therapeutic practices.

Key Existential Themes and Propositions: Applications to Therapeutic Practice

Proposition 1: Self-Awareness

Human beings possess the capacity for self-consciousness, which allows them to transcend the immediate situation and forms the basis for the distinctly human activity of thinking and choosing.

Human beings are distinct from other animals in that they possess an awareness of themselves. They can stand outside themselves and can reflect on their own existence. In a sense, the more consciousness one possesses, the more alive one is as a person, or, as Kierkegaard put it, "The more consciousness the more self." Responsibility is based on the capacity for consciousness. Because one is conscious, one can become aware of the responsibility to choose. As May (1953) put it, "Man is the being who can be conscious of, and therefore responsible for, his existence."

Thus to expand one's awareness is to increase one's capacity to fully experience human living. At the core of human existence, awareness discloses the following to all of us:

1. We are finite, and we do not have forever to actualize our potentials.
2. We have the potential to take action or not to take action.
3. We have some measure of choice in what our actions will be, and therefore we can partially create our own destiny.
4. We are basically alone, yet we have a need to relate ourselves to other beings; we recognize that we are separate from, yet related to, other beings.
5. Meaning is something that is not automatically bestowed on us but is the product of our searching and of our creating a unique purpose.
6. Existential anxiety is an essential part of living, for, as we increase our awareness of choice potentials, we also increase our responsibility for the consequences of these choices.

7. Anxiety results from accepting the uncertainty of our future.
8. We can experience conditions of loneliness, meaninglessness, emptiness, guilt, and isolation, for awareness is the capacity that allows us to know these conditions.

Awareness can be conceptualized in the following way: Picture yourself walking down a long hallway with many doors on each side of the hallway. Let yourself imagine that you can choose to open some of the doors either a crack or fully, or to leave them closed. Perhaps if you open one of the doors you'll not like what you see—it might be fearsome or ugly. On the other hand, you might discover a room filled with beauty. You might debate with yourself whether to leave a door shut or attempt to pry it open.

I believe we can choose to expand our consciousness or to limit our self-knowledge. I witness the struggle between the opposing desires in almost every counseling situation. Since the concept of self-awareness is at the root of most other human capacities, the decision to expand self-awareness is fundamental to human growth. What follows is a list of some dawning awarenesses that individuals experience in both individual and group counseling:

1. They become aware that, in desperately seeking to be loved, they really miss the experience of feeling loved.
2. They see how they trade the security of dependence for the anxieties that accompany deciding for themselves.
3. They recognize how they attempt to deny in themselves their inconsistencies and how they do not want to accept in themselves what they consider unacceptable.
4. They begin to see that their identity is anchored in someone else's definition of them; that is, they seek approval and confirmation of their being in others instead of looking to themselves for their confirmation.
5. They learn that they are in many ways kept as prisoner by some of their past experiences and decisions.
6. They discover a multitude of facets within them and come to realize that, as they repress one side of their being, they repress another. For example, if they repress tragedy, they seal themselves off from joy; if they deny their hate, they deny their capacity to love; if they cast out their devils, they also cast out their angels.
7. They can learn that they are not condemned to a future similar to the past, for they can learn from their past, and by understanding their past they can reshape the future.
8. They can realize that they are so preoccupied with death and dying that they fail to appreciate living.
9. They are able to accept their limitations yet still feel worthwhile, for they understand that they do not need to be perfect to feel worthy.
10. They can come to realize that they fail to live in the present moment because of either preoccupation with the past, or planning the future, or trying to do too many things at once.

In a real sense, increasing self-awareness, which includes awareness of alternatives, of motivations, of factors shaping the person, and of personal goals, is a goal of all counseling. I don't believe, however, that the therapist's job is to seek out unaware persons and tell them that they need to expand their awareness. Perhaps those persons are content and are not the slightest bit interested in consciousness-raising. When a person does come for therapy, or seeks a group experience, or asks for counseling, then it is a far different matter.

I believe also that it is a therapist's task to indicate to the client that a price must be paid for increased awareness of self. As one becomes more aware, one finds it more difficult to "go back home again." Ignorance of one's condition might bring contentment along with a feeling of partial deadness, but, as one opens the doors in one's world, one can expect more struggle as well as the potential for more fulfillment.

Proposition 2: Freedom and Responsibility

The human being is self-determining in that he or she possesses the freedom to choose among alternatives. Because humans are essentially free, they must accept the responsibility for directing their lives and shaping their destinies.

The existential approach puts freedom, self-determination, willingness, and decision at the very center of human existence. If consciousness and freedom are stripped from human beings, they no longer exist as humans, for it is precisely those capacities that give them humanness. The existential view is that the individual, by his or her decisions, shapes his or her own destiny and carves out his or her own existence. The individual becomes what he or she decides to become and must accept the responsibility of the course of his or her life. Tillich remarked "Man becomes truly human only at the moment of decision." Sartre said "We are our choices." Nietzsche described freedom as "the capacity to become what we truly are." Kierkegaard's phrase "choosing one's self" implies that one is responsible for one's life and existence. Jaspers said "We are deciding beings."

Freedom is the capacity to take a hand in one's own development and to choose among alternatives. To be sure, freedom has limits, and choices are restricted by outside factors, but we do have an element of choice. We are not simply bounced around like billiard balls. As Rollo May (1961) stated, "No matter how great the forces victimizing the human being, man has the capacity to know that he is being victimized and thus to influence in some way how he will relate to his fate" (pp. 41–42). Viktor Frankl continually emphasizes man's freedom and responsibility. As Frankl (1959) put it, "Life ultimately means taking the responsibility to find the right answer to its problems and to fulfill the tasks which it constantly sets for each individual" (p. 122). The very thing that can never be taken from a person is his or her freedom. We can at least choose our attitude in any given set of circumstances. We are self-determining beings who become what we choose to become.

Perhaps the central issue in counseling and psychotherapy is that of freedom and responsibility. The core existential theme is that we create ourselves. By virtue of making choices, we are the architects of our own present and future. In fact, we are condemned to freedom and to the anxiety that accompanies this freedom to choose for ourselves. The existentialist sees no basis for counseling and therapy without recognition of the freedom and responsibility each individual possesses. The therapist's tasks are to assist clients in discovering ways they avoid full acceptance of their freedom and to encourage them to learn to risk trusting the results of using their freedom. Not to do so is to cripple clients and make them neurotically dependent on the therapist. Therapists need to teach clients that they can begin to exercise choice, even though they might have devoted most of their lives to escaping the freedom to do so.

Proposition 3: Need for Center and Need for Others

Every individual has the need to preserve his or her uniqueness and centeredness; yet at the same time the individual has the need for going outside himself or herself and for relating to other beings and to nature. Failure to relate to others and to nature results in loneliness, alienation, estrangement, and depersonalization.

Each of us has a strong need to discover a self—that is, to find our personal identity. But finding out who we are is not an automatic process; it takes courage. Paradoxically, we also have a strong need to go outside our own existence. We need to discover our relationship to other beings. We must give of ourselves to others and be concerned with them. Many existential writers discuss loneliness, uprootedness, and alienation, which can be seen as the failure to develop ties with others and with nature. This failure becomes an acute problem for the individual in an industrialized and urbanized society, where, in a desperate attempt to escape from loneliness, the individual has become the outer-directed person in the lonely crowd that Riesman speaks of. As a result of inward emptiness and hollowness and the lack of a personal sense of being, the individual attempts to immerse himself or herself in the anonymous crowd.

The Courage to Be. It does take courage to discover our core, and to learn how to live from the inside. We struggle to discover, to create, and to maintain the core deep within our being. One of the greatest fears of clients is that they will discover that there is no core, no self, and no substance and that they are merely reflections of everyone's expectations of them. A client might say "My fear is that I'll discover I'm nobody, that there really is nothing to me, and that I have no self. I'll find out that I'm an empty shell, hollow inside, and nothing will exist if I shed my masks."

Existential therapists might begin by asking their clients to allow themselves to intensify the feeling that they are nothing more than the sum of others' expectations and that they are merely the introjects of parents and parent substitutes. How do they feel now? Are they condemned to stay this way forever? Is there a way out? Can they create a self if they find that they are without a self? Where can they begin? Once clients have demonstrated the courage to simply recognize this fear, to put it into words and share it, the fear does not seem so overwhelming. I find that the place to begin to work is by inviting clients to accept the ways in which they have lived outside of themselves and to explore ways in which they are out of center with themselves.

The trouble with so many of us is that we have sought directions, answers, values, and beliefs in the important people in our worlds. Rather than trusting ourselves to search within and find our own answers to the conflicts in our lives, we sell out by becoming what others expect of us. Our being becomes rooted in their being, and we become strangers to ourselves.

The need for the self relates to the need to have meaningful relationships with other persons. If we live in isolation and have no real connection to others, we experience a sense of abandonment, estrangement, and alienation. Perhaps one of the functions of therapy is to help clients distinguish between a neurotically dependent attachment to another and a therapeutic relationship wherein both persons in the relationship are enhanced. A therapist's function could be to challenge clients to examine what they get from their relationships, how they avoid intimate contact, how they prevent themselves from having equal relationships, and ways they might create therapeutic, healthy, and mature human relationships.

The Experience of Aloneness. The existentialists postulate that part of the human condition is the experience of aloneness. However, we can derive strength from the experience of looking to ourselves and sensing our aloneness and separation. The sense of isolation comes when we recognize that we cannot depend on anyone else for our own confirmation; that is, we alone must give a sense of meaning to our lives, we alone must decide how we will live, we alone must find our own answers, and we alone must decide whether we will be or not be. If we are unable to tolerate ourselves when we are alone, then how can we expect anyone else to be enriched by our company? Before we can have any solid relationship with another, we must have a relationship with ourselves. We must learn to listen to ourselves. We have to be able to stand alone before we can truly stand beside another.

There is a paradox in the proposition that humans are existentially both alone and related, but this very paradox describes the human condition. To think that we can cure the condition, or that it should be cured, is a mistake. Ultimately we are alone. We experience existential loneliness when we recognize and accept that we bear the responsibility for our choices and their outcomes, that total communication from one individual to another can never be attained, that we are individuals separate from others, and that we identify ourselves as unique.

The Experience of Relatedness. We humans are relational beings in that we depend on relationships with others for our humanness. We have a need to be significant in another's world, and we need to feel that another's presence is important in our world. When we allow another person to matter in our world, we experience a sense of meaningful relatedness. When we are able to stand alone and dip within ourselves for our own strength, our relationships with others are based on our fulfillment, not our deprivation. If we feel personally deprived, however, we can expect little but a clinging, parasitic, symbiotic relationship with someone else.

Proposition 4: Search for Meaning

A distinctly human characteristic is the struggle for a sense of significance and purpose in life. Human beings are by nature in search of meaning and personal identity.

In my experience, the underlying conflicts that bring people into counseling and therapy are the dilemmas centered in the existential questions Why am I here? What do I want from life? What gives my life purpose? Where is the source of meaning for me in life?

Existential therapy can provide the conceptual framework for helping the client challenge the meaning in his or her life. Questions that the therapist might ask are: Do you like the direction of your life? Are you pleased with what you now are and what you are becoming? Are you actively doing anything to become closer to your self-ideal? Do you even know what you want? If you are confused regarding who you are and what you want for yourself, what are you doing to get some clarity?

The Problem of Discarding Old Values. One of the problems in therapy is discarding traditional values (and values that were imposed on the person) without finding other, suitable values to replace them. What does the therapist do when the client no longer clings to values that were never really challenged or internalized and now experiences a vacuum? The client reports that he or she feels like a boat without a rudder. The client seeks new guidelines and values that are appropriate for newly discovered facets of himself or herself, and yet for a time he or she is without them. Perhaps the task of the therapeutic process is to assist the client in creating a value system based on a way of living that is consistent with the client's way of being.

The therapist's job might well be to trust the capacity of the client eventually to discover an internally derived value system that does provide a meaningful life. The client will no doubt flounder for a time and experience anxiety as a result of the absence of clear-cut values. The therapist's trust in the client is an important variable in teaching the client to trust in his or her own capacity to discover from within a new source of values.

Learning to Challenge the Meaning in Life. Founded by Viktor Frankl, logotherapy is designed to help the person find a meaning in life. According to Frankl (1959), challenging the meaning in life is a mark of being human.

"The will to meaning" is the individual's primary striving. Life is not meaningful in itself; the individual must create and discover meaning.

I think that it is important to realize that the issue of meaning changes at various stages in life. Children attempt to discover the sense of the universe on one level. During adolescence, new quests for meaning emerge. Healthy adolescents question their values, challenge the sources of their values, and look critically at inconsistencies in their world. They struggle to discover their uniqueness. Persons in declining years meet another crisis in life. Now that most of their projects are completed and the vitality of living is on the decline, what significance of living do they find? Do their lives really matter? Do they count in anyone else's life? I remember a man in one of our groups who captured precisely the idea of personal significance when he said "I feel like another page in a book that has been quickly turned, and nobody bothered to read the page."

From the existentialist's view, a central task of counseling is deeply exploring issues pertaining to hopelessness, despair, loss of meaning and significance, and existential emptiness. In fact, some existentialists assert that out of a meaningless and absurd world we find the wellsprings of creativity. The absurdity and nothingness of life allow us to create our meaning in the world. The task of the therapeutic process is to confront the issue of meaninglessness and help the client make sense out of a chaotic world.

Frankl (1959) contended that the therapist's function is not to tell the client what his or her particular meaning in life should be but to point out that the client can discover meaning even in suffering. This view does not share the pessimistic flavor of existential philosophy but holds that human suffering (the tragic and negative aspects of life) can be turned into human achievement by the stand an individual takes in the face of suffering. Frankl also contended that people can face pain, guilt, despair, and death and, in the confrontation, challenge the despair and thus triumph. Meaninglessness and the existential vacuum are central problems that the process of therapy must face.

The Existential View of Psychopathology. Existentialists see neurosis as the loss of the sense of being, which entails limitations of awareness and a locking up of potentials that are manifestations of being. They also cite "existential frustration," or the "existential vacuum," as the result of failing to find a meaning in life. Meaninglessness of life leads to emptiness and hollowness. Men and women are haunted by the emptiness of their lives; hence they withdraw from the struggle of developing and actualizing their unique potentials.

Existential guilt is related to the concept of pathology. Existential guilt grows from a sense of incompleteness, or the realization that one is not what one might have become. It is the awareness that one's actions and choices express less than one's full range as a person. To the degree that one restricts one's becoming, one becomes sick. Narrowing one's life, which does help one cope with the unknown, results in restricting one's development as a person.

Psychological health is the utilization of all one's potentials. To the extent that one does not fulfill one's potentials, one becomes sick. Pathology, viewed as something one learns, is the result of frustration of one's inner nature, or the failure to become what one is able to become.

Proposition 5: Anxiety as a Condition of Living

Anxiety is a basic human characteristic. It is not necessarily pathological, for it can be a strong motivational force toward growth. Anxiety is the result of the awareness of the responsibility for choosing.

Anxiety as a Source of Growth. As a basic human characteristic, anxiety is a reaction to threat. It strikes at the core of existence. It is what is felt when the existence of self is threatened.

Anxiety can be a stimulus for growth in that we experience anxiety as we become increasingly aware of our freedom and the consequences of accepting or rejecting our freedom. In fact, when we make a decision that involves reconstruction of our lives, the accompanying anxiety can be a signal that we are ready for personal change. The signal is constructive, for it tells us that all is not well. If we learn to listen to the subtle messages of anxiety, we can dare to take steps necessary to change the direction of our lives.

Escape from Anxiety. As pointed out above, anxiety is a by-product of change. The constructive form of anxiety (existential anxiety) is a function of our acceptance of our aloneness, and, even though we can find meaningful relationships with others, still we are fundamentally alone. Existential anxiety results also from the guilt we experience when we fail to actualize our potentials.

Yet so many clients who seek counseling want solutions that will enable them not to suffer from anxiety. Although attempts to avoid anxiety by creating the illusion that there is security in life may help us cope with the unknown, we really know on some level that we are deceiving ourselves when we think we've found fixed security. We can blunt anxiety by constricting our lives and thus reducing choices. Opening up to new life, however, means opening up to anxiety, and we pay a steep price when we short-circuit anxiety.

People who have the courage to face themselves are, nonetheless, frightened. I am convinced that those who are willing to live with their anxiety for a time are the ones who profit from personal therapy. Those who flee too quickly into comfortable patterns might experience a temporary relief but in the long run seem to experience the frustration of being stuck in their old ways.

Counseling Implications of Anxiety. Most people seek professional help because they experience anxiety or depression. Many clients enter a counseling office with the expectation that the counselor will remove their suffering or at least provide some formula for the reduction of their anxiety. The existentially oriented counselor is not, however, devoted to mere removal of symptoms or to anxiety reduction per se. In fact, the existential counselor does not view anxiety as undesirable. He or she might work in such a way that the client might experience increased levels of anxiety for a time. Some questions that might be posed are: How is the client coping with anxiety? Is the anxiety a function of growth, or is it a function of clinging to neurotic behaviors? Is the anxiety in proportion to the threat to the client's well-being? Does the client demonstrate the courage to allow himself or herself to experience the anxiety of the unknown?

Anxiety is the material for productive therapy sessions in either individual counseling or group work. If clients experienced no anxiety, their motivation for change would be low. Anxiety can be transformed into the needed energy for enduring the risks of experimenting with new behavior. Thus the existentially oriented therapist can help the client recognize that learning how to tolerate ambiguity and uncertainty and how to live without props can be a necessary phase in the journey from living dependently to becoming a more autonomous person. The therapist and client can explore the possibility that, although breaking away from crippling patterns and building new life-styles might be fraught with anxiety for a while, as the client experiences more satisfaction with newer ways of being, anxiety will diminish. As the client begins to learn a confidence in self, his or her anxiety that results from an expectation of catastrophe becomes less.

Proposition 6: Awareness of Death and Nonbeing

Awareness of death is a basic human condition that gives significance to living.

The existentialist does not view death negatively. A distinguishing characteristic of the human being is to be able to grasp the concept of the future and the inevitability of death. The very realization of eventual nonbeing gives meaning to existence because it makes every human act count.

The existentialist contends that life has meaning because it has a time limitation. If we had eternity to actualize our potentials, no urgency would exist. Because of our temporal nature, however, death does jar us into taking life seriously. To deny the inevitability of death limits the possibility of the richness of life. This does not mean that it is healthy to live in constant terror of dying, nor does it mean that we must be preoccupied with death. The message is that, because of our finite nature, the present moment becomes important to us. The present is precious, for it is all we really have.

The fear of death and the fear of life are correlated. The fear of death looms over those of us who are afraid to outstretch our arms and fully embrace life. If we affirm life and attempt to live in the present as fully as possible, however, we are not obsessed with the termination of life. Those of us who fear death also fear life, as though we were saying "We fear death because we have never really lived."

Because some of us are afraid of facing the reality of our own deaths, we might attempt to escape the fact of our eventual nonbeing. However, when we do try to flee from the confrontation with nothingness, we must pay a price. As May (1961) put it, "The price for denying death is undefined anxiety, self-alienation. To completely understand himself, man must confront death, become aware of personal death" (p. 65).

Frankl (1959) agrees with May and teaches that death gives meaning to human existence. If we were immortal, we could put off acting forever, but, because we are finite, what we do now takes on special significance. For Frankl, it is not how long one lives that determines the meaningfulness of life; rather, the key is how one lives.

Counseling Implications. I have come to appreciate that dying and living are counterpoints. In order to grow we must be willing to let go of some of our past. Parts of us must die if new dimensions of our being are to emerge. We cannot cling to the neurotic aspects of our past and at the same time expect a more creative side of us to flourish.

One group technique that I have found useful is to ask people to fantasize themselves in the same room with the same people in the group ten years hence. I ask them to imagine that they have not followed through with their decisions and that they have failed to accept opportunities to change themselves in ways they said they most wanted to change. They are to imagine that they have not faced the parts of themselves they fear, that their unfinished business remains unfinished, that they have not carried out their projects, and that they have chosen to remain as they are rather than take risks for more. Then I ask them to talk about their lives as if they knew they were going to die. This exercise can mobilize clients to take seriously the time they have, and it can jar them into accepting the possibility that they could accept a zombie-like existence in place of a fuller life.

Proposition 7: Striving for Self-Actualization

Human beings strive for self-actualization, which is the tendency to become all that they are able to become.

All individuals have an inborn urge to become a person; that is, they have the tendency toward developing their uniqueness and singularity, discovering their personal identities, and striving for the full actualization of their potentials. To the extent that they fulfill their potentials as persons, they experience the deepest joy that is possible in human experience, for nature has intended them to do so.

Becoming a person is not an automatic process, yet every person has the desire to become his or her potential. Whereas acorns grow automatically into oak trees, we human beings become the kind of people we choose to become. Nature almost says to us "You must become all that you can become." It takes courage to be, and whether we want to be or not to be is our choice. There is a constant struggle within us. Although we want to grow toward maturity, independence, and actualization, we realize that expansion is a painful process. Hence the struggle is between the security of dependence and the delights and pains of growth.

What are the characteristics of a self-actualizing person? Abraham Maslow's (1968, 1970) findings based on his research with healthy subjects gives us a perspective for understanding the nature of self-actualization. Maslow speaks of the "psychopathology of the average." So-called normals never extend themselves to become what they are capable of becoming. Maslow argued that healthy people differ from "normals" in kind as well as in degree and that a study of both the healthy and the "average" generates two different kinds of psychology. He also criticized the Freudian orientation of psychology for its preoccupation with the sick and crippled side of human nature. Maslow contended that, if we base our findings on a sick population, we will have a sick psychology. According to Maslow, too much attention has been given to man's anxiety, hostility, neuroses, and immaturities.

In his quest to create a humanistic psychology that would focus on what man might become, Maslow designed a study that utilizes self-actualizing subjects. Some of the characteristics that Maslow (1968, 1970) found in self-actualizing people were: the capacity to tolerate and even welcome uncertainty in their lives, acceptance of self and others, spontaneity and creativity, a need for privacy and solitude, autonomy, the capacity for deep and intense interpersonal relationships, a genuine caring for others, a sense of humor, an inner-directedness (as opposed to a tendency to live by others' expectations), and the absence of artificial dichotomies within themselves (such as work/play, love/hate, weak/strong).

Maslow's self-actualization proposition has definite implications for the practice of counseling psychology because the tendency toward growth and actualization accounts for the primary force underlying the therapeutic process. By nature, the human being has a strong positive drive for actualization and seeks more than a secure static existence. The basic tendency is to fulfill the highest potential, even in the face of internal problems and external resistances.

Carl Rogers (1961), a major figure in creating a humanistic psychotherapy, builds his entire theory and practice of therapy on the concept of the "fully functioning person," who is much like Maslow's "self-actualizing" person. Rogers believes in a basic trustworthiness of human nature and sees the movement toward full functioning as a basic need. According to Rogers, when human beings are functioning freely, their basic nature is both constructive and trustworthy.

Summary and Evaluation

One of the criticisms of the existential approach to therapeutic practice is that it lacks a systematic statement of the principles and practices of psychotherapy. The approach is most frequently criticized for lacking rigor in methodology. Some criticize it because of its mystical language and concepts, and some object to it as a fad based on a reaction against the scientific and positivistic approach. Those who prefer a counseling practice based on research would contend that the concepts should be empirically sound, that definitions should be operational, and that the hypotheses should be testable.

Although there are some justifiable grounds on which to criticize existential-humanistic therapy, the approach does emphasize unique aspects that the other therapeutic approaches ignore. Greening (1971) summarized well the essence of existential humanism as a distinctive orientation when he wrote the following:

> Existential humanism as a psychological orientation combines aspects of both existentialism and humanism in a way that recognizes the contributions of both approaches while attempting to avoid some of their limitations. Thus it is more affirmative than much of existentialism but more cognizant of the finiteness and contingency accompanying man's self-actualization than are some joy-and-growth-centered humanists. Existential humanism includes existentialism's recognition of the chaos, absurdity, contingency, despair, and "thrownness" of man's being in the world where he alone is responsible for his becoming. It also includes that humanistic postulate that man has a huge potential to transform himself as an unsuppressible drive to experience fulfillment in testing the limits of that potential against the obstacles inherent in existence [p. 9].

The focus on human nature, the importance of the relationship between the therapist and the client, and the freedom of the client to decide his or her own destiny are significant aspects. The existential-humanistic approach does not reduce people to a bundle of instincts or to the product of conditioning. Instead, it provides a philosophy on which to base a therapeutic practice.

The existential approach has brought back the person into central focus. It has given a picture of people at their highest levels of being. It has shown that people are constantly becoming and that they are continually actualizing and fulfilling their potential. The existential approach has focused sharply on the central facts of human existence—self-consciousness and the consequent freedom. To the existentialist goes the credit for giving a new view of death as a positive thing, not a morbid prospect to fear, for death gives life its meaning. Further, the existentialist has contributed a new dimension to the understanding of anxiety, guilt, frustration, loneliness, and alienation.

In my judgment, one of the major contributions of the existential-humanistic approach is its emphasis on the human-to-human quality of the therapeutic relationship. This aspect of the approach lessens the chances of dehumanizing psychotherapy by making it a mechanical process. Also, I find the philosophy underlying existential-humanistic therapy very exciting. I particularly like the emphasis on freedom and responsibility and the person's capacity to redesign his or her life by choosing with awareness. From my viewpoint, this model provides a sound philosophical base on which to build a personal and unique style of the practice of therapy because it addresses itself to the core struggles of the contemporary person.

On the other hand, I think this theory also has some distinct limitations. There are many lofty and abstract concepts in existentialism that are often difficult to grasp and even more difficult to apply in practice. The broad, elusive concepts and vocabulary unnecessarily complicate the therapeutic process. That few techniques are generated by this approach makes it essential for the practitioner to develop his or her own innovative procedures or to borrow from other schools of therapy. Finally, although I think this model has much to offer clients who function psychologically and socially at a relatively high level, I think it is severely limited in its applicability to clients who function at low levels, to clients in crisis states, and to clients in poverty conditions. In short, clients who struggle to meet their basic survival needs are really not that interested in self-actualization or in the existential meanings of life.

Questions for Evaluation

Since the existential-humanistic approach to counseling and psychotherapy is based on a philosophy of the human condition and on the encounter between the client and the therapist, it would be well to ask yourself some of the basic questions that your clients may struggle with in therapy. Most of the issues underlying the questions deal with personal freedom and responsibility and the anxiety that is the result of choosing for oneself. I assume that as counselors and therapists we cannot help clients come to grips with those issues unless we have faced them in our own lives.

1. What does personal freedom mean to you? Do you believe that you are what you are now largely as a result of your choices, or do you believe that you are the product of your circumstances?
2. As you reflect on some critical turning points in your life, what appear to be some decisions that have been crucial to your present development?
3. Are you able to accept and exercise your own freedom and make significant decisions alone? Do you attempt to escape from freedom and responsibility? Are you inclined to give up some of your autonomy for the security of being taken care of by others?
4. Do you agree that basically each person is alone? What are the implications for counseling practice? In what ways have you attempted to avoid your experience of aloneness?
5. What is your experience with anxiety? Does your anxiety result from the consideration that you must choose for yourself, the realization that you are alone, the fact that you will die, and the realization that you must create your own meaning and purpose in life? How have you dealt with anxiety in your own life?
6. Do you believe that, unless you take death seriously, life has little meaning?
7. What are some specific things that you value most? What would your life be like without them? What gives your life meaning and a sense of purpose?

8. Have you experienced an "existential vacuum"? Is your life at times without substance, depth, and meaning? What is this experience of emptiness like for you, and how do you cope with it?

9. Do you believe that anxiety is a motivational force toward growth and that personal growth and change usually entail anxiety? What are the implications for the practice of counseling?

10. What is your concept of a self-actualizing person? In what specific areas of your life do you experience a gap between the way you actually see yourself and the way you would like to experience yourself?

References and Suggested Readings

*Arbuckle, D. Counseling and psychotherapy: An existential-humanistic view. Boston: Allyn & Bacon, 1975.

*Bugental, J. F. T. The search for authenticity: An existential-analytic approach to psychotherapy. New York: Holt, Rinehart and Winston, 1965.

Bugental, J. (Ed.). Challenges of humanistic psychology. New York: McGraw-Hill, 1967.

*Bühler, C., & Allen, M. Introduction to humanistic psychology. Monterey, Cal.: Brooks/Cole, 1972.

Carkhuff, R., & Berenson, B. Beyond counseling and therapy. New York: Holt, Rinehart and Winston, 1967.

*Corey, G. The struggle toward realness: A manual for therapeutic groups. Dubuque, Iowa: Kendall/Hunt, 1974.

Corlis, R., & Rabe, P. Psychotherapy from the center: A humanistic view of change and of growth. Scranton, Pa.: International Textbook, 1969.

Fabry, J. The pursuit of meaning. Boston: Beacon Press, 1968.

*Frankl, V. Man's search for meaning. New York: Washington Square Press, 1959.

Frankl, V. The doctor and the soul. New York: Knopf, 1963.

Gendlin, E. Experiential psychotherapy. In R. Corsini (Ed.), Current psychotherapies. Itasca, Ill.: Peacock, 1973.

Greening, T. (Ed.). Existential humanistic psychology. Monterey, Cal.: Brooks/Cole, 1971.

Hodge, M. Your fear of love. New York: Doubleday, 1967.

Jourard, S. Disclosing man to himself. New York: Van Nostrand Reinhold, 1968.

*Jourard, S. The transparent self (Rev. ed.). New York: Van Nostrand Reinhold, 1971.

Keen, E. Three faces of being: Toward an existential clinical psychology. New York: Appleton-Century-Crofts, 1970.

*Kubler-Ross, E. On death and dying. New York: Macmillan, 1969.

Kubler-Ross, E. Death: The final stages of growth. Englewood Cliffs, N.J.: Prentice-Hall, 1975.

Lyon, W. Let me live! North Quincy, Mass.: Christopher, 1970.

Marshall, B. (Ed.). Experiences in being. Monterey, Cal.: Brooks/Cole, 1971.

*Maslow, A. Toward a psychology of being (Rev. ed.). New York: Van Nostrand, 1968.

Maslow, A. Motivation and personality (Rev. ed.). New York: Harper & Row, 1970.

Maslow, A. The farther reaches of human nature. New York: Viking, 1971.

*May, R. Man's search for himself. New York: New American Library (Signet), 1953.

*May, R. (Ed.). Existential psychology. New York: Random House, 1961.

May, R. Psychology and the human dilemma. New York: Van Nostrand Reinhold, 1967.

May, R. Love and will. New York: Norton, 1969.

May, R., & Ellenberger, H. F. (Eds.). Existence: A new dimension in psychiatry and psychology. New York: Basic Books, 1958.

*Moustakas, C. *Loneliness and love*. Englewood Cliffs, N.J.: Prentice-Hall, 1972.

Moustakas, C. *The touch of loneliness*. Englewood Cliffs, N.J.: Prentice-Hall, 1975.

Patterson, C. H. *Theories of counseling and psychotherapy* (Rev. ed.). New York: Harper & Row, 1973.

Rogers, C. *On becoming a person*. Boston: Houghton Mifflin, 1961.

Sutich, A., & Vich, M. *Readings in humanistic psychology*. New York: Free Press, 1969.

Van Kaam, A. Counseling and psychotherapy from the viewpoint of existential psychology. In D. Arbuckle (Ed.), *Counseling and psychotherapy: An overview*. New York: McGraw-Hill, 1967.

CHAPTER FOUR
THE
CLIENT-CENTERED
APPROACH

Introduction

Carl Rogers developed client-centered therapy as a reaction against what he considered the basic limitations of psychoanalysis. Essentially, the client-centered approach is a specialized branch of humanistic therapy that highlights the experiencing of a client and his or her subjective and phenomenal world. The therapist functions mainly as a facilitator of personal growth by helping the client discover his or her own capacities for solving problems. The client-centered approach puts great faith in the client's capacity to lead the way in therapy and find his or her own direction. The therapeutic relationship between the therapist and the client is the catalyst for change; the client uses the unique relationship as a means of increasing awareness and discovering latent resources that he or she can use constructively in changing his or her life.

Key Concepts

View of Human Nature

The client-centered view of human nature rejects the concept of the individual's basic negative tendencies. Whereas some approaches assume that human beings are by nature irrational and destructive of self and others unless they are socialized, Rogers exhibits a deep faith in human beings. He sees people as socialized and forward-moving, as striving to become fully functioning, and as having at the deepest core a positive goodness. In short, people are to be trusted, and, as they are basically cooperative and constructive, there is no need to control their aggressive impulses.

This positive view of human nature has significant implications for the practice of client-centered therapy. Because of the philosophical view that the individual has inherent capacity to move away from maladjustment toward a state of psychological health, the therapist places the primary responsibility for the process of therapy on the client. The client-centered model rejects the concept of the therapist as the authority who knows best and that of the passive client who merely follows the dictates of the therapist. Therapy is thus rooted in the client's capacity for awareness and the ability to make decisions.

Characteristics of the Client-Centered Approach

Rogers has not presented the client-centered theory as a fixed and completed approach to therapy. He has hoped that others would view his theory as a set of tentative principles relating to how the therapy process develops and not as dogma. Rogers (1974, pp. 213–214) describes the characteristics that distinguish the client-centered approach from other models. An adaptation of this description follows.

The client-centered approach focuses on the client's responsibility and capacity to discover ways to more fully encounter reality. The client, who knows himself or herself best, is the one to discover more appropriate behavior for himself or herself.

The client-centered approach emphasizes the phenomenal world of the client. With accurate empathy and an attempt to apprehend the client's internal frame of reference, the therapist concerns himself or herself mainly with the client's self-perception and perception of the world.

The same principles of psychotherapy apply to all persons—"normals," "neurotics," and "psychotics." Based on the concept that the urge to move toward psychological maturity is deeply rooted in human nature, the principles of client-centered therapy apply to those who function at relatively normal levels as well as to those who experience a greater degree of psychological maladjustment.

According to the client-centered approach, psychotherapy is only one example of all constructive personal relationships. The client experiences psychotherapeutic growth in and through the relationship with another person who helps the client do what the client cannot do alone. It is the relationship with a congruent (matching external behavior and expression with internal feelings and thoughts), accepting, and empathic counselor that serves as the agent of therapeutic change for the client.

Rogers proposes the hypothesis that there are certain attitudes on the therapist's part (genuineness, nonpossessive warmth and acceptance, and accurate empathy) that constitute the necessary and sufficient conditions for therapeutic effectiveness to occur within the client. Client-centered therapy incorporates the concept that the therapist's function is to be immediately present and accessible to the client and to focus on the here-and-now experience created by the relationship between the client and the therapist.

Perhaps more than any other single approach to psychotherapy, client-centered theory has developed through research on the process and outcomes of therapy. The theory is not a closed one but one that has grown through years of counseling observations and that continues to change as new research yields increased understanding of human nature and the therapeutic process.

Thus client-centered therapy is not a set of techniques, nor is it a dogma. Rooted in a set of attitudes and beliefs that the therapist demonstrates, the client-centered approach is perhaps best characterized as a way of being and as a shared journey in which both therapist and client reveal their humanness and participate in a growth experience.

The Therapeutic Process

Therapeutic Goals

According to Rogers (1961), the question Who am I? brings most people into psychotherapy. They seem to ask: How can I discover my real self? How can I become what I deeply wish to become? How can I get behind my facades and become myself?

A basic goal of therapy is to provide a climate conducive to helping the individual become a fully functioning person. Before one is able to work toward that goal, one must first get behind the masks one wears. One develops pretenses and facades as defenses against threat. One's games keep one from becoming fully real with others, and, in the process of attempting to deceive others, one eventually becomes a stranger to oneself.

When the facades are worn away during the therapeutic process, what kind of person emerges from behind the pretenses? Rogers (1961) described the characteristics of the person who is moving in the direction of becoming increasingly actualized: (1) an openness to experience, (2) a trust in one's organism, (3) an internal locus of evaluation, and (4) the willingness to be a process. These characteristics constitute the basic goals of client-centered therapy.

Openness to Experience

Openness to experience entails seeing reality without distorting it to fit a preconceived self-structure. The opposite of defensiveness, openness to experience implies becoming more aware of reality as it exists outside oneself. It also means that one's beliefs are not rigid; one can remain open to further knowledge and growth and can tolerate ambiguity. One has an awareness of oneself in the present moment and the capacity to experience oneself in fresh ways.

Trust in One's Organism

One goal of therapy is to help clients establish a sense of trust in themselves. Often, in the initial stages of therapy, clients trust themselves and their own decisions very little. They typically seek advice and answers outside themselves for they basically do not trust their own capacities to direct their own lives. As clients become more open to their experiences, their sense of trust in self begins to emerge.

An Internal Locus of Evaluation

Related to self-trust, an internal locus of evaluation means looking more to oneself for the answers to the problems of existence. Instead of looking outside oneself for validation of personhood, one increasingly pays attention to one's own center. One substitutes self-approval for the universal approval of others. One decides one's own standards of behavior and looks to oneself for the decisions and choices to live by.

Willingness to Be a Process

The concept of self in the *process of becoming,* as opposed to the concept of self as a *product,* is crucial. Although clients might enter therapy seeking some kind of formula for building a successful and happy state (an end product), they come to realize that growth is a continuing process. Rather than being fixed entities, clients in therapy are in a fluid process of challenging their perceptions and beliefs and opening themselves to new experiences and revisions.

The goals of therapy as just described are broad goals that provide a general framework for understanding the direction of therapeutic movement. The therapist does not choose specific goals for the client. The cornerstone of the client-centered theory is that clients in relationship with a facilitating therapist have the capacity to define and clarify their own goals. Many counselors, however, will experience difficulty in allowing clients to decide for themselves their specific goals in therapy. Although it is easy to give lip service to the concept of clients' finding their own way, it takes considerable respect for clients and courage on the therapist's part to encourage clients to listen to themselves and follow their own directions—particularly when clients make choices that might not be the choices the therapist would hope for.

The Therapist's Function and Role

The role of the client-centered therapist is rooted in his or her ways of being and attitudes, not in the implementation of techniques designed to get the client to "do something." Research on client-centered therapy seems to indicate that the attitudes of the therapist, rather than his or her knowledge, theories, or techniques, initiate personality change in the client. Basically, the therapist uses himself or herself as an instrument of change. By encountering the client on a person-to-person level, the therapist's "role" is to be without roles. The therapist's function is to establish a therapeutic climate that facilitates the client's growth along a process continuum.

The client-centered therapist thus creates a helping relationship in which the client will experience the necessary freedom to explore areas of his or her life that are now either denied to awareness or distorted. The client becomes less defensive and more open to possibilities within himself or herself and in the world.

First and foremost, the therapist must be willing to be real in the relationship with the client. Instead of perceiving the client in preconceived diagnostic categories, the therapist meets the client on a moment-to-moment experiential basis and helps the client by entering the client's world. Through the therapist's attitudes of genuine caring, respect, acceptance, and understanding, the client is able to loosen his or her defenses and rigid perceptions and move to a higher level of personal functioning.

The Client's Experience in Therapy

With the client-centered model, therapeutic change depends on the client's perception both of his or her own experience in therapy and of the counselor's basic attitudes. If the counselor creates a climate conducive to self-exploration, then the client has the opportunity to experience and explore the full range of his or her feelings, many of which may be denied to the client's awareness at the outset of therapy. What follows is a general sketch of the experience of the client in therapy.

The client comes to the counselor in a state of incongruence; that is, a discrepancy exists between the client's self-perception and his or her experience in reality. For example, a college student may see himself as a future physician, and yet most of his grades, which are below average, might exclude him from medical school. The discrepancy between how the client sees himself (self-concept) or how the client would *like* to view himself (ideal-self-concept) and the reality of his poor academic performance might result in anxiety and personal vulnerability, which can provide the necessary motivation to enter therapy. The client must perceive that a problem exists, or at least that he is uncomfortable enough with his present psychological adjustment to want to explore possibilities for change.

Clients initially may expect the counselor to provide answers and direction or view the counselor as the expert who can provide magical solutions. One of the reasons clients seek therapy might be the feeling of basic helplessness, powerlessness, and inability to make decisions or effectively direct their own lives. Clients may hope to find "the way" through the teachings of the therapist. Within the client-centered framework, however, they soon learn that they are responsible for themselves in the relationship and that they can learn to be freer by using the relationship to gain greater self-understanding.

During the beginning stages of therapy, the client's behavior and feelings might be characterized by extremely rigid beliefs and attitudes, much internal blockage, a lack of centeredness, a sense of being out of touch with his or her own feelings, an unwillingness to communicate deeper levels of the self, a fear of intimacy, a basic distrust in the self, a sense of fragmentation, and a tendency to externalize feelings and problems, just to mention a few. In the therapeutic climate created by the counselor, the client is able to explore in a safe and trusting environment the hidden aspects of his or her personal world. The therapist's own realness, unconditional acceptance of the client's feelings, and ability to assume the client's internal frame of reference allow the client gradually to peel away layers of defenses and come to terms with what is behind the facades.

As therapy progresses, the client is able to explore a wider range of his or her feelings. Now the client is able to express fears, anxiety, guilt, shame, hatred, anger, and other feelings that he or she had deemed too negative to accept and incorporate into the self-structure. Now the client constricts less, distorts less, and moves to a greater degree of willingness to accept and integrate some conflicting and confusing feelings related to self. Gradually, the client discovers aspects, negative and positive, of the self that had been kept hidden. The client moves in the direction of being more open to all experience, less defensive, more in contact with what he or she feels at the present moment, less bound by the past, less determined, freer to make decisions, and increasingly trusting in himself or herself to effectively manage his or her own life. In short, the client's experience in therapy is like throwing off the deterministic shackles that had kept him or her in a psychological prison. With increased freedom the client tends to become more mature psychologically and more actualized.

The Relationship between Therapist and Client

Rogers (1961) summarized the basic hypothesis of client-centered therapy in one sentence: "If I can provide a certain type of relationship, the other person will discover within himself the capacity to use that relationship for growth and change, and personal development will occur" (p. 33). Rogers (1967) hypothesized further that "significant positive personality change does not occur except in a relationship" (p. 73).

What are the characteristics of the therapeutic relationship? What are the key attitudes of the client-centered therapist that are conducive to creating a suitable psychological climate in which the client will experience the freedom necessary to initiate personality change? According to Rogers (1967), the following six conditions are necessary and sufficient for personality changes to occur:

1. Two persons are in psychological contact.
2. The first, whom we shall term the client, is in a state of incongruence, being vulnerable or anxious.
3. The second person, whom we shall term the therapist, is congruent or integrated in the relationship.
4. The therapist experiences unconditional positive regard for the client.
5. The therapist experiences an empathic understanding of the client's internal frame of reference and endeavors to communicate this experience to the client.
6. The communication to the client of the therapist's empathic understanding and unconditional positive regard is to a minimal degree achieved [p. 73].

Rogers hypothesizes that no other conditions are necessary. If the six conditions exist over some period of time, then constructive personality change will occur. The conditions do not vary according to client type. Further, they are necessary and sufficient for all approaches to therapy and apply to all personal relationships, not just to psychotherapy. The therapist need not have any specialized knowledge. Accurate psychological diagnosis is not necessary and may more often than not interfere with effective psychotherapy. Rogers admits that his theory is striking and radical. His formulation has generated considerable controversy, for Rogers asserts that many conditions that other therapists commonly regard as necessary for effective psychotherapy are nonessential.

Three personal characteristics, or attitudes, of the therapist that form a central part of the therapeutic relationship, and thus of the therapeutic process, are as follows: (1) congruence, or genuineness, (2) unconditional positive regard, and (3) accurate empathic understanding.

Congruence, or Genuineness

Of the three characteristics, congruence is the most important, according to Rogers' recent writings. Congruence implies that the therapist is real; that is, the therapist is genuine, integrated, and authentic during the therapy hour. He or she is without a false front, his or her inner experience and outer expression of that experience match, and he or she can openly express feelings and attitudes that are present in the relationship with the client. The authentic therapist is spontaneous and openly being the feelings and attitudes, both negative and positive, that flow in him or her. By expressing (and accepting) any negative feelings, the therapist can facilitate honest communication with the client. Through the person-to-person relationship, the therapist works toward his or her own becoming and self-actualization as well as toward the client's growth. Through authenticity the therapist serves as a model of a human being struggling toward greater realness. Being congruent might necessitate the therapist's expression of anger, frustration, liking, attraction, concern, boredom, annoyance, and a range of other feelings in the relationship. This does not mean that the therapist should impulsively share all feelings, for self-disclosure must also be appropriate. Nor does it imply that the client is the cause of the therapist's boredom or anger. The therapist must, however, take responsibility for his or her own feelings and explore with the client persistent feelings that block the therapist's ability to be fully present with the client.

The goal of therapy is not, of course, for the therapist to continually discuss his or her own feelings with the client. Client-centered therapy does, however, stress the value of a nonexploitive, authentic, personal relationship and the potential value of open and honest feedback when meaningful communication is blocked. It also stresses that counseling will be inhibited if the counselor feels one way about the client but acts in a different way. Hence, if the counselor either dislikes or disapproves of the client but feigns acceptance, therapy will not occur.

The concept of therapist congruence does not imply that only a fully self-actualized therapist can be effective in counseling. Since the therapist is human, he or she cannot be expected to be fully authentic. The client-centered model assumes that, if the therapist is congruent in the relationship with the client, then the process of therapy will get under way. Congruence exists on a continuum rather than on an all-or-none basis.

Unconditional Positive Regard

The second attitude that the therapist needs to communicate to the client is a deep and genuine caring for the client as a person. The caring is unconditional in that it is not contaminated by evaluation or judgment of the client's feelings, thoughts, and behavior as good or bad. The therapist values and warmly accepts the client without placing stipulations on the acceptance. It is not an attitude of "I'll accept you when"; rather, it is one of "I'll accept you as you are." The therapist communicates through his or her behavior that he or she values the client as the client is and teaches the client that he or she is free to have his or her own feelings and experiences without risking the loss of the therapist's acceptance. Acceptance is the recognition of the client's right to have feelings; it is not the approval of all behavior. All overt behavior need not be approved or accepted.

It is important also that the therapist's caring be nonpossessive. If the caring stems from the therapist's own needs to be liked and appreciated, the change in the client is inhibited.

The concept of unconditional positive regard does not imply an all-or-none characteristic. Like congruence, unconditional positive regard is a matter of degree on a continuum. The greater the degree of liking, caring, and warmly accepting the client, the greater the opportunity to facilitate change in the client.

Accurate Empathic Understanding

One of the main tasks of the therapist is to understand sensitively and accurately the client's experience and feelings as they are revealed during the moment-to-moment interaction during the therapy session. The therapist strives to sense the client's subjective experience, particularly the here-and-now experience. The aim of empathic understanding is to encourage the client to get closer to himself or herself, to experience feelings more deeply and intensely, and to recognize and resolve the incongruity that exists within the client.

The concept implies the therapist's sensing the client's feelings as if they were his or her own without becoming lost in those feelings. By moving freely in the world as experienced by the client, the therapist not only can communicate to the client an understanding of what is already known to the client but can also voice meanings of experience of which the client is only dimly aware. It is important to understand that high levels of accurate empathy go beyond recognition of obvious feelings to a sense of the less obvious and less clearly experienced feelings of the client. The therapist helps the client expand his or her awareness of feelings that are only partially recognized.

Empathy is more than a mere reflection of feeling. It entails more than reflecting content to the client, and it is more than an artificial technique that the therapist routinely uses. It is not simply objective knowledge ("I understand what your problem is"), which is an evaluative understanding *about* the client from the outside. Instead, empathy is a deep and subjective understanding *of* the client *with* the client. It is a sense of personal identification with the client. The therapist is able to share the client's subjective world by tuning into his or her own feelings that might be like the client's feelings. Yet the therapist must not lose his or her own separateness. Rogers believes that, when the therapist can grasp the present experiencing of the client's private world, as the client sees and feels it, without losing the separateness of his or her own identity, then constructive change is likely to occur.

As do the other two concepts, accurate empathic understanding exists on a continuum; it is not an all-or-nothing matter. The greater the degree of therapist empathy, the greater the chance that the client will move forward in therapy.

Application: Therapeutic Techniques and Procedures

The Place of Techniques in the Client-Centered Approach

Earlier formulations of Rogers' view of psychotherapy placed more stress on techniques. The development of this approach involved a shift of focus away from therapeutic techniques toward the therapist's personhood, beliefs, and attitudes and toward the therapeutic relationship. The therapeutic relationship, then, is the critical variable, not what the therapist says or does. In the client-centered framework, the "techniques" are expressing and communicating acceptance, respect, and understanding and sharing with the client the attempt to develop an internal frame of reference by thinking, feeling, and exploring. As seen from the client-centered approach, the therapist's use of techniques as gimmicks would depersonalize the relationship. The techniques must be an honest expression of the therapist; they cannot be used self-consciously, for then the counselor would not be genuine.

Periods of Development of Client-Centered Therapy

To give the reader an understanding of the place of techniques in the client-centered approach, the following discussion outlines the evolution of Rogers' theory. Hart (1970) divided the periods of development into three phases:

> *Period 1 (1940–1950): Nondirective psychotherapy.* This approach emphasized the therapist's creation of a permissive and noninterventive climate. Acceptance and clarification were the main techniques. Through nondirective therapy the client would achieve insight into himself or herself and into his or her life situation.
> *Period 2 (1950–1957): Reflective psychotherapy.* The therapist mainly reflected the feelings of the client and avoided threat in the relationship. Through reflective therapy the client was able to develop a greater degree of congruence between self-concept and ideal self-concept.
> *Period 3 (1957–1970): Experiential therapy.* The therapist's wide range of behavior to express basic attitudes characterizes this approach. Therapy focuses on the client's experiencing and the expression of the therapist's experiencing. The client grows on a continuum by learning to use immediate experiencing.*

Over the past 30 years client-centered therapy has shifted in the direction of bringing more of the therapist's personhood into the therapeutic process. In the earliest period, the nondirective therapist conspicuously avoided interaction with the client. The therapist functioned as a clarifier but submerged his or her own personhood. During this period directive techniques such as questioning, probing, evaluating, and interpreting and directive procedures such as taking a case history, psychological testing, and diagnosis were not a part of the therapeutic process because they were based on external reference points; client-centered therapy relied mainly on the innate growth urge of the client.

Later, therapy shifted away from the cognitive emphasis to clarification, which was to lead to insight. Characteristic of the period of reflective psychotherapy, the change in the actual practice of psychotherapy was the

*Adapted from Table 1.1 in *New Directions in Client-Centered Therapy,* by J. Hart. Copyright 1970 by Houghton Mifflin Co. Reprinted by permission.

therapist's emphasis on responding sensitively to the affective, rather than semantic, meaning of the client's expression (Hart, 1970, p. 8). The therapist's role was reformulated and elaborated to emphasize his or her responsiveness to the client's feelings. Instead of merely clarifying a client's comments, the therapist reflected feelings. To implement the client's reorganization of self-concepts, the therapist's basic job was to remove sources of threat from the therapeutic relationship and function as a mirror so that the client might better understand his or her own world (Hart, 1970). The therapist as a person was still largely left out of this formulation.

The next transition of experiential therapy emphasized certain "necessary and sufficient" conditions for personality change to occur. This period introduced the crucial elements of the therapist's attitudes of congruence, positive regard and acceptance, and empathic understanding as prerequisites to effective therapy. Then, the focus of the approach shifted from the therapist's reflection of the client's feelings to the therapist's expression of his or her own immediate feelings in relationship with the client. The current formulation allows for a wider range and greater flexibility of therapist behavior, including expressions or opinions, feelings, and so forth that in earlier periods were undesirable.

The focus on the therapist's immediate experiencing leads the therapist to express his or her feelings to the client when appropriate, and it allows the therapist, more than in earlier conceptions of the model, to bring in his or her own personhood. The early formulations of the client-centered view stipulated that the therapist was to refrain from intruding his or her own values and biases into the counseling relationship. The therapist was to forego commonly used procedures such as setting goals, giving advice, interpreting behavior, and selecting topics for exploration. The modern formulation, however, addresses itself less to prohibitions and allows the therapist greater freedom to participate more actively in the relationship in order to create an atmosphere in which the client feels fully received regardless of the techniques or style that a particular therapist employs.

Application to Schools:
The Teaching/Learning Process

The philosophy underlying client-centered theory has direct application to the teaching/learning process. Rogers' interest in the nature of the learning process involved in counseling has also carried over to a concern for what occurs in education. In *Freedom to Learn* (1969), Rogers dealt with issues that are basic to humanistic education and proposed a philosophy for student-centered learning. Basically, this philosophy of education is the same as his view of counseling and therapy, for he believes that the student can be trusted to discover significant problems that are related to the student's existence. The students can become involved in meaningful learning, which can best occur when the teacher creates a climate of freedom and trust. The teacher's function is like that of the client-centered therapist: the teacher's genuineness, openness, honesty, acceptance, understanding, empathy, and willingness to allow students to explore personally meaningful material create the atmosphere in which significant, rather than apparent, learning can occur. Rogers advocates a reformation in education, and he contends that, if even one teacher in 100 would have student-centered classrooms where students were permitted genuine freedom to pursue personally relevant issues, education could be revolutionized in this country.

In my book *Teachers Can Make a Difference* (1973), I examined the key messages that are transmitted to learners within the framework of traditional education. Briefly, the messages so frequently broadcast in a conventional classroom that almost exclusively focuses on content and curriculum include the following:

1. Discover what the teacher wants and strive to please the teacher.
2. Never question the teacher's authority.
3. Learning is the result of external motivation.
4. Learners should always search for the one right answer.
5. Learners should be passive.
6. Learning is a product rather than a process.
7. School learning is separate from living.
8. The self is ignored in education.
9. Learners are objects, not persons.
10. Feelings are not important in education.
11. Teachers ought to keep at a distance from students.
12. Schools teach us to be dishonest.
13. Students are not to be trusted.*

I believe that humanistic education, which is rooted in much of the client-centered approach, is a viable alternative to the sterile results of most conventional education. In my book I describe four "humanistic" teachers, who are unique and work quite differently from one another but who, in addition to teaching concepts and knowledge, share a concern for the development of students' personhood. A teacher who is psychologically oriented can in many ways counsel students, both individually and in groups. Rather than being separated from content learning, counseling can be integrated into the curriculum. Rather than exclude issues related to the self and to the learner's values, experiences, feelings, and real concerns and interests, the teaching/learning process can put the learner in a central place. Unfortunately, many teachers believe that, if education is directed toward the personal development of learners, then content-mastery suffers. On the contrary, much evidence supports the value of a meaningful and personal curriculum that involves issues relevant to the learners. Many critics have charged that traditional learning produces only the illusion of real learning, which soon fades away.

*From *Teachers Can Make a Difference*, by Gerald F. Corey. Copyright 1973 by Charles E. Merrill Publishing Co. Reprinted by permission.

Summary and Evaluation

Client-centered therapy is based on a philosophy of human nature that holds that we have an innate striving for self-actualization. Further, Rogers' view of human nature is phenomenological; that is, one structures oneself according to one's perceptions of reality. One is motivated to actualize oneself in the reality that one perceives.

Rogers' theory is based on the postulate that the client possesses within himself or herself the capacity to understand the factors in his or her life that are causing unhappiness. The client also has the capacity for self-direction and constructive personal change. Personal change will occur if a congruent therapist is able to establish with the client a relationship characterized by warmth, acceptance, and accurate empathic understanding. Therapeutic counseling is based on an I-thou, or person-to-person, relationship in the safety and acceptance of which the client drops his or her rigid defenses and comes to accept and integrate into his or her self-system aspects that he or she formerly denied or distorted.

Client-centered therapy places the primary responsibility for the direction of therapy on the client. The general goals are: becoming more open to experience, trusting in one's organism, developing an internal locus of evaluation and a willingness to become a process, and in other ways moving toward higher levels of self-actualization. The therapist does not impose specific goals and values on the client; the client decides on his or her own specific values and life goals.

The client-centered model is not a fixed theory. Rogers intended to develop a set of working principles that could be stated in the form of tentative hypotheses regarding the conditions facilitating personal growth. This is an open system, one that, after 30 years, is still in evolution. Formulations continue to be revised in light of new research findings.

The client-centered approach emphasizes the personal relationship between client and therapist; the therapist's attitudes are more critical than techniques, knowledge, or theory. If the therapist demonstrates and communicates to the client that the therapist is (1) a congruent person, (2) warmly and unconditionally accepting of the feelings and personhood of the client, and (3) able to sensitively and accurately perceive the internal world as the client perceives it, then the client will use this relationship to unleash his or her growth potential and become more of the person he or she chooses to become.

The Contributions of the Client-Centered Approach

Perhaps one of the dominant modes used in counselor education is the client-centered approach. One reason for this is its built-in safety features. It emphasizes active listening, respecting the client, adopting the internal frame of reference of the client, and staying with the client as opposed to getting ahead of the client with interpretations. Client-centered therapists typically reflect content and feelings, clarify messages, help clients to muster their own resources, and encourage clients to find their own solutions. Hence, this approach is far safer than many models of therapy that put the therapist in the directive position of making interpretations, forming diagnoses, probing the unconscious, analyzing dreams, and working toward more radical personality changes. For a person with limited background in counseling psychology, personality dynamics, and psychopathology, the client-centered approach offers more realistic assurance that prospective clients will not be psychologically harmed.

The client-centered approach contributes in other ways to both individual and group counseling situations. It offers a humanistic base from which to understand the subjective world of clients. It provides clients the rare opportunity to be really listened to and heard. Further, if clients feel that they are heard, they most likely will express their feelings in their own ways. They can be themselves, since they know that they will not be evaluated or judged. They can feel free to experiment with new behavior. They are expected to take responsibility for themselves, and it is *they* who set the pace in counseling. They decide what areas they wish to explore, on the basis of their own goals for change. The client-centered approach provides the client with immediate and specific feedback of what he or she has just communicated. The counselor acts as a mirror, reflecting the deeper feelings of a client. Thus the client has the possibility of gaining sharper focus and deeper meaning to aspects of his or her self-structure that were previously only partially known to him or her. The client's attention is focused on many things that he or she has not attended to before. The client is thus able to increasingly own his or her total experiencing.

Another major contribution to the field of psychotherapy has been Rogers' willingness to state his formulations as testable hypotheses and to submit his hypotheses to research efforts. Even his critics give Rogers credit for having conducted and inspired others to conduct the most extensive research on counseling process and outcome of any school of psychotherapy. Rogers' theory of therapy and personality change have had tremendous heuristic effect, and, though much controversy surrounds this approach, Rogers' work has challenged practitioners and theoreticians to examine their own therapeutic styles and beliefs.

Client-centered therapy has not been confined to one-to-one psychotherapy. Rogers indicates that his theory has had implications for education, business, industry, and international relations. Rogers devoted considerable effort to the group-counseling movement and is one of the fathers of the "basic encounter group" (Rogers, 1970). He has long been interested in student-centered teaching and has pioneered humanistic education (Rogers, 1969). His efforts contributed to the establishment of the Association for Humanistic Psychology. Clearly, the client-centered approach has implications for psychotherapy, for training mental-health workers and paraprofessionals, for family living, and for all interpersonal relationships (Rogers, 1961).

The Limitations of Client-Centered Therapy

A vulnerability of the client-centered approach lies in the manner in which some practitioners misinterpret or simplify the central attitudes of the client-centered position. Not all counselors can practice client-centered therapy, for some do not really believe in the underlying philosophy. Many of Rogers' followers have attempted to be carbon copies of Rogers himself and have misunderstood some of Rogers' basic concepts. They limit their own range of responses and counseling styles to reflections and empathic listening. Surely there is value in listening to and really hearing a client and in reflecting and communicating understanding to the client. But psychotherapy is, one hopes, more than this. Perhaps listening and reflecting constitute a requisite for establishing a therapeutic relationship, but they should not be confused with therapy itself.

One limitation of the approach is the way some practitioners become "client centered" and lose a sense of their own personhood and uniqueness. Paradoxically, the counselor may focus on the client to such an extent that he or she diminishes the value of his or her own power as a person and thus loses the impact and influence of his or her personality on the client. The therapist may highlight the needs and purposes of the client, and yet at the same time feel free to bring his or her own personality into the therapeutic hour.

Thus one must be cautioned that this approach is something more than merely a listening and reflecting technique. It is based on a set of attitudes that the therapist brings to the relationship, and, more than any other quality, the therapist's genuineness determines the power of the therapeutic relationship. If the therapist submerges his or her unique identity and style in a passive and nondirective way, he or she may not be harming many clients but also may not be really affecting clients in a positive way. Therapist authenticity and congruence are so vitally related to this approach that the therapist who practices within this framework must feel natural in doing so and must find a way to express his or her own reactions to clients. If not, a real possibility is that client-centered therapy would be reduced to a bland, safe, and ineffectual mode of working with clients.

Questions for Evaluation

Client-centered therapy is rooted in assumptions regarding the capacities of the client and the basic attitudes of the therapist. One real problem with the approach is that therapists sometimes give lip service to the basic concepts of the client-centered approach, but, because they do not deeply believe in some of these attitudes, their behavior as therapists reflects a conception different from their philosophy of counseling. What follows are some questions designed to help you test and challenge the degree to which you accept a client-centered philosophy and thus would be able genuinely to incorporate it into your own counseling practice.

1. The relationship that the therapist creates with the client is the cornerstone of client-centered therapy. Do you accept Rogers' "necessary and sufficient" conditions for therapeutic change? Is it enough that the therapist have unconditional positive regard for the client, possess an accurate empathic understanding, and be genuine in the relationship? Do you believe that other therapeutic procedures and techniques might be essential for change to occur?
2. Do you think that diagnosis and case history are important prerequisites for therapy? Could you proceed without having information about the client? Do you think that gathering data on the client's past experiences is useful?
3. Would you want to interpret the meaning of your client's behavior, or would you let the client form his or her own meanings?
4. Might you feel compelled to give your own opinions or even to persuade your client to a certain action? Might you strongly suggest certain activities if you really believed they were in your client's best interest? Would you want to give advice?
5. Would you be able to refrain from making value judgments if your client had a life-style that was radically different from yours? What if your client's values and beliefs contradicted your own?
6. Would you be able to accept your client? What would you do if you did not feel accepting of a certain person? Do you see any conflict between the concepts of genuineness and acceptance?
7. How congruent or real could you be if you withheld your own values, feelings, and attitudes from your client? If you feel like making suggestions but refrain from doing so, are you being inauthentic?
8. What factors might interfere with your being genuine with a client? What about your need for the client's approval? Is there a danger that you might avoid a confrontation because you want to be liked?
9. What within yourself might make accurate empathic understanding difficult for you? Do you have broad enough life experiences that will help you identify with your client's struggles?
10. Can you empathize with clients and understand their subjective worlds without losing your own separateness and overidentifying with them?

References and Suggested Readings

*Axline, V. *Dibs: In search of self.* New York: Ballantine Books, 1964.

Carkhuff, R., & Berenson, B. *Beyond counseling and therapy.* New York: Holt, Rinehart and Winston, 1967.

*Corey, G. *Teachers can make a difference.* Columbus, Ohio: Merrill, 1973.

*Evans, R. *Carl Rogers: The man and his ideas.* New York: Dutton, 1975.

Hart, J., & Tomlinson, T. *New directions in client-centered therapy.* New York: Houghton Mifflin, 1970.

Jourard, S. *The transparent self* (Rev. ed.). New York: Van Nostrand Reinhold, 1971.

Martin, D. G. *Introduction to psychotherapy*. Monterey, Cal.: Brooks/Cole, 1971.

*Martin, D. G. *Learning-based client-centered therapy*. Monterey, Cal.: Brooks/Cole, 1972.

*Nye, R. *Three views of man*. Monterey, Cal.: Brooks/Cole, 1975.

Patterson, C. H. *Theories of counseling and psychotherapy* (2nd ed.). New York: Harper & Row, 1973.

Rogers, C. *Counseling and psychotherapy*. Boston: Houghton Mifflin, 1942.

Rogers, C. *Client-centered therapy*. Boston: Houghton Mifflin, 1951.

*Rogers, C. *On becoming a person*. Boston: Houghton Mifflin, 1961.

Rogers, C. The conditions of change from a client-centered viewpoint. In B. Berenson & R. Carkhuff (Eds.), *Sources of gain in counseling and psychotherapy*. New York: Holt, Rinehart and Winston, 1967.

*Rogers, C. *Freedom to learn*. Columbus, Ohio: Merrill, 1969.

*Rogers, C. *On encounter groups*. New York: Harper & Row, 1970.

Rogers, C. *Becoming partners: Marriage and its alternatives*. New York: Delacorte, 1972.

Rogers, C., & Meador, B. Client-centered therapy. In R. Corsini (Ed.), *Current psychotherapies*. Itasca, Ill.: Peacock, 1973.

Rogers, C., & Wood, J. Client-centered theory: Carl Rogers. In A. Burton (Ed.), *Operational theories of personality*. New York: Brunner/Mazel, 1974.

CHAPTER FIVE

GESTALT

THERAPY

Introduction

Developed by Frederick Perls, Gestalt therapy is a form of existential therapy based on the premise that individuals must find their own ways in life and accept personal responsibility if they hope to achieve maturity. As it works mainly on the principle of awareness, the Gestalt approach focuses attention on the *what* and *how* of behavior and experience in the here-and-now by integrating the fragmented and unknown parts of personality.

The basic assumption of Gestalt therapy is that individuals can themselves deal effectively with their life problems. The central task of the therapist is to assist clients toward fully experiencing their being in the here-and-now by helping them become aware of how they prevent themselves from feeling and experiencing in the present. Therefore, the approach is basically noninterpretive, and, as much as possible, clients carry out their own therapy. They make their own interpretations, create their own direct statements, and find their own meanings. Finally, clients are encouraged to experience directly in the here-and-now their struggles with unfinished business from their past. By experiencing their conflicts instead of merely talking about them, they gradually expand their own levels of awareness.

Key Concepts

View of Human Nature

The Gestalt view of human nature is rooted in existential philosophy and phenomenology. It stresses concepts such as expanding awareness, accepting personal responsibility, the unity of the person, and experiencing the ways that awareness is blocked. In its therapy, the approach focuses on the restoration of awareness and on integrating the polarities and dichotomies within the self. Therapy aims not at analysis but at integration, which proceeds step-by-step in therapy until the client becomes strong enough to facilitate his or her own personal growth.

The Gestalt view is that the individual has the capacity to assume personal responsibility and live fully as an integrated person. Because of certain problems in development, the individual forms various ways of avoiding a problem and, therefore, reaches an impasse in his or her personal growth. Therapy provides the necessary intervention and challenge that help the individual gain knowledge and awareness as he or she proceeds toward integration and growth. As the individual recognizes and experiences blocks to maturity, his or her awareness of the blocks increases, and he or she can then muster the potential for a more authentic and vital existence.

The Now

For Perls, nothing exists except the "now." Since the past is gone and the future has not yet arrived, only the present is significant. One of the main contributions of the Gestalt approach is its emphasis on the here-and-now and on learning to appreciate and experience fully the present moment. Focusing on the past is viewed as one way of avoiding coming to terms with the full experience of the present.

In speaking of the "now ethos," Polster and Polster (1973) developed the thesis that "power is in the present." Their view is that "a most difficult truth to teach is that only the present exists now and that to stray from it distracts from the living quality of reality" (p. 7). For so many people the power of the present is lost; instead of being in the present moment, they invest their energies in bemoaning their past mistakes and ruminating about how life could and should have been different, or they engage in endless resolutions and plans for the future. As they direct their energy toward what was or what might have been, their capacity to capitalize on the power of the present diminishes.

Perls (1969a) described anxiety as "the gap between the now and the later." According to Perls, when individuals stray from the present and become preoccupied with the future, they experience anxiety. In thinking of the future they might experience "stage fright," for they become filled with "catastrophic expectations of the bad things that will happen or anastrophic expectations about the wonderful things that will happen" (p. 30). Rather than living in the now, they attempt to fill the gap between the now and the later with resolutions, plans, and visions.

To help the client make contact with the present moment, the Gestaltist asks "what" and "how" questions but rarely asks "why" questions. In order to promote "now" awareness, the therapist encourages a dialogue in the present tense by asking such questions as: What is happening now? What is going on now? What are you experiencing as you sit there and attempt to talk? What is your awareness at this moment? How are you experiencing your fear? How are you attempting to withdraw at this moment? Perls (1969a) contended that without an intensification of feelings the person would speculate *why* he or she felt this way. According to Perls, "why" questions lead only toward rationalizations and "self-deceptions" and away from the immediacy of experiencing. "Why" questions lead to an endless and heady rumination about the past that only serves to encourage resistance to present experience.

The Gestalt therapist actively points out how easily clients can escape from the now into the past or the future. Most people can stay in the present for only a short while. They are inclined to find ways of interrupting the flow of the present. Instead of experiencing their feelings in the here-and-now, they often *talk about* their feelings, almost as if their feelings were detached from their present experiencing. Perls' aim was to help persons make contact with their experience with vividness and immediacy rather than merely talk about the experience. Thus if a client begins to talk about sadness, pain, or confusion, the therapist makes every attempt to have the client experience that sadness, pain, or confusion *now*. Talking about problems can become an endless word game that leads to unproductive discussion and exploration of hidden meanings. It is one way of resisting growth and also a way of engaging in self-deception; clients attempt to trick themselves into believing that, because they are facing their problems and talking about them, they are resolving their problems and growing as persons. To lessen the danger of this, attempts are made to intensify and exaggerate certain feelings. Thus, in a group setting, for example, the therapist may ask a client who reports how conscious he or she is of pleasing others and meeting others' expectations to strive at that very moment to please each person in the group.

Is the past ignored in the Gestalt approach? It is not accurate to say that Gestaltists have no interest in a person's past; the past is important when it is related in some way to significant themes in the individual's present functioning. When the past seems to have a significant bearing on one's present attitudes or behavior, it is dealt with by bringing it into the present as much as possible. Thus, when clients speak about their pasts, the therapist asks them to bring the past into the now by reenacting it as though they were living it now. The therapist directs clients to "be there" in fantasy and to relive some of the feelings they experienced earlier. For example, rather than talking *about* a past childhood trauma with his or her father, the client becomes that hurt child and talks directly to the father in fantasy and, it is hoped, relives and reexperiences that hurt.

Perls believes that individuals tend to hang onto the past in order to justify their unwillingness to take responsibility for themselves and their growth. They play blaming games to discount their own responsibility. He sees most persons as having a difficult time in staying in the now. They get caught up in a whirl by making resolutions and by rationalizing their half-dead state. They would rather do anything than become conscious of how they prevent themselves from being fully alive.

Unfinished Business

In Gestalt theory a key concept is unfinished business, which generally involves unexpressed feelings such as resentment, rage, hatred, pain, anxiety, grief, guilt, abandonment, and so on. Even though the feelings are unexpressed, they are associated with distinct memories and fantasies. Because the feelings are not fully experienced in awareness, they linger in the background and are carried into present life in ways that interfere with effective contact with oneself and others. Unfinished business persists until the individual faces and deals with the unexpressed feelings. In speaking of the effects of unfinished business, Polster and Polster (1973) maintained that "These incomplete directions *do seek* completion and when they get powerful enough, the individual is beset with preoccupation, compulsive behavior, wariness, oppressive energy and much self-defeating behavior" (p. 36).

An example of how unfinished business nags at one and manifests itself in current behavior can be seen in the man who never really felt loved and accepted by his mother. He might develop resentment for his mother, for no matter how he sought her approval he was always left feeling that he was not adequate. In an attempt to deflect the direction of this need for maternal approval, he might look to women for his confirmation of worth as a man. In developing a variety of games to get women to approve of him, he reports that he is still not satisfied. The unfinished business has prevented him from authentic intimacy with women. His behavior thus becomes a compulsive search for the love that he never received from his mother. He needs to experience closure of the unfinished business before he can experience real satisfaction—that is, he needs to return to the old business and express his unacknowledged feelings.

How does unfinished business hamper a person's creativity and spontaneity? Polster and Polster (1973) indicated how unfinished business interrupts a spontaneous flow:

> Whenever unfinished business forms the center of one's existence, one's effervescence of mind becomes hampered. Ideally, the unencumbered person is free to engage spontaneously with whatever interests him and to stay with it until this lively interest subsides and something else draws his attention. This is a natural process and a person who lives according to this rhythm experiences himself as flexible, clear, and effective. [p. 37].

According to Polster and Polster, two polar hindrances interfere with the process. One is an obsession or compulsion that leads to a rigid need to complete unfinished business. The other is the grasshopper experience, wherein the focus is so fleeting that any closure is prevented.

Unacknowledged feelings create unnecessary emotional debris that clutter present-centered awareness. According to Perls (1969a), resentment is the most frequent source and the worst kind of unfinished business. In his view, when people are resentful they become stuck, for they can neither let go nor engage in authentic communication until they express the resentment. Thus Perls contended that it is imperative to express resentments. Unexpressed resentment frequently converts to guilt. Perls' advice is "Whenever you feel guilty, find out what you are resenting and express it and make your demands explicit" (p. 49).

The Therapeutic Process

Therapeutic Goals

Gestalt therapy has several different important aims. A basic aim is to challenge the client to move from "environmental support" to "self-support." According to Perls (1969a), the aim of therapy is "to make the patient *not* depend upon others, but to make the patient discover from the very first moment that he can do many things, *much* more than he thinks he can do" (p. 29).

In keeping with the existential-humanistic spirit, Perls believes that the average person uses only a fraction of his or her potential. This view is like Maslow's concept of the "psychopathology of the average": our lives are patterned and stereotyped; we play the same roles again and again and find very few ways to really reinvent our existence. Perls contends that, if we find out how we prevent ourselves from realizing the full measure of our human potential, we have ways to make life richer. This potential is based on the attitude of living each moment freshly. A major goal of therapy, therefore, is to help the client live a fuller life.

The goal of Gestalt therapy is *not* adjustment to society. Perls considers the basic personality in our time to be neurotic because, as he believes, we are living in an insane society. He sees that we have a choice of becoming part of the collective sickness or taking the risks of becoming healthy. A goal of therapy then is to help each individual find his or her center within. Perls (1969a) said "If you are centered in yourself, then you don't adjust any more—then, whatever happens becomes a passing parade and you assimilate, you understand, and you are related to whatever happens" (p. 30).

An underlying aim of Gestalt therapy is the attaining of awareness. Awareness, by and of itself, is seen as curative. Without awareness, clients do not possess the tools for personality change. With awareness, they have the capacity to face and accept denied parts of their beings and to get in touch with subjective experiences and with reality. Clients can become unified and whole. When clients are aware, their most important unfinished business will always emerge so that it can be dealt with in therapy.

The Function and Role of the Therapist

Gestalt therapy focuses on the client's feelings, awareness at the moment, body messages, and blocks to awareness. Perls' dictum is to "lose your mind and come to your senses."

Gestalt therapy is being in touch with the obvious, according to Perls (1969a), who contended that the neurotic does not see the obvious: "He doesn't see the pimple on his nose" (p. 38). Thus the therapist's job is to challenge clients. In this way clients learn to use their senses fully. They can avoid the obvious or they can be open to what is there now. Perls believes that the total being of a person is before the therapist. Gestalt therapy uses the eyes and ears of the therapist to stay in the now. The therapist avoids abstract intellectualization, diagnosis, interpretation, and excessive verbiage. On the issue of the simplicity of Gestalt therapy, Polster and Polster (1973) agree with Perls. They point out that interpretations and clever diagnoses are not necessary and that what is crucial is to provide a climate where the clients tap their own developmental processes and become more clearly focused on their changing awareness from moment to moment.

> Life *is* as plain as the nose on your face when you are willing to stay with that which is presently clear, moving from one moment of actual experience to the next, discovering something new in each, something which moves forward, developing the theme of its own movement and culminating in illuminations which were inaccessible in the beginning [p. 46].

Although the Gestalt approach is concerned with the obvious, the simplicity of the approach should not be taken to mean that the Gestalt therapist's job is easy. In my judgment, one vulnerability of the approach is the danger of slipping into an impersonal and technical role whereby the therapists hide their own personhood from clients and become directors of endless exercises and games. If therapists do not use their personhood as an instrument of therapeutic change, then they become little more than responders, catalysts, and technicians who play therapeutic games with clients. Developing a variety of Gestalt gimmicks is easy, but employing the techniques in a mechanical fashion is another way that allows the clients to continue inauthentic living. If clients are to become authentic, they need contact with an authentic therapist.

Polster and Polster (1973, pp. 18–22) discussed the concept of the "therapist as his own instrument." Like artists who need to be in touch with what they are painting, the therapist is an "artistic participant in the creation of new life." Polster and Polster implore the therapist to use his or her own experience as an essential ingredient in the therapy process. According to them, therapists are more than mere responders, givers of feedback, or catalysts that do not change themselves. The data of the therapeutic encounter are grounded in the mutual experiences of both the client and the therapist. If therapists are to function effectively, they must be in tune with the persons before them, and they must also be in tune with themselves. Thus therapy is a two-way engagement on a genuine I-Thou basis. Not only does the client change but so does the therapist. If the therapist is not sensitively tuned in to his or her own qualities of tenderness, toughness, and compassion and to reactions to the client, then "he becomes a technician, ministering to another person and not living the therapy with the full flavor that is available."

How does Gestalt therapy proceed, and what are the functions of the therapist in the process? What follows are Perls' (1969a) key ideas about the role of the therapist. To begin with, the therapist's aim is the client's maturation and the removal of "blocks that prevent a person from standing on his own feet." The therapist's job is to help the client make the transition from external to internal support, and this is done by locating the impasse. The impasse is the point at which individuals avoid experiencing threatening feelings because they feel uncomfortable. It is a resistance to facing one's self and to changing. People often express resistance by saying "I feel frustrated—like I'm spinning my wheels and getting nowhere"; "I don't know where to go from here"; "I can't do thus and so"; "I feel stuck." According to Perls, people experience "being stuck" because of their "catastrophic expectations." They imagine that something terrible will occur. Their catastrophic fantasies prevent them from fully living, and, because of their unreasonable fears, they refuse to take the necessary risks for becoming more mature. Typically, "catastrophic expectations" take the form of statements such as "If I am a certain way, or have certain feelings, then I won't be loved, or accepted, or approved of. I'll be stupid. I'll perish. I'll feel like a fool. I'll be abandoned."

At the moment of impasse, clients attempt to maneuver their environments by playing phony roles of weakness, helplessness, stupidity, and foolishness. The therapist's task is to help clients get through the impasse so that growth is possible. This is a difficult task, for at the point of impasse clients believe that they have no chance of survival and that they won't find the means for survival within. The therapist assists clients in recognizing and working through the impasse by providing situations that encourage clients to experience fully their conditions of being stuck. By fully experiencing the blockage, clients are able to get into contact with their frustrations. Perls believes that frustration is essential for growth, for without frustration persons have no need to muster their own resources and to discover that they can well do on their own what they are manipulating others to do for them. If the therapist is not careful, he or she too will be sucked into the client's manipulations.

Perls (1969a, p. 36) shows that the way to keep from being manipulated by clients is to let them find their own missing potentials. Clients use the therapist as a "projection screen" and look to the therapist to provide them with what they think is missing in themselves. Perls maintains that all people have "holes" in their personalities. Clients' holes might include their giving up their eyes or ears; instead of doing their own seeing and hearing, they look to others to do their seeing and hearing for them. According to Perls (1969a, p. 37) the holes are apparent. The therapist, then, must provide a situation for growth to occur by confronting clients to the point that they face a decision of whether or not they will develop their potentials. Frustration results in the discovery that the impasse doesn't exist in reality but only in fantasy. Clients have persuaded themselves that they don't have the resources to cope, and, out of their fears of "catastrophic expectations," they prevent themselves from utilizing their resources. When they face and work through their fears, their neurotic anxiety converts to a sense of positive excitement. As Perls (1969a) put it, "We apply enough skillful frustration so that the patient is forced to find his own way, discover that *what he expects from the therapist, he can do just as well himself*" (p. 37).

An important function of the Gestalt therapist is paying attention to the client's body language. The client's nonverbal cues provide the therapist with rich information, since they often betray feelings of which the client is unaware. Perls (1969a) says that a client's posture, movements, gestures, voice, hesitations, and so on tell the real story. He warns that verbal communication is usually a lie and that if therapists are content-oriented they miss the essence of the person. Real communication is beyond words. "The sounds tell you everything. Everything a person wants to express is all there—not in words. What we say is mostly either lies or bullshit. But the voice is there, the gesture, the posture, the facial expression, the psychosomatic language" (p. 54).

Thus the therapist needs to be alert to splits in attention and awareness, and he or she needs to watch for incongruities between verbalizations and what the clients are doing with their bodies. Clients demonstrate from moment to moment how they avoid being in full contact with their present-centered actuality. Thus the therapist might direct clients to speak for and become their gestures or body parts. Gestaltists often ask: What do your eyes say? If your hands could speak at this moment what would they say? Can you carry on a conversation between your right and left hands? Clients might verbally express anger and at the same time smile. Or they may state that they are in pain and at the same time laugh. The therapist could ask them to recognize that their laughter covers up their pain. Clients might be asked to become aware of how they use their laughter to mask feelings of anger or pain. Attention to the messages that clients send nonverbally are grist for the mill, and the therapist needs to focus on the nonverbal cues.

The Client's Experience in Therapy

Perls (1969a) expresses his skepticism about those who seek therapy and indicates that not very many people really want to invest themselves in the hard work involved in changing. As he points out, "Anybody who goes to a therapist has something up his sleeve. I would say roughly ninety percent don't go to a therapist to be cured, but to be more adequate in their neurosis. If they are power mad, they want to get more power. If they are intellectual, they want to have more elephantshit. If they are ridiculers, they want to have a sharper wit to ridicule, and so on" (p. 75).

Although Perls may sound pessimistic, not all clients want only the "improvement of their neurosis." Clients in the Gestalt therapeutic experience decide for themselves what they want and how much they want. Perls' caution can be used in confrontation with clients to help them examine how much change they really desire. I believe that, if clients have the courage to honestly face the issue that all they may want is to improve their manipulative skills, there is a greater chance that they might use therapy productively for something other than supporting the status quo of their defense systems. Thus one of the first of the clients' responsibilities is to decide what they want for themselves from therapy. If they state that they are confused and don't know or if they attempt to have the therapist decide goals for them, then this is a place to begin. The therapist can explore with clients their avoidance of accepting this responsibility.

The general orientation of Gestalt therapy is toward the clients' assumption of more and more responsibility for themselves—for their thoughts, feelings, and behavior. The therapist confronts clients with the ways in which they are now avoiding their personal responsibilities and asks them to make decisions about continuing therapy, about what they wish to learn from it, and about how they want to use their therapy time. Other issues that can become the focal point of therapy might include the relationship between the client and the therapist and the ways clients relate similarly to the therapist and to others in their outside environments. Clients in Gestalt, then, are the active participants who make their own interpretations and meanings. It is they who achieve increasing awareness and decide what they will or will not do with their personal learning.

The Relationship between Therapist and Client

As an existential brand of therapy, effective Gestalt practice involves a person-to-person relationship between the therapist and the client. The therapist's experiences, awareness, and perceptions provide the background while the client's awareness and reactions constitute the forefront of the therapy process. It is important that the therapist actively share his or her own present perceptions and experiences as he or she encounters clients in the here-and-now. Further, the therapist gives feedback, particularly as it relates to what clients are doing with their bodies. Feedback gives clients tools to develop awareness of what they are actually doing. The therapist must encounter clients with honest and immediate reactions and they must challenge clients' manipulations without rejecting the clients as persons. The therapist needs to explore with clients their fears, catastrophic expectations, blockages, and resistances.

Perls (1969a), Polster and Polster (1973), and Kempler (1973) all emphasize the importance of the therapist's personhood, not merely the acquisition of techniques, as the vital ingredient in the therapy process. Perls (1969a, p. 1) objects to people using techniques as gimmicks that prevent growth and become a brand of "phony therapy." Polster and Polster (1973, pp. 18–23) caution that, if the therapist ignores his or her personal qualities as an instrument in therapy, he or she becomes a mere technician. They encourage a wide range of behavior on the therapist's part and warn of the dangers of becoming identified with a limited range of techniques. They call on the therapist to tap his or her spontaneity and draw on the relationship with the client for therapeutic technique. Kempler (1973) considers the actual

relationship between the client and the therapist as the core of the therapeutic process, and he cautions against the "use of tactics which might obscure
the real identity of the therapist to his patient" (p. 261). Kempler contends
that the use of role-playing can be a temptation for the therapist to keep his
or her personal responses hidden. Although role-playing might be an effective means, it is not the end of therapy. He asserts that techniques are often
valuable as adjuncts to the therapeutic process but puts the emphasis on the
process of the client-therapist relationship, for it is the quality of their relationship that determines what happens to both of them.

Application: Therapeutic Techniques and Procedures

Techniques of Gestalt Therapy

In the preceding section I stressed that Gestalt therapy consists of
more than a collection of techniques and "games." Whereas the personal
interaction between the therapist and the client is the core of the therapeutic
process, however, techniques can be useful tools to help the client gain fuller
awareness, experience internal conflicts, resolve inconsistencies and dichotomies, and work through an impasse that prevents completion of unfinished business. The following Gestalt techniques are presented in the
style that is personally fitting to the therapist.

Levitsky and Perls (1970, pp. 144–149) provide a brief description of a
number of games that can be used in Gestalt therapy, including (1) games of
dialogue, (2) making the rounds, (3) unfinished business, (4) "I take responsibility," (5) "I have a secret," (6) playing the projection, (7) reversals, (8) the
rhythm of contact and withdrawal, (9) "rehearsal," (10) "exaggeration," (11)
"May I feed you a sentence?" (12) marriage-counseling games, and (13) "Can
you stay with this feeling?" The discussion of the following Gestalt
techniques is based on the games described by Levitsky and Perls (1970),
although I have modified the material and added suggestions for implementing these techniques.

The Game of Dialogue

As was mentioned earlier, a goal of Gestalt therapy is to effect integrated functioning and the acceptance of aspects of one's personality that
have been disowned and denied. Gestalt therapists pay close attention to
splits in personality function. A main division is between the "top dog" and
the "underdog." Often therapy focuses on the war between the top dog and
the underdog.

The top dog is righteous, authoritarian, moralistic, demanding, bossy,
and manipulative. This is the "critical parent" that badgers with "shoulds"
and "oughts" and manipulates with threats of catastrophe. The underdog
manipulates by playing the role of victim, by being defensive, apologetic,

helpless, and weak, and by playing powerless. This is the passive side, the one without responsibility, and the one that finds excuses. The top dog and the underdog are engaged in a constant struggle for control. The struggle helps to explain why one's resolutions and promises often go unfulfilled and why one's procrastination persists. The tyrannical top dog demands that one be thus-and-so while the underdog defiantly plays the role of disobedient child. As a result of this struggle for control, the individual becomes fragmented into controller and controlled. The civil war between the two sides is never really complete, for both sides are fighting for their existence.

The conflict between the two opposing poles in the personality is rooted in the mechanism of introjection, which involves incorporating aspects of another, usually parents, into one's ego system. Perls implies that the taking in of values and traits is both inevitable and desirable; the danger is in the uncritical and wholesale acceptance of another's values as one's own, which makes becoming an autonomous person difficult. It is essential that one become aware of one's introjects, especially the toxic introjects that poison the system and prevent personality integration.

The empty-chair technique is one way of getting the client to externalize the introject. In this technique two chairs are placed in the center of the room. The therapist asks the client to sit in one chair and be fully the top dog and then to shift to the other chair and become the underdog. The dialogue can continue between both sides of the client. Essentially, empty-chair is a role-playing technique, whereby all the parts are played by the client. In this way the introjects can surface, and the client can experience the conflict more fully. The conflict can be resolved by the client's acceptance and integration of both sides. This technique helps the client get in touch with a feeling or a side of himself or herself that he or she might be denying; rather than merely talking about a conflicted feeling, the client intensifies the feeling and experiences it fully. Further, by helping clients realize that the feeling is a very real part of themselves, the technique discourages clients from disassociating the feeling. The technique can help clients identify distasteful parental introjects. For example, a client might say "That sounds exactly like my father in me!" Parental introjections can keep a "self-torture" game alive as the client swallows parental injunctions and uses them to punish and control himself or herself.

The dialogues between opposing tendencies have as their aim the promotion of a higher level of integration between the polarities and conflicts that exist in everyone. The aim is not to rid oneself of certain traits but to learn to accept and live with the polarities. Perls believes that other therapeutic approaches place too much emphasis on change. He contended that change cannot be forced but that, through the acceptance of polarities, an integration can occur and the client can stop the badgering self-torture game. There are many examples of common conflicts that lend themselves to the game of dialogue. Some common conflicts that I find applicable to the dialogue approach include (1) the parent inside versus the child inside, (2) the responsible one versus the impulsive one, (3) the puritanical side versus the sexy side, (4) the "good boy" versus the "bad boy," (5) the aggressive self versus the passive self, and (6) the autonomous side versus the resentful side.

The dialogue technique can be used in both individual and group counseling. Let me describe one example of a common conflict between the top dog and underdog that I have found to be a powerful agent in helping a client become more intensely aware of the internal split and of which side would become dominant. The client, in this case a woman, plays the weak, helpless, dependent game of "poor me." She complains that she is miserable and that she hates and resents her husband, yet she fears that if he leaves her she will disintegrate. She uses him as the excuse for her impotence. She continually puts herself down, always saying "I can't," "I don't know how," "I am not capable." If she decides that she is miserable enough to want to change her dependent style, I'd probably ask her to sit on one chair in the center of the room and become fully the underdog martyr and to exaggerate this side of herself. Eventually, if she got disgusted with this side, I'd ask her to be the other side—that is, the top-dog side that puts her down—and talk to the "poor me." Then I might ask her to pretend that she is powerful, strong, and independent and to act as if she weren't helpless. I might ask "What would happen if you were strong and independent and if you gave up your clinging dependency?" That technique can often energize clients into really experiencing the roles they continue to play, the result frequently being the reinvention of the autonomous aspects of self.

Making the Rounds

Making the rounds is a Gestalt exercise that involves requesting a person in a group to make the rounds to others in the group and either speak to or do something with each person. The purpose of the technique is to confront, to risk, and to disclose the self, to experiment with new behavior, and to grow and change. I have employed the technique when I've sensed that a participant needs to face each person in the group with some theme. For example, a group member might say "I've been sitting here for a long time wanting to participate but holding back because I'm afraid of trusting people in here. And besides, I don't think I'm worth the time of the group anyway." I might counter with "Are you willing to do something right now to get yourself more invested and to begin to work on gaining trust and self-confidence?" If the person answers affirmatively, my suggestion could well be "Go around to each person and finish this sentence: I don't trust you because. . . ." Any number of exercises could be invented to help the individual involve himself or herself and choose to work on the things that keep him or her frozen in fear.

Some other related illustrations and examples that I find appropriate for the "making the rounds" technique are reflected in clients' comments such as "I would like to reach out to people more often"; "I'm bored by what's going on in this group"; "Nobody in here seems to care very much"; "I'd like to make contact with you, but I'm afraid of being rejected (or accepted)"; "It's hard for me to accept good stuff. I always discount good things people say to me"; "It's hard for me to say negative things to people. I want to be nice always"; "I'd like to feel more comfortable in touching and getting close."

The Exercise of "I Take Responsibility for . . ."

In this game, the therapist asks the client to make a statement and then add "and I take responsibility for it." Some examples are "I'm feeling bored, and I take responsibility for my boredom"; "I'm feeling excluded and lonely, and I take responsibility for my feelings of exclusion"; "I don't know what to say now, and I take responsibility for my not knowing." This technique is an extension of the continuum of awareness, and it is designed to help the individuals recognize and accept their feelings instead of projecting their feelings onto others. Whereas this technique may sound mechanical, it is one that can be very meaningful.

"I Have a Secret"

This technique permits exploration of feelings of guilt and shame. The therapist asks clients to fantasize about a well-guarded personal secret, not to share the secret but to imagine how they would feel, and how others would react to them, if they were to reveal the secret. In group settings I have asked participants to allow themselves to imagine standing before the entire group and revealing aspects of themselves that they invest a lot of energy in hiding from others. Then I ask them to imagine what each person in the group might say to them if they were to share their secrets. This technique can also be used as a method of building trust in order to explore why clients might not reveal their secrets and to explore their fears of revealing material they feel ashamed or guilty about.

Playing the Projection

The dynamics of projection consist of one's seeing clearly in others the very things one does not want to see and accept within oneself. One can invest much energy in denying feelings and imputing motives to others. Often, especially in a group setting, the statements an individual makes toward and about others are in fact projections of attributes he or she possesses.

In the "playing the projection" game, the therapist asks the person who says "I can't trust you" to play the role of the untrustworthy person—that is, to become the other—in order to discover the degree to which the distrust is an inner conflict. In other words, the therapist asks the person to "try on for size" certain statements he or she makes to others in the group.

Reversal Technique

Certain symptoms and behavior often represent reversals of underlying or latent impulses. Thus the therapist could ask a person who claims to suffer from severe inhibitions and excessive timidity to play the role of an exhibitionist in the group. I remember the "super nice" lady in one of our groups who had difficulty in being anything but sugary sweet. I asked her to reverse her typical style and be as bitchy as she could be. The reversal worked well; soon she was playing her part with real gusto and later was able to recognize and accept her "bitch side" as well as her "lady side."

The theory underlying the reversal technique is that clients take the plunge into the very thing that is fraught with anxiety and make contact with those parts of themselves that have been submerged and denied. This technique can thus help clients begin to accept certain personal attributes that they have tried to deny.

Another illustration of the use of reversal technique is the time I asked one of the women in a group to become an evil witch. I asked her to go around to all the others in the group to place her curse on them, to wish evil upon them, and to tell them the very thing they feared most. As part of her act she delivered a chilling, evil lecture. This was a woman who, because she had never really been allowed to recognize her demonic side, had repressed her devils. She stored up hostility and resentment as by-products of repression. When she was encouraged to release her personal demons, to become fully the witch she had never been allowed to express, the results were dramatic. She felt intensely her denied side and gradually was able to integrate that side into her personality.

The Rehearsal Game

According to Perls, much of our thinking is rehearsing. We rehearse in fantasy for the role we think we are expected to play in society. When it comes to the performance, we experience stage fright, or anxiety, because we fear we will not play our roles well. Internal rehearsal consumes much energy and frequently inhibits our spontaneity and willingness to experiment with new behavior.

The members of the therapy group play the game of sharing their rehearsals with one another in order to become more aware of the many preparatory means they use in bolstering their social roles. They become increasingly aware of how they try to meet the expectations of others, of the degree to which they want to be approved, accepted, and liked, and of the extent to which they go to attain acceptance.

The Exaggeration Game

This game is related to the concept of becoming more aware of the subtle signals and cues one sends through body language. Movements, postures, and gestures may communicate significant meanings, yet the cues may be incomplete. The person is asked to exaggerate the movement or gesture repeatedly, which usually intensifies the feeling attached to the behavior and makes the inner meaning clearer.

Some examples of behavior that lends itself to the exaggeration technique are habitually smiling while expressing painful or negative material, trembling (shaking hands, legs), slouched posture and bent shoulders, clenched fists, tight frowning, facial grimacing, crossed arms, and so forth. If a client reports that his or her legs are shaking, for instance, the therapist might ask the client to stand up and exaggerate the shaking. Then the therapist might ask the client to put words to the shaking limbs.

As a variation from body language, verbal behavior also lends itself to the exaggeration game. The therapist can ask a client to repeat a statement that he or she had glossed over and to repeat it each time louder and louder. The effect frequently is that clients begin to really listen to and hear themselves.

Staying with the Feeling

This technique can be used at key moments when a client refers to a feeling or a mood that is unpleasant and from which he or she has a great urge to flee. The therapist urges the client to stay with, or retain, the feeling.

Most clients desire to escape from fearful stimuli and to avoid unpleasant feelings. The therapist may ask a client to remain with whatever fear or pain he or she is experiencing at present and encourage the client to go deeper into the feeling and behavior he or she wishes to avoid. Facing, confronting, and experiencing feelings not only take courage, but to do so is also a mark of the willingness to endure the pain necessary for unblocking and making way for newer levels of growth.

The Gestalt Approach to Dream Work

In psychoanalysis dreams are interpreted, intellectual insight is stressed, and free association is used as one method of exploring the unconscious meanings of dreams. The Gestalt approach does not interpret and analyze a dream. Instead, the intent is to bring the dream back to life, to re-create the dream, and to relive the dream as though it were happening now. The dream is not told as a past event but is acted out in the present, and the dreamer becomes a part of his or her dream. The suggested format for working with dreams includes making a list of all the details of the dream, remembering each person, event, and mood in the dream, and then becoming each of these parts in the dream by transforming oneself, acting as fully as possible and inventing dialogue; since each part of the dream is assumed to be a projection of oneself, one creates scripts for encounters between various characters or parts; all of the different parts of a dream are expressions of one's own contradictory and inconsistent sides. Thus, by engaging in a dialogue between these opposing sides, one gradually becomes more aware of the range of one's own feelings.

The concept of projection is central in Perls' theory of dream formation. According to him, every person and every object in the dream represents a projected aspect of the dreamer. Perls (1969a) suggests that "we start with the impossible assumption that whatever we believe we see in another person or in the world is nothing but a projection" (p. 67). Perls believes that the recognition of the senses and the understanding of projections go hand in hand. Thus Perls does not interpret dreams, nor play intellectual guessing games, nor tell the client the meaning of his or her dreams. Instead, the client takes responsibility for his or her dream, brings it back to life in the present, and relives it as though it were happening now. The client becomes each aspect of a dream by reenacting all the details of the dream. The client does not think about or analyze the dream but writes a script and acts out the dialogue among the various parts of the dream. Because the client is able to act out a fight between opposing contradictory sides, eventually he or she can appreciate and accept his or her inner differences and integrate the opposing forces. Whereas Freud called the dream the royal road to the unconscious, Perls (1969a) believed it was the "royal road to integration" (p. 66).

According to Perls (1969a), the dream is the most spontaneous expression of the existence of the human being. The dream represents an unfinished situation but is more than an unfinished situation or an unfulfilled wish. Every dream contains an existential message of oneself and one's current struggle. Everything is to be found in dreams if all the parts are understood and assimilated. Each piece of work done on a dream leads to some assimilation. Perls asserted that, if dreams are properly worked with, the existential message becomes clearer. According to him, dreams serve as an excellent way to discover personality voids by revealing missing parts and the client's methods of avoidance. If people do not remember dreams, they are refusing to face what is wrong with their lives. At the very least, the Gestaltist asks clients to talk to their dreams.

The preceding brief account of dream work is intended to acquaint the reader with the general manner in which dreams are a useful technique in Gestalt therapy. For the reader who wishes an in-depth treatment of the issue, I suggest Downing and Marmorstein's book *Dreams and Nightmares*, which is possibly the most detailed work on Gestalt approaches to dreams.

Application in Individual and Group Therapy

Gestalt therapy can be practiced in a variety of ways, whether it is in an individual or a group setting. In counseling, it can be applied in a strict Gestalt fashion whereby the client's interaction with the therapist is minimal. The client translates his or her immediate experience into an ongoing, role-playing situation in which he or she personifies all aspects of his or her awareness. In this puristic form even the client's reactions to the therapist are a part of the client's fantasy projections.

Individual therapy might also proceed in a less puristic form, characterized by a dialogue between the client and the therapist. The therapist might suggest experiments to help the client gain sharper focus on what he or she is doing in the present, but the therapist also brings his or her own reactions into the dialogue and thus is more than a director of individual therapy. Polster and Polster (1973) and Kempler (1973), leading figures in the Gestalt approach, call for an active, self-disclosing, involved human approach on the therapist's part.

Kempler (1973, pp. 270–271) urged "full personal expression" of the therapist during the therapeutic hour: "The therapist's responsibility is to live it and not merely preach it by interpreting the other person's behavior." Kempler suggested that the therapist express everything he or she thinks or feels "that he expects to be of value or that would diminish his ability to participate if he withheld it." Kempler allows for a wide range of behavior on the therapist's part during the individual encounter. The therapist might suggest, shout, or cry, talk about himself or herself, explore his or her own embarrassment, or admonish a client. According to Kempler, "No behavior is exclusive property of the patient alone. If the patient-therapist process is to be kept alive, it depends as much on the full participation of the therapist as it does on his demand for his patient's full commitment." Clearly, Kempler believes that the success of individual therapy is a function of the joint participation of two humans. The therapist must do more than ask questions, make interpretations, and give suggestions. The therapist's own conflicted process is a vital part of the therapy process.

In a group setting, Gestalt practice can also take a puristic form or, alternatively, encourage members to spontaneously become involved in interactions with one another. Perls worked with a group in the puristic way. His contact was focused on a single client at a time, and he diverted the client's attention away from the group and toward the client's internal reactions. Essentially, in that manner, the therapist and client work together, with the other members as observers. When a particular client is finished working, the therapist usually asks members to give feedback or to relate what occurred to their own experiences. With this model of Gestalt group therapy, a member of the group volunteers and accepts the invitation to work. The volunteer takes the "hot seat" and focuses as much as possible on his moment-to-moment, here-and-now awareness. A variety of Gestalt techniques, which I described earlier, encourage intensification of the client's experience. The direct and spontaneous interchanges between the members and the client on the hot seat are absent. At certain times the therapist might call other members of the group, although it is usually in a structured way that is aimed at furthering the therapist's work with the client on the hot seat.

As can individual therapy, group therapy can be practiced within a Gestalt context but less puristically. More freedom can be given. Group members can have more freedom to interact spontaneously, and the therapist can encourage more member-to-member interaction. The important variable is to decide whether the intervention is helpful or distracting. Some member interaction distracts from the quality of work and diffuses the energy of the group. In short, as Kempler (1973) indicates, "the Gestalt therapist is identified more by who he is than by what he does" (p. 273). The therapist, whether doing individual or group work, thus has latitude to employ psychotherapeutic techniques with a wider range than those originally developed by Perls in his workshops. Perls' "hot seat" pattern of working suited his own style and needs. As Kempler (1973) pointed out, this pattern put Perls in the top-dog position. Kempler indicates that Perls was his own person and developed a unique style that cannot be mechanically imitated with effective results. "That Fritz followed himself is the essence of him and hopefully also this will be the core of the Gestalt Movement" (p. 253). Thus the practice of Gestalt can assume flexible dimensions so that, it is hoped, the therapist will develop a style of leadership that is consistent with his or her personhood and not fall into the trap of merely mimicking Fritz Perls.

Factors related to the appropriate application of Gestalt techniques are (1) when, (2) with what kind of population, and (3) in what setting. Shepherd (1970) addressed herself to those factors and the underlying issues they reflect:

> In general, Gestalt therapy is most effective with overly socialized, restrained, constricted individuals—often described as neurotic, phobic, perfectionistic, ineffective, depressed, etc.—whose functioning is limited or inconsistent, primarily due to their internal restrictions, and whose enjoyment of living is minimal. Most efforts of Gestalt therapy are therefore directed toward persons with these characteristics [pp. 234–235].*

According to Shepherd (1970), Gestalt techniques, particularly confrontive or reenacting techniques, are contraindicated for use with a psychotic population. She indicates that more severely disturbed clients need considerable support before they can undertake the in-depth experience of reliving overwhelming rage, pain, and despair underlying the psychotic processes. Rather than involve the client with role-playing that releases intense feelings, "it is helpful to use techniques to facilitate the patient's reclaiming freedom to use eyes, hands, ears, body; in general, to increase sensory, perceptual, and motor capacities toward self-support and mastery of his environment" (p. 235).

Applications to Schools:
The Teaching/Learning Process

Gestalt methodology has direct application to working with children and adolescents in schools. Janet Lederman's moving book *Anger and the Rocking Chair* is a dramatic account of her adaptation of Gestalt methods for her work with children with emotional and behavioral problems in special-

*From "Limitations and Cautions in the Gestalt Approach," by I. Shepherd. In J. Fagan and I. Shepherd (Eds.), *Gestalt Therapy Now.* Copyright 1970 by Science and Behavior Books, Inc. This and all other quotations from this source are reprinted by permission of the publisher.

education classrooms. She vividly describes the feelings of powerlessness and apathy that both the children and their parents often experience. Lederman applies Gestalt concepts in confronting the children with the specific ways in which they are avoiding using their personal power, and she demands, by virtue of her own personhood and her real relationship with the children, that they accept responsibility for what they are doing. She meets children who are filled with hate, rage, and feelings of helplessness and who see themselves as failures. She accepts and recognizes the reality of their feelings, and she does not pretend to discount their anger and rebellion.

Teachers are typically afraid of their students' explosive emotions and generally ignore their reality. Instead, teachers insist that children submerge their aggressive and angry feelings as well as their behavior. They demand that children think civilized, feel civilized, and act civilized. Hence, in doing so, they ignore the reality of the child's being and his or her world. So often teachers believe that, unless "negative" feelings are repressed, chaos will reign in the classroom.

By contrast, Lederman not only recognizes strong emotions but encourages the expressions of feelings and at the same time demands that the children accept responsibility for the consequences of their behavior. Chaos does not reign in her classroom. Sometimes she is tough and demanding; at other times she is gentle. But she always works toward having the children discover insights into themselves. In short, she knows full well that the children will not learn subject matter until they have effectively dealt with the emotional turmoil that prevents them from focusing on any learning task.

Brown (1971) has developed humanistic approaches to the teaching/learning process based on Gestalt awareness techniques that are applicable to both elementary and secondary schools. Workshops conducted by the Ford-Esalen staff were aimed at in-service education of teachers to help them learn how to integrate the central concerns of learners with the subject matter. The goal was not to discard the conventional curriculum but to demonstrate to teachers the possibilities of applying the conventional curriculum to the lives of the learners. The emphasis was not solely on the feelings of the learner but on the integration of the cognitive and affective aspects of learning.

Alternative ways of learning that incorporate the feelings, ambitions, goals, values, attitudes, and life space of the learner are the focus of confluent education. In his book *Human Teaching for Human Learning*, Brown (1971) described a variety of Gestalt affective techniques that are appropriate for classroom use, including inner and outer groups designed to help people stay in the "now," fantasy groups and fantasy exercises, aggression exercises, touching, improvisational-theater techniques, fantasy body trips, personal life maps, trust walks, mirroring, Gestalt projection games, trust circles, animal fantasy, Gestalt trust and contact techniques, Gestalt teacher/pupil techniques, imagination games, Gestalt teacher-role awareness techniques, Gestalt responsibility techniques, and many other verbal and nonverbal Gestalt awareness techniques that are applicable to the first grade through high school. Brown described specific ways of implementing these techniques for all grade levels. He reported that the use of affective learning techniques integrated with the cognitive material resulted in better learning of cognitive material, increased motivation, greater appreciation of self, others, and nature, and increased pupil responsibility. In summary, Brown has shown a way of applying the Gestalt approach to the teaching/learning situation that resulted in positive behavioral changes of students and that not only made them better students but also assisted them in enhancing their human relations.

Summary and Evaluation

Gestalt therapy is an experiential therapy stressing here-and-now awareness. This major focus is on the *what* and *how* of behavior and the role of unfinished business from the past that prevents effective functioning in the present. Some of the key concepts of the approach include accepting personal responsibility, living in the immediate moment, direct experiencing as opposed to abstract talking about experiences, avoidance, unfinished business, and dealing with the impasse.

A central therapeutic aim is to challenge the client to move from environmental support to self-support. Expansion of awareness, which is viewed as curative by and of itself, is a basic goal. With awareness, clients are able to reconcile polarities and dichotomies within themselves and thus proceed toward the reintegration of all aspects of themselves.

In this approach, the therapist assists clients to experience more fully all feelings and this enables them to make their own interpretations. The therapist avoids making interpretations and instead focuses on how the client is behaving. Clients identify their own unfinished business, and they work through the blockages impeding their growth. They do this largely by reexperiencing past situations as though they were happening in the present. The therapist has many techniques at his or her disposal, all of which have one thing in common: they are designed to intensify direct experiencing and to integrate conflicting feelings.

I like many of the Gestalt techniques and make frequent use of them in my work with clients, both in individual therapy and in groups. I am impressed with the action approach, and I find that direct experiencing yields far better results than merely abstractly discussing a client's historical account or fishing for causes for present behavior. I have discovered that clients do report that they can feel their conflicts, develop a new awareness of their struggles, and learn to accept and integrate the various factions within themselves. The following are the specific characteristics of Gestalt therapy that I find valuable:

1. It is a confrontive and active approach.
2. It deals with the past by bringing relevant aspects of one's past into the present.

3. The approach encourages direct contact and expression of feelings, and deemphasizes abstract intellectualizing *about* one's problems.
4. Attention is given to nonverbal and body messages.
5. It refuses to accept helplessness as an excuse for not changing.
6. It puts the emphasis upon the client to find his or her own meanings and make his or her own interpretations.
7. In a very brief time, clients can intensely experience their feelings via some of the Gestalt exercises.

What are some of the limitations of Gestalt therapy? I have several criticisms of the way I often see Gestalt therapy being practiced:

1. This approach is not grounded in a solid theory.
2. It tends to be anti-intellectual to the point that cognitive factors are discounted. I believe that *both* feeling and thinking functions are of critical importance in therapy, and I see this approach as leaving little room for clients to conceptualize and think about their experiencing.
3. Philosophically, there is a real danger in accepting an "I do my thing, and you do your thing" life-style. I believe that we are responsible for ourselves, but I also believe that we have responsibility to and for others. Our behavior does have impact on the feelings of others, and therefore we are partly responsible for others. Gestalt (at least as described by Perls) stresses responsibility to ourselves but at the same time denies our responsibility to others.
4. There is a real danger that the practitioner will grab a bag of techniques and, by using them in a mechanical way, remain hidden as a person.
5. This approach can be dangerous because of the therapist's power to manipulate the client with techniques. The therapist can misuse his or her power and thus prevent a client from becoming autonomous.
6. People often react negatively to some of the Gestalt techniques, for they think they are foolish. It behooves the therapist to lay the necessary groundwork so that the techniques do not appear as mere gimmicks.

Although I am enthusiastic about many of the Gestalt concepts and techniques, I am not selling this as the only or as the best type of therapy. I strongly recommend that you experience for yourself several Gestalt group workshops, preferably led by different Gestalt therapists so that you experience the possible uses and limitations of this method for yourself. In my opinion, there is much to be learned about yourself personally, and much can be gained in your professional know-how if you approach this orientation with openness. In addition to experiencing several Gestalt workshops, I recommend viewing the films that Fritz Perls made on Gestalt therapy and reading Perls' *Gestalt Therapy Verbatim*, perhaps his autobiography, *In and Out of the Garbage Pail*, and Fagan and Shepherd's *Gestalt Therapy Now*. If you are interested in the applications of the Gestalt approach to education, I suggest two books: Lederman's *Anger and the Rocking Chair*, which describes her application of the Gestalt principles to children in a special-education classroom, and Brown's *Human Teaching for Human Learning*, which describes

Gestalt exercises applicable to the elementary and secondary classroom and discusses how several elementary and secondary teachers have implemented humanistic principles of confluent education into their own classrooms.

I'd like to conclude with a few more words of caution. Gestalt therapy worked dramatically well for Frederick Perls because he invented it. If you read his autobiography, *In and Out of the Garbage Pail,* you'll get some sense of why and how it worked for him. Unfortunately, many therapists have become so enthralled with his dynamic personality and style that they mimic only his style, without fully understanding and incorporating the conceptual framework of the Gestalt approach. Learning the Gestalt jargon and getting the techniques down pat do not automatically make one an effective Gestalt therapist.

Questions for Evaluation

Following are some questions for self-examination that might help you to apply some of the Gestalt concepts to yourself personally and thus show you a way of integrating this approach with your counseling practice.

1. Do you live in the past, thinking of what you could or should have done? Or do you look toward the future and make resolutions and plans for how you want things to be? Are you able to live fully in the here-and-now? What interferes with your fully being present? How do you distract yourself from living in the present?
2. Perls said that anxiety comes from a preoccupation with the future, for we become struck with catastrophic expectations. What are your catastrophic expectations?
3. Are you aware of talking about your feelings? Do you talk about your sadness and pain, or are you able to experience these feelings?
4. A major concept in Gestalt is that of unfinished business. What are some kinds of specific unfinished business in your life? How do you think your unfinished business might hamper your effectiveness in counseling others? What prevents you from completing the unfinished business?
5. According to Perls, getting to the impasse is the crucial point in therapy. This is the point where the clients believe that they have no chance of survival and that they cannot find the means of surviving within themselves. What is your own experience with the impasse? Do you go through the impasse, or do you choose to maintain the status quo?
6. Are you aware of a "top dog" and "underdog" conflict in your life? What are some of your unresolved polarities and conflicts?
7. A therapeutic goal is to become aware. According to Gestalt theory, when awareness is present our most important unfinished business will always emerge to be dealt with in therapy. In your life do you find that awareness of what and how you are doing is enough? Do you take action? Is awareness without action therapeutic?
8. A suggestion: take one of your dreams and apply the Gestalt method

of taking the role of each person in your dream and experiencing that role as fully as possible. What meaning do you attach to your dream? What does it tell you about yourself?

9. Do you think that Gestalt, with its emphasis on experiencing moment-by-moment feelings, tends to discount the valid place of thinking in therapy?

10. What is your reaction to the underlying philosophy of Gestalt that one is responsible only to and for oneself? Is this viewpoint responsible? Do you believe that you are also responsible to and for others?

References and Suggested Readings

*Brown, G. *Human teaching for human learning*. New York: Viking, 1971.

Downing, J., & Marmorstein, R. (Eds.). *Dreams and nightmares: A book of Gestalt therapy sessions*. New York: Harper & Row, 1973.

Fagan, J. The tasks of the therapist. In J. Fagan & I. Shepherd (Eds.), *Gestalt therapy now*. New York: Harper Colophon, 1970.

*Fagan, J., & Shepherd, I. *Gestalt therapy now*. New York: Harper Colophon, 1970. (a)

Fagan, J., & Shepherd, I. *Life styles in Gestalt therapy*. New York: Harper & Row, 1970. (b)

Fagan, J., & Shepherd, I. *What is Gestalt therapy?* New York: Harper & Row, 1970. (c)

*James, M., & Jongeward, D. *Born to win: Transactional Analysis with Gestalt experiments*. Reading, Mass.: Addison-Wesley, 1971.

Kempler, W. Gestalt therapy. In R. Corsini (Ed.), *Current psychotherapies*. Itasca, Ill.: Peacock, 1973.

*Lederman, J. *Anger and the rocking chair*. New York: McGraw-Hill, 1969.

Levitsky, A., & Perls, F. The rules and games of Gestalt therapy. In J. Fagan & I. Shepherd (Eds.), *Gestalt therapy now*. New York: Harper Colophon, 1970.

Patterson, C. H. *Theories of counseling and psychotherapy* (2nd ed.). New York: Harper & Row, 1973.

*Perls, F. *Gestalt therapy verbatim*. Moab, Utah: Real People Press, 1969. (a)

Perls, F. *In and out of the garbage pail*. Moab, Utah: Real People Press, 1969. (b)

Perls, F., Hefferline, R., & Goodman, P. *Gestalt therapy: Excitement and growth in the human personality*. New York: Dell, 1951.

*Polster, E., & Polster, M. *Gestalt therapy integrated*. New York: Brunner/Mazel, 1973.

Rhyne, J. *The Gestalt art experience*. Monterey, Cal.: Brooks/Cole, 1973.

Shaffer, J., & Galinsky, M. D. *Models of group therapy and sensitivity training*. Englewood Cliffs, N.J.: Prentice Hall, 1974.

Shepherd, I. Limitations and cautions in the Gestalt approach. In J. Fagan & I. Shepherd (Eds.), *Gestalt therapy now*. New York: Harper Colophon, 1970.

CHAPTER SIX

TRANSACTIONAL

ANALYSIS

Introduction

Transactional Analysis (TA) is an interactional psychotherapy that can be used in individual therapy but that is particularly appropriate for the group approaches. This approach is set apart from most other therapies in that it is both contractual and decisional. It involves a contract, developed by the client, that clearly states the goals and direction of the therapy process. It also focuses on early decisions that each person makes, and it stresses the capacity of the person to make new decisions. It emphasizes the cognitive-rational-behavioral aspects and is oriented toward increasing awareness so that the client will be able to make new decisions and alter the course of his or her life.

Developed by Eric Berne, this approach is based on a personality theory related to structural and transactional analysis. The theory supplies a framework for the analysis of three separate ego states: Parent, Adult, and Child. Clear-cut operational statements characterize the approach. It utilizes several key words and offers a framework that can be easily understood and learned. The key words are *Parent, Adult, Child, decision, redecision, game, script, racket, strokes, discounting,* and *stamps*. Because of the operational nature of TA, including a contract, a client's degree of change can be established.

The contractual nature of the psychotherapeutic process tends to equalize the power of the therapist and the client. It is the client's responsibility to decide what he or she will change. To make the changes a reality, the client changes behavior in an active manner. During the course of therapy, the client evaluates the direction of his or her life, comes to understand some very early decisions that he or she made, and realizes that he or she can now redecide and initiate a new direction in life. In essence, then, TA assumes that people can learn to trust themselves, think and decide for themselves, and express their feelings.

Key Concepts

View of Human Nature

Transactional Analysis is rooted in a philosophy that is antideterministic and asserts that human beings are capable of transcending their conditioning and early programming. Further, this theory rests on the assumptions that persons are capable of understanding their past decisions and that they can choose to redecide. It places faith in the person's capacity to rise above habit patterns and to select new goals and behavior. This does not imply that people are free from the influences of social forces, nor does it mean that people arrive at crucial life decisions totally by themselves. It does mean, however, that they were influenced by the expectations and demands of significant others, especially since their early decisions were made at a time in life when they were highly dependent on others. But decisions can be reviewed and challenged, and, if early decisions are no longer appropriate, new decisions can be made.

Harris (1967) agrees that humans have choices and are not bound by their pasts. "Although the early experiences which culminated in the position cannot be erased, I believe the early positions can be changed. *What was once decided can be undecided*" (p. 66).* Although Berne (1970) believed that human beings have the capacity to choose, he felt that few people achieve the degree of awareness necessary for becoming autonomous:

> Man is born free, but one of the first things he learns is to do as he is told, and he spends the rest of his life doing that. Thus his first enslavement is to his parents. He follows their instructions forevermore, retaining only in some cases the right to choose his own methods and consoling himself with an illusion of autonomy [p. 194].

This view of human nature has definite implications for the practice of TA therapy. The therapist recognizes that one reason a person is in therapy is because he or she has entered into conspiracies and game-playing with others. The therapist does not, however, allow the same conspiratorial relationship to develop in therapy. The therapist will not accept "I tried"; "I

*From *I'm OK—You're OK*, by T. Harris. Copyright 1967 by Harper & Row, Publishers, Inc. This and all other quotations from this source are reprinted by permission.

couldn't help it"; and "Don't blame me, because I'm stupid." Because of the basic premise that the person can make choices, can make new decisions, and can act, excuses, or "cop-outs," are not accepted in the therapeutic practice of TA. Holland (1973) commented that "a therapist who quickly and crudely refuses to accept a prospective patient's favorite cop-out soon finds himself without that patient, unless the patient is strongly and sincerely committed to change" (p. 38).* Therefore, if clients are not allowed to perpetuate their cop-out style in the therapeutic relationship, there is a good chance that they will discover their own internal strengths and capacities to use their freedom in redesigning their lives in new and effective ways.

The Ego States

Transactional Analysis is a system of therapy based on a personality theory utilizing three distinct patterns of behavior or ego states: Parent, Adult, and Child (P-A-C).

The Parent ego state is the part of the personality that is an introject of the parents and parental substitutes. In the Parent ego state we reexperience what we imagined were our own parents' feelings in a situation, or we feel and act toward others the same way our parents felt and acted toward us. The Parent ego state contains "shoulds" and "oughts." The Parent in each of us can be the "Nurturing Parent" or the "Critical Parent."

The Adult ego state is the processor of data and information. It is the objective part of the personality, and it is the part of the personality that knows what is going on. It is not emotional, nor is it judgmental, but it works with the facts and with external reality. Based on available information, it produces the best solution to a particular problem.

The Child ego state consists of feelings, impulses, and spontaneous acts. The "Child" in each of us might be the "Natural Child," the "Little Professor," or the "Adapted Child." The Natural Child is the impulsive, untrained, spontaneous, expressive infant in each of us. The Little Professor is the unschooled wisdom of a child. It is manipulative and creative. It is that part of the Child ego state that is intuitive, the part that plays on hunches. The Adapted Child exhibits a modification of the Natural Child's inclinations. The modifications are the result of traumatic experiences, demands, training, and decisions about how to get strokes.

Life Scripts and the Basic Psychological Positions

Life scripts are the early parental teachings that we learn and early decisions that we make as children and continue to carry around with us as adults. We receive messages—and thus learn and decide—about how we are

*From "Transactional Analysis," by G. Holland. In R. Corsini (Ed.), *Current Psychotherapies.* Copyright 1973 by F. E. Peacock Publishers, Inc. This and all other quotations from this source are reprinted by permission of the publisher, F. E. Peacock Publishers, Inc., Itasca, Illinois.

at an early age from those in our environments. Our parents' verbal and nonverbal messages communicate how they see us and how they feel about us. We make some early decisions that contribute to feeling like a winner (feeling "OK") or a loser (feeling "Not OK").

Parental injunctions are a part of our life scripting, which includes "shoulds," "oughts," "do's," "don'ts," and parental expectations. We learn these injunctions early in life, and we also make decisions about how we will respond to others and how we feel about our own worth. In adult life much of our present behavior grows out of how we were "scripted" and out of the results of our early decisions.

Related to the concepts of life scripting, parental messages and injunctions, and early decisions is the concept in TA of the four basic positions in life: (1) "I'm OK—You're OK"; (2) "I'm OK—You're Not OK"; (3) "I'm Not OK—You're OK"; and (4) "I'm Not OK—You're Not OK." Each of the positions is based on the decisions one makes as a result of early experience in childhood. Once a person has made a decision, he or she generally stays with it unless there is some intervention (in therapy or in life) to change it. The healthy position is that of the winner, or the I'm OK—You're OK position. Here both people can feel like winners and can have straight-across relationships. I'm OK—You're Not OK is the position of people who project their problems onto others and blame others. It is an arrogant position that distances one from others and keeps one aloof. The I'm Not OK—You're OK position is that of a depressed person, one who feels powerless in comparison to others and who tends to withdraw or serve other people's needs rather than his or her own. I'm Not OK—You're Not OK is the futile position of those who have given up all hope, who have lost interest in living, and who see life as without any promise.

The Human Need for Strokes

People need to be touched, both physically and emotionally. Humans (and animals) hunger for strokes, and, if their stroking needs are unmet, ample evidence indicates that they do not develop in a healthy manner, either emotionally or physically. TA thus pays attention to how people structure their time to get strokes. The script decisions people make define the kinds of strokes they allow themselves to obtain. Stroking can be either positive or negative, and the kinds of early strokes one receives condition one to behave in certain ways. According to TA, it behooves us to understand how we get strokes, to learn to ask for the strokes we want, and to take responsibility for the rewards or punishments.

Positive stroking is essential for the development of psychologically healthy persons with a sense of feeling OK. If the strokes we receive are authentic and if they come from the I'm OK—You're OK position, we are nourished. Positive strokes, which can take the form of expressions of affection or appreciation, can be transmitted by words, a touch, a look, or a gesture.

Negative stroking by parents leads to thwarting a child's growth. Negative strokes take the form of messages (verbal and nonverbal) that rob a person of dignity and leave a person feeling discounted and insignificant. Negative stroking, which sends the message "You're Not OK," involves diminishing, humiliating, ridiculing, abusing, and treating a person like an object. However, even negative strokes seem to be preferable to receiving no strokes at all—that is, to being ignored.

TA adopts the view of human motivation that basic needs are directly related to observable daily behavior. Some basic needs include stroke hunger, structure hunger, excitement hunger, and recognition hunger. TA theory asserts that much human behavior can be understood in the context of the way one structures one's time. According to Berne (1961, 1964) and Harris (1967), the six types of transactions that occur between people are withdrawal, rituals, activities, pastimes, games, and intimacy. The first five of these ways of spending time can keep people apart, although to some degree each of them is useful and necessary for advancing the script and providing strokes. Games, by their very nature, are manipulative and prevent intimacy and lead to "not OK" feelings. TA theory proposes that humans have a need to make contact, which is done best by intimacy. Harris (1967) contended that an intimate relationship between two people may be thought of as independent of the first five ways—withdrawal, pastimes, activities, rituals, and games—of structuring time. "It is based upon the acceptance of both people of the I'm OK—You're OK position. It rests, literally, in an accepting love where defensive time structuring is made unnecessary. Giving and sharing are spontaneous expressions of joy rather than responses to socially programmed rituals. Intimacy is a game-free relationship, since goals are not ulterior" (pp. 151–152). Thus one way TA theory describes human behavior is in terms of structuring time, which involves a variety of ways of getting strokes from other people. These ways exist on a continuum from the recognition one gets from others through rituals, pastimes, and games to the quality of strokes involved in a meaningful and intimate personal relationship.

Games We Play

TA proponents encourage people to identify and understand their ego states. Their contention is that, by recognizing and accepting them, people free themselves from outdated Child decisions and irrational Parent messages that complicate their lives. TA teaches the individual which part he or she is using to make important life decisions. Further, TA proponents say that people can understand their internal dialogues between Parent and Child. They can hear and also understand their relationships with others. They can be aware of when they are straight and when they are crooked with others. Using the principles of TA, people can become aware of the kind of strokes they were reared on, and they can change the strokes they respond to from negative to positive. They are able to ask for the strokes they need, but if they are reluctant to do so they can bet that their Critical Parent is dictating to them that they "shouldn't" be so stuck on themselves. In short, one of the aims of TA is to help persons understand the nature of their transactions with others so that they can respond to others with directness, wholeness, and intimacy. Game playing is then reduced.

TA views games as exchanges of strokes that lead to pay-offs of bad feelings and advance the script. Games might give the appearance of intimacy, but people who engage in game-playing transactions create distances between themselves by impersonalizing each other. It takes at least two to play a game, so that one way of aborting game transactions is for one of the players to become aware of the game he or she is in and then to decide not to play anymore. The first step is to gain awareness of the subtle nature of the game. Common games include "Poor Me," "Martyr," "Yes, but," "If It Weren't for You," "Look What You Made Me Do!" "Harassed," "Uproar," and "Wooden Leg." Parents often resort to a battery of games to control their children, and children counter with a thesaurus of games that are even more highly developed; for example, children are masterful at inventing games to avoid doing chores. The problem with a game is that the ulterior motive for it is buried, and the players end up feeling not OK.

The Karpman Drama Triangle (see Figure 6-1) is a useful device to help people understand games. The triangle has a "Persecutor," a "Rescuer," and a "Victim." For example, a family drama might include the interplay of family members, each operating from a different point on the Drama Triangle. The Victim plays the "Kick Me" game by inviting another person to kick him or her. Often the Victim persecutes another person until he or she kicks the Victim. To complete the Triangle, another family member may rush in to save the poor, helpless, kicked Victim from the ruthless Persecutor. It is not uncommon for the Victim to persecute the Rescuer. The Rescuer, in the guise of being helpful, works to keep others in dependent positions. The feature that distinguishes a game from a straight transaction is the "switch" from one position in the triangle to another such as the switch from rescuer to persecutor or from victim to persecutor, as illustrated in Figure 6-1.

The Therapeutic Process

Therapeutic Goals

The basic goal of Transactional Analysis is to assist the client in making new decisions regarding his or her present behavior and the direction of his or her life. Its aims are to have the individual gain awareness of how freedom of choice has been restricted by following early decisions about his or her life position and to provide options to sterile and deterministic ways of living. The essence of therapy is to substitute an autonomous life-style characterized by awareness, spontaneity, and intimacy for a life-style characterized by manipulative game playing and self-defeating life scripts.

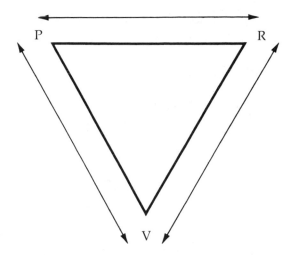

Figure 6-1 The Karpman Drama Triangle

Harris (1967) sees the goal of Transactional Analysis as enabling the individual "to have freedom of choice, the freedom to change at will, to change the responses to recurring and new stimuli" (p. 82). The "restoration of the freedom to change" is based on knowledge of the Parent and the Child and of how these ego states feed into present-day transactions. The therapeutic process essentially involves freeing the Adult of the contaminating and troublemaking influences of the Parent and Child. As Harris (1967) put it, "The goal of treatment is to *cure* the presenting symptom, and the method of treatment is freeing up of the Adult so that the individual may experience freedom of choice and the creation of new options above and beyond the limiting influences of the past" (p. 231). According to Harris, the goal is achieved by teaching the client the basics of P-A-C. Clients in a group setting learn how to recognize, identify, and describe the Parent, Adult, and Child as each appear in transactions in the group.

Berne (1964) implied that the basic objective of Transactional Analysis is the attainment of autonomy, which is manifested by the release and recovery of three characteristics: awareness, spontaneity, and intimacy.

Like Berne, James and Jongeward (1971) view achieving autonomy as the ultimate goal of TA, which for them means "being self-governing, determining one's own destiny, taking responsibility for one's own actions and feelings, and throwing off patterns that are irrelevant and inappropriate to living in the here and now" (p. 263). They make the point that courage is necessary to be a "real winner" at responding to life. It takes courage to accept the freedom that comes with autonomy, courage to choose intimate and direct encounters, courage to accept the responsibility of choosing, and "courage to be the very unique person you really are." They sum up the goal of becoming a healthy person as follows: "The path of an ethical person who is autonomously aware, spontaneous, and able to be intimate is not always easy; but, if such a person recognizes his 'losing streak' and decides against it, he is likely to discover that he was born with what it takes to win" (p. 274).

The Therapist's Function and Role

Transactional Analysis is designed to gain both emotional and intellectual insight, but, as the focus is clearly on rational aspects, the role of the therapist is largely to pay attention to the didactic and emotional issues. Harris (1967) sees the therapist's role as that of a "teacher, trainer, and resource person with heavy emphasis on involvement" (p. 239). As a teacher, the therapist explains concepts such as structural analysis, transactional analysis, script analysis, and game analysis. The therapist assists the client in discovering the disadvantageous conditions of the past under which the client made certain early decisions, adopted life plans, and developed strategies in dealing with people that the client might now wish to reconsider. The therapist helps the client gain more realistic awareness and find alternatives for living more autonomously.

Whereas the therapist has an expert knowledge of structural analysis, transactional analysis, and script analysis, he or she does not function in the role of a detached, aloof, superior expert who is there to cure the "sick patient." Most TA theorists—for example, Claude Steiner—stress the importance of an "equal relationship" and point to the contract for therapy as evidence that the therapist and the client are partners in the therapeutic process. Hence the therapist's job is to bring his or her knowledge to bear in the context of a clear, specific contract that the client initiates.

The therapist's job basically is to help the client acquire the tools necessary for change. The therapist encourages and teaches the client to rely on his or her own Adult rather than on the therapist's Adult, to examine old decisions, and to make new decisions. This process is implicit in the contract idea. Holland (1973) captures the process well in the following words:

> The therapist's willingness to allow this separation, strictly in accord with the initial contract, is the last bit of assurance the patient receives that he has indeed been in helpful company and that he has "permission" to "go it" on his own. This is the final act of the therapeutic relationship. The patient takes away with him not just an education in the principles of Transactional Analysis, but also a new experience in the nature of relationships, and a new image of himself as an "OK" person, capable of doing whatever needs to be done for himself [p. 386].

The Client's Experience in Therapy

One basic prerequisite for being a TA client is the capacity and willingness to understand and accept a therapeutic contract. The treatment contract contains a specific and concrete statement of objectives that the client will attain and the criteria to determine how and when these goals are effectively met. Any transactions that are not related to the contract between the client and the therapist are excluded. This means that the therapist will not go on unauthorized fishing expeditions in the client's life history. In this way the client knows what he or she is coming to the therapist for, and, when the terms of the contract are completed, the relationship is terminated unless a new contract is established.

The contract implies that clients are active agents in the therapeutic process. From the outset, clients clarify and state their own therapeutic goals in the form of a contract. To implement these goals the client and therapist may design "assignments" to carry out within a therapy session and in everyday life. For example, Treva Sudhalter, a TA therapist in southern California, designs with her clients "Rehearsals for Change." Clients experiment with new ways of behaving, and thus they can determine whether they prefer the old or the new behavior. They decide whether or not they want to change, and, if they decide to change, they then specify new behavior plans in terms of the changes desired. In this way, the therapeutic process does not become an interminable one in which clients become dependent on the wisdom of the therapist. Clients demonstrate their willingness to change by actually doing, not by merely "trying" and not by endlessly exploring the past and talking about insights. For therapy to continue, clients act to effect desired changes.

Harris (1967) raises the question of what makes people want to change. He gives three reasons why a person might become a client and why the person might want to change:

1. One is that they hurt sufficiently. . . . They have invested in the same slot machines without a pay-off for so long that they are finally willing either to stop playing or to move on to others.
2. Another thing that makes people want to change is a slow type of despair called ennui, or boredom. When the person asks the ultimate—"*So What?*"—he is ready for change.
3. A third thing that makes people want to change is the sudden discovery that they can [p. 85].

According to Harris (1967), the goal is "to make every person in treatment an expert in analyzing his own transactions" (p. 229). The client's role is to learn the fundamentals of P-A-C; then the client can use the TA group to experience differently from the old ways. Harris described the essence of a cure: "If a patient can put into words why he does what he does and how he has stopped doing it, then he is cured, in that he knows what the cure is and can use it again and again" (p. 238).

The Relationship between Therapist and Client

TA is a contractual form of therapy. A contract in TA implies that a person will change. The contract should be specific, clearly defined, and briefly stated. The contract states what the client will do, how the client will go about accomplishing his or her stated goals, and when the client will know when the contract is fulfilled. Subject to modification, contracts can be made in steps. A therapist will support and work with a contract that is therapeutic for the client.

The emphasis upon specific contracts is one of TA's major contributions to counseling and therapy. It is easy in therapy to wander aimlessly without looking at goals or without taking personal responsibility for effecting desired personal changes. Many clients seek a therapist as the source of a cure-all, and they begin therapy in a passive and dependent stance. One of their difficulties is that they have avoided assuming responsibility, and they attempt to continue their life-styles by shifting responsibility to their therapist. The contractual approach of TA is based on the expectation that clients focus on their goals and make a commitment. It emphasizes the division of responsibility and provides a point of departure for working.

Omnibus contracts, such as "I want to be happy," "I want to understand myself," or "I hope to become better adjusted," are not accepted. The contract must be more specific and must delineate the ways of actually working on the contract in personal therapy or in a group setting. If a client says "I feel lonely and I'd like to get closer to people," a contract might include a specific exercise or task to actually begin to get close. For example, the client might be asked to experience closeness with other members of the group by spending 15 minutes exploring these feelings with each person in the group.

Some clients complain that they do not know what they want, or that they are too confused to form a clear contract. They can begin by deciding on short-term or easier contracts, perhaps by merely coming for three individual sessions to decide what, if anything, they want from therapy. It is important to keep in mind that a contract is not an end in itself but a means of helping a person accept responsibility for becoming autonomous.

The contract approach clearly implies a joint responsibility. Through sharing responsibility with the therapist the client becomes a colleague in his or her treatment. An expert does not do something to him or her while he or she remains passive; rather, both the client and the therapist are active in the relationship. There are several implications of this concept in regard to the relationship. First, there is not an unbridgeable gap of understanding between the client and the therapist. Both share the same vocabulary and concepts, and both have a similar comprehension of the situation. Second, the client has full and equal rights while in therapy. This means that the client is not forced to make any disclosures he or she chooses not to make. Further, the client is assured that he or she will not be observed or recorded without his or her knowledge and consent. Third, the contract reduces the status differential and emphasizes equality between the client and the therapist.

In speaking of client-therapist equality, Holland (1973) made it clear that at no time is the client excluded from the "councils of the mighty." The client learns the basic principles and concepts of TA so that the possible differences regarding understanding the client's problem will be minimized and a common frame of reference for working insured. As Harris (1967) put it, "The Transactional Analytic approach to therapy via the establishing of a contractual relationship has the impact of elevating the patient to the status of the therapist's peer, the terms 'patient' and 'therapist' then serving to distinguish different roles in the therapeutic relationship rather than differences in value, status, or other forms of worthiness" (p. 384).

In a similar vein, Harris (1967) implies that all persons can analyze their own transactions, for TA is basically a learning process by which a person discovers how to evaluate the data that are used in decision making. Therefore "there is no magic applied by an omnipotent expert. The therapist uses words to convey what he knows and uses in his own transactions to the person who comes into treatment, so he can know and use the same technique" (p. 229). According to Harris, the psychoanalytic concepts of transference and resistance retard the progress of therapy and therefore TA does not use these terms. Transference, according to this view, is unlikely to occur, because of the format of mutual participation and the content of P-A-C. In Harris' judgment, the client should find in the therapist "a human being interested in advancing the patient's knowledge of himself at once so that, as quickly as possible, he can become his own analyst" (p. 230).

Application: Therapeutic Techniques and Procedures

Application to Groups

The concepts and techniques of Transactional Analysis are particularly suited for group situations. TA was originally devised as a form of group treatment, and the therapeutic procedures yield results in a group setting. In the group setting people are able to observe other people changing, which gives them more models for increasing their own options. They come to understand the structure and functioning of their individual personalities and learn how they transact with others. They are quickly able to identify the games they play and the scripts they act out. They are able to focus on their early decisions, which may never have been subject to scrutiny. Interaction with other group members gives them ample opportunities to practice assignments and fulfill their contracts. The transactions in the group enable the members to increase their awareness of both self and others and thus focus the changes and redecisions they will make in their lives.

Harris (1967) agrees that "the treatment of individuals in groups is the method of choice by Transactional Analysts" (p. 234). He views the beginning phase of a TA group as a teaching and learning process and places significance on the didactic role of the group therapist. As he puts it, "Since the essential characteristic of the group is that of teaching, learning, analyzing, the effectiveness of the Transactional Analyst rests in his enthusiasm and ability as a teacher and his alertness in keeping abreast of every communication or signal in the group, verbal or otherwise" (p. 239). Harris discusses several advantages of a group approach over the traditional one-to-one approach to therapy, some of which are the following: (1) the variety of ways the Parent manifests itself in transactions can be observed; (2) the characteristics of the Child in each individual in the group can be experienced; (3) people can be experienced in a natural milieu, characterized by an involvement with other people; (4) mutual confrontation of games can naturally occur; and, (5) patients move faster and get well sooner in group treatment. Harris clarifies the last advantage: "By 'get well' I mean achieving the goals stated in the initial hour contract, one of which is the alleviation of the presenting symptom and the other of which is to learn to use P-A-C accurately and effectively" (p. 238).

Therapeutic Procedures

In Transactional practice techniques from a variety of sources, particularly from Gestalt therapy, are used. In fact, there are exciting procedures that can result in the marriage between Transactional Analysis and Gestalt. James and Jongeward (1971) combine concepts and processes from TA with Gestalt experiments and, with the combined approach, demonstrate a promising avenue toward self-awareness and autonomy.

The remainder of this section is devoted to a brief description of some of the more commonly used processes, procedures, and techniques in TA practice. Most of these therapeutic methods and processes can be applied to individual psychotherapy as well as to group treatment. However, as pointed out earlier, even though TA can effectively work on a one-to-one basis, the group itself is a significant vehicle for educational and therapeutic change.

Structural Analysis

Structural analysis is a tool by which a person becomes aware of the content and functioning of his or her ego states of Parent, Adult, and Child. TA clients learn how to identify their own ego states. Structural analysis helps the individual resolve patterns that he or she feels stuck with. It allows a person to find out which ego state his or her behavior is based on. With that knowledge, the person can figure out what his or her options are.

Two types of problems related to the structure of personality can be considered by structural analysis: contamination and exclusion. Contamination exists when the contents of one ego state are mixed with those of another ego state. Either the Parent or the Child, or both, intrudes within the boundaries of the Adult ego state and interferes with the clear thinking and functioning of the Adult (see Figure 6-2). Contamination from the Parent ego state typically is manifested through prejudiced ideas and attitudes. Contamination from the Child ego state involves distorted perceptions of reality. When contamination of the Adult by the Parent or the Child, or both, exists, "boundary work" is called for so that the demarcation of each ego state is clearly drawn. When the ego-state boundaries are realigned, the person understands his or her Child and Parent rather than being contami-

The Parent
Contaminating
the Adult

The Child
Contaminating
the Adult

Both the Parent
and the Child
Contaminating
the Adult

Figure 6-2   Contamination

nated by them. Examples of statements reflecting contamination from the Parent are "Don't mix with people that are not of our kind"; "You can't trust those damned minorities"; "Always be on the lookout for those mechanics because they'll cheat you every time"; and "You can't trust teen-agers." Examples of statements reflecting contamination from the Child are "Everyone's always picking on me, and nobody treats me good"; "Anything I want I should get right now"; "Who could possibly ever want me for a friend?" and "The entire universe should revolve around me."

Exclusion exists when an Excluding-Child ego state can "block out" the Parent or when an Excluding-Parent ego state can "block out" the Child—that is, when rigid ego-state boundaries do not allow for free movement.

The Constant Parent
Exclusion of Adult
and Child by Parent

The Constant Adult
Exclusion of Parent
and Child by Adult

The Constant Child
Exclusion of Parent
and Adult by Child

Figure 6-3 Exclusion

The person might be relating primarily as Parent, or as Child, or as Adult. The Constant Parent excludes the Adult and Child and can typically be found in the person who is so duty-bound and work-oriented that he or she cannot play. This person may be judgmental, moralistic, and demanding of others. He or she often behaves in a domineering and authoritarian manner.

The Constant Child excludes the Adult and Parent and, at the extreme, is the sociopath without a conscience. The person operating mainly from the Constant Child is perpetually childlike—one who refuses to grow up. He or she doesn't think or decide for himself or herself but attempts to remain dependent in order to escape the responsibility for his or her own behavior. This individual seeks someone who will take care of him or her. The Constant Adult, who excludes the Parent and the Child, is objective—that is, involved and concerned with facts. The Constant Adult is an individual who appears robot-like, with little feeling and little spontaneity.

Didactic Methods

Since TA emphasizes the cognitive domain, teaching/learning procedures are basic to the approach. Members of TA groups are expected to become thoroughly acquainted with structural analysis by mastering the fundamentals of P-A-C. Books are often recommended as an adjunct to therapy. Useful books for the layman include Eric Berne's *Games People Play* and *What Do You Say after You Say Hello?*, Thomas Harris' *I'm OK–You're OK*, Claude Steiner's *Scripts People Live*, and Muriel James and Dorothy Jongeward's *Born to Win*. In addition to readings, there are available introductory courses in TA, which are often recommended as preparation for TA therapy. Also recommended for members of an ongoing TA group is participation in special workshops, conferences, and educational events related to TA.

Transactional Analysis

Transactional analysis is basically a description of what people do and say to one another. Whatever happens between people involves a transaction between their ego states. When messages are sent, a response is expected. There are three types of transactions: complementary, crossed, and ulterior. Complementary transactions occur when a message sent from a specific ego state gets the predicted response from a specific ego state of the other person. An example is the playful Child-Child transaction illustrated in Figure 6-4. Crossed transactions occur when an unexpected response is made to a message that a person sends out, as shown in Figure 6-5. Ulterior transactions are complex in that they involve more than two ego states, and a disguised message is sent, as is illustrated in Figure 6-6.

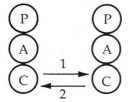

1. "I'd love to go sledding in the snow with you."

2. "Hey, that sounds like fun! Let's go!"

Figure 6-4 Complementary Transactions

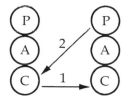

1. "I'd love to go sledding with you in the snow."

2. "Oh, grow up and act your age! I don't have time to waste on foolishness like that!"

Figure 6-5 Crossed Transactions

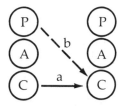

He to her: "Would you like to go out in the snow and play, or maybe we should finish all this work we should be doing in the house!" He is sending a mixed message, which she can hear as (a) Let's go out and play in the snow (Child ⟶ Child) *or* (b) Let's be responsible and finish our work (Parent ⟶ Child).

Figure 6-6 Ulterior Transactions

Empty Chair

"Empty chair" is a procedure that works well with structural analysis. How does it work? Assume the client is having difficulty coping with his or her boss (a Parent ego state). The client is asked to imagine that person in the chair before him or her and carry on a dialogue with him or her. This procedure allows the client to express many thoughts, feelings, and attitudes as he or she assumes the roles of the ego states involved. The client sharpens not only his or her awareness of, in this case, the Parent ego state but of the other two ego states (Child and Adult), which usually have certain characteristics in relation to the imagined state. The empty-chair technique can be useful for people who struggle with strong internal conflicts to get a sharper focus and a concrete grasp on a resolution.

McNeel (1976) describes the two-chair technique as an effective tool to assist clients in resolving old conflicts with their parents or people who were in their environment as they were growing up. The goal of the two-chair work is to make closure by completing unfinished business from the past. McNeel contends "that those therapists who do not make interventions and who sit on the sideline watching the reenactment of an old scene and waiting for the client to make a resolution in this process do not achieve very high results" (p. 62). In order to help clients stop waiting for some unresolved scene in the past to change, it is necessary for therapists to know how to potently intervene in the two-chair work. McNeel provides guidelines for issues to watch for in two-chair work, and he suggests the use of "heighteners" to clarify the issues involved. For example, a client may present himself as a helpless victim when he says "My father never really loved me, so now I don't know how to love anyone else and I don't know what to do about this." An appropriate "heightener" the therapist may use is "So maybe you can stay as you are until you die, unless your father finally decides to love you!"

Role-Playing

TA procedures can also be beneficially combined with psychodrama and role-playing techniques. In group therapy, role-playing situations can involve other members. Another group member becomes the ego state that a client is having problems with, and the client talks to that member. Also, group members may rehearse with another group member certain kinds of behaviors that they would like to try out in their outside lives. Another possibility is to exaggerate characteristic styles of Constant Parent, Constant Adult, or Constant Child or certain games so that a client can get feedback on present behavior in the group.

Family Modeling

Family modeling, another approach to working with structural analysis, is particularly useful in working with a Constant Parent, a Constant Adult, or a Constant Child. The client is asked to imagine a scene including as many significant persons in his or her past as possible, including himself or herself. The client becomes the director, producer, and actor. He or she defines the situation and uses other members of the group as substitutes for his or her family members. The client places them in the way he or she remembers the situation. The subsequent discussion, action, and evaluation can then heighten the awareness of a specific situation and the personal meanings it still holds for the client.

Analysis of Rituals, Pastimes, and Games

Analysis of transactions includes identification of rituals, pastimes, and games that are used in the structuring of time. Time structuring is important material for discussion and examination because it reflects the decisions of the script about how to transact with others and how to get strokes. A person who fills his or her time chiefly with rituals and pastimes is probably experiencing stroke deprivation, and thus he or she lacks intimacy in his or her transactions with others. Because ritual and pastime transactions have low stroke value, the person's social transacting may lead to complaints such as emptiness, boredom, lack of excitement, feeling unloved, and a sense of meaninglessness.

Analysis of Games and Rackets

The analysis of games and rackets is an important aspect of understanding the nature of transactions with others. Berne (1964) described a game as "an ongoing series of complementary ulterior transactions progressing to a well-defined, predictable outcome" (p. 48). A pay-off for most games is a "bad" feeling that the player experiences. It is important to observe and understand why the games are played, what pay-offs result, what strokes are received, and how these games maintain distance and interfere with intimacy. Learning to understand a person's "racket" and how the racket relates to the person's games, decisions, and life scripts is an important process in TA therapy.

A racket consists of the collection of feelings that one uses to justify one's life script and, ultimately, one's decisions. A person can develop an "anger racket," a "hurt racket," a "guilt racket," or a "depression racket." For example, if a person saves up feelings of depression, the games he or she plays with others most often have depression as the pay-off, and, when he or she has finally gathered enough feelings of depression, he or she feels justified in suicide, which is the action called for to conclude the life script. This is true of the person who has bought the "don't be" message. A racket is an old, familiar, bad feeling, such as resentment, guilt, fear, hurt, and inadequacy.

Rackets involve the "collection of stamps" that are later traded for a psychological prize. The individual collects archaic feelings (stamp collecting) by manipulating others to make himself or herself feel rejected, angry, depressed, abandoned, guilty, and so on. The person invites others to play certain roles. For example, a group member may invite other group members to react to him or her with anger. He or she could program this reaction by being extremely closed and hostile, and by persuading himself or herself that nobody could ever understand, much less care for, him or her. Any genuine approach from others would be rebuffed by his or her refusal to accept anything from anyone. Eventually, the person would collect enough stamps to prove to the entire group that he or she was right all along, and then he or she could say "See, I told you at the beginning that nobody really cares for me and that I'd wind up feeling isolated from and rejected by all of you!"

When people manipulate others to reexperience and collect archaic feelings, they are collecting bad feelings, and a racket consists of that kind of collection. Rackets are as important as games in manipulating others, for they are the primary method of masking a person from the real world. It takes a competent therapist to distinguish between anger, tears, and fears that are used as a racket and the honest expression of emotions. The competent and skillful therapist squarely challenges a client's racket in such a manner that the client becomes aware of his or her behavior without being driven off.

Script Analysis

A person's lack of autonomy is related to the person's involvement with his or her scripting—that is, with a life plan decided on at an early age as a means of meeting the person's needs in the world as he or she sees it from the vantage point of his or her life position. The life script, or the plan for a lifetime, which is based on a series of decisions and adaptations, is much like a dramatic stage production. The individual experiences certain life events, accepts and learns definite roles, and rehearses and acts out these roles according to the script. There are a cast of characters, scenes, dialogues, plots, and actions leading to a finale. The psychological life script outlines where the person is going in life and what he or she will do on arrival. An important aspect of the life script is the compelling quality that drives the person to play it out.

Scripting initially occurs nonverbally in infancy, from parents' messages. During the early years of development, one learns about one's worth as a person and one's place in life. Later, scripting occurs in direct as well as indirect ways. For example, in a family, such messages as the following may be picked up: "In this family, the man is the boss of the house"; "Children are to be seen, but not heard"; "We always expect the best from you"; "The way you are, you'll never amount to a hill of beans"; and "Never question our authority, and always strive to be respectful and obedient." Because a person's life script forms the core of his or her personal identity and destiny, life experiences may lead a person to conclude "I'm really dumb because nothing I do ever turns out right. I suppose I'll always be stupid," or "I can do almost anything that I really decide I want to do. I know I can attain my goals if I channel my efforts in a direction I want to go in."

Script analysis is a part of the therapeutic process by which the life pattern that a person follows is identified. It can demonstrate to the person the process by which he or she acquired the script and the ways he or she justifies his or her script actions. When a person becomes aware of his or her life script, he or she is in a position to do something about changing the programming. A person is not condemned to be a victim of early scripting, for, through awareness, redecision is possible. Script analysis opens up new alternatives from which to choose as the person goes through life; he or she need no longer feel compelled to play games to collect pay-offs to justify a certain action that is called for in his or her life script.

Script analysis can be carried out by means of a script checklist, which contains items related to life positions, rackets, and games—all of which are key functional components of a person's life script. Holland (1973) asserted that autonomy and intimacy can replace script and games through script and game analysis:

> The only interesting alternative to living a game-playing, racket-ridden life script is to live an autonomous, self-chosen life pattern which can be changed to a more interesting and rewarding pattern at any time, including the possibility of true intimacy with another person. This is the alternative that script and game analysis makes possible, since it provides the patient with the possibility of shutting down a familiar but unsatisfying life pattern in order to put a newer and more interesting show on the road [p. 398].

The Gouldings (1976) make the point that clients are not "scripted" and that "injunctions are not placed in people's heads like electrodes." According to them, "each child makes decisions in response to real or imagined injunctions, and thereby 'scripts' her/himself" (p. 42). A list of behavioral, thinking, and feeling injunctions has been developed by the Gouldings (1976) and includes the injunctions "Don't be" or "Don't exist," "Don't be you (the sex you are)," "Don't be a child," "Don't grow," "Don't make it," "Don't be important," "Don't belong," "Don't be close," and "Don't trust."

Through a combination of TA, Gestalt, and behavior modification, the Gouldings discovered, clients changed without years of analysis. They emphasize the concept of redecisions by challenging clients to realize that it is a myth that scripts were implanted into their heads. The Gouldings indicate that, when clients perceive that they were the ones who made certain decisions, then they also use their power to change their early decisions. In other words, clients decided to be aloof, nontrusting, or childlike; thus they are the ones who through redecision can change all that. This redecision process is facilitated by working in the here and now and by avoiding talking about the past.

Summary and Evaluation

I want to share some personal reactions to TA as a method of therapy or counseling. First, I find the contract method very useful, and I believe that any orientation to counseling can incorporate this aspect that, in my judgment, helps the client assume more personal responsibility for the outcomes of the counseling experience. The analysis of the games that we all play, another contribution of TA, teaches clients to become more aware of game structures, and in TA clients have the opportunity to search for ways to free themselves from game-playing behavior. They can move from manipulative behavior to more authentic behavior.

Another contribution of TA that I value and that I have incorporated into my style of counseling is challenging clients to become more aware of the early decisions that they made at one time in their childhood because of psychological survival motives but that are now, in adult life, not only inappropriate but archaic. A lot of people drag behind them their early decisions about their self-worth and personal power, and they fail to come to terms with their power because they cling to parental messages that they rehearse over and over in their heads. I favor asking people to talk out loud and to share their inner rehearsals of the messages, many of which keep them in an emotional straitjacket. The TA insistence on examining here-and-now transactions with others to determine what people get from some of their behavior styles is another useful concept that I have incorporated into my counseling practice.

Further, the integration of TA concepts and practices with certain concepts from Gestalt therapy is extremely useful. A good example of how these two approaches can be blended together can be found in James and Jongeward's *Born to Win*, which I think is essential reading for any counselor.

I frequently use some of the concepts from TA, such as working with early parental messages or the subtle ways people behave as their own parents behaved, as catalysts for role-playing or psychodrama. For example, instead of allowing a group participant to carry on a lengthy monologue about why he or she has difficulty expressing affection to those he or she cares about, I'll request that the client reenact some early scene with his or her parents that depicts how he or she learned that "You aren't supposed to get too close." Psychodrama, which can tap the deeper feelings of a current difficulty, tends to be far more meaningful than having the person talk about an early decision. The above, then, are a few of the concepts and techniques that I find meaningful and useful in my counseling style.

Now, what about the limitations of TA? First, since I encourage my students not to subscribe to any approach exclusively, I am somewhat uncomfortable with some proponents of TA who seem to believe that psychotherapy begins and ends with Eric Berne's model and who follow to the letter Berne's terminology and methodology. The emphasis on the many TA terms and jargon disturbs me. While this seems to be characteristic of amateur TA therapists, I do not think that a good TA therapist restricts himself or herself to structure and terminology. The emphasis on the structure, to the degree that I find structure in TA, is another disquieting aspect for me. I believe that it is very possible for a person who is well schooled in TA to become an expert in diagnosing game patterns, indicating to the client what type of transaction the client is now in, labeling every bit of behavior with some cliché phrase, detecting to what degree a person is "OK," and sorting out all kinds of scripting and yet still practice therapy in such a manner that he or she leaves himself or herself (his or her values, feelings, reactions to the client, and so on) out of the transaction with a client. In other words, I don't see in TA a great emphasis on the authenticity of the therapist or on the quality of the person-to-person relationship with the client. As the Rogerian therapist can hide under the blanket of passivity and refrain from directing the client to any degree, the TA therapist can hide under the blanket of categories, structures, labeling, transaction analysis, and the figurative job of directing traffic. The danger is that TA can be primarily an intellectual experience whereby, as the client who has undergone years of psychoanalysis, the TA client can understand intellectually all sorts of things but perhaps not also feel and experience those aspects of himself or herself. Is the client in TA encouraged to work toward a synthesis of head and gut? Reliance on TA as an exclusive way of growth seems to be limiting in that it stresses understanding on a cognitive level. In my opinion, one of the shortcomings of the Gestalt approach is that it deemphasizes intellectual factors. In Gestalt one is frequently called to task if one thinks and is told that one is "bullshitting" or, even worse, "elephantshitting"! In TA, however, one of the shortcomings is its deemphasis of the affective domain. Thus it is the marriage of many of the concepts and techniques of Gestalt with those of TA that is most useful. It should be added, however, that contemporary TA stresses the integration of the cognitive and emotional domains.

Questions for Evaluation

Below are questions that are based on the TA framework. I suggest you apply them to yourself and use them as guidelines for your evaluation of Transactional Analysis and its implications for you.

1. What are some values and standards that you have taken from your parents? What kinds of values do you hold that are in contrast to your parents' values? To what degree have you thought through these values and made them your own or modified them?

2. What are some games and strategies you used as a child with your family and that you are aware of still using in your present relationships with people? What do these games do for you?

3. Can you trace some of the basic early decisions that you made about yourself during your childhood? Are those decisions still operating in your present behavior? Are you aware of changing any of your basic decisions? If so, which ones?

4. What are some parental injunctions that you can identify in your life? Can you identify with any of the following? Don't play. Don't think. Don't touch. Don't talk. Don't stare. Don't be close. Don't succeed. Don't fail. Don't let us down. Don't enjoy. Don't trust. Don't be you. Don't be sexy. Don't be rude. Don't fight. Don't be selfish. Don't be.

5. What are some "do's," "ought's," and "should's" in your life? Which of the following fit for you? Be perfect. You should be productive. You ought to work to your potential. You should do what is expected of you. You ought to be responsible. Succeed at everything. Be tough. Do what is right.

6. Can you see how some injunctions that you have internalized might have some effect on you as you counsel others? For example, if you have trouble being spontaneous or being childlike, how might you be affected in working with clients who are impulsive and tend to live for the moment?

7. How do you get your strokes? Are they mainly negative or mainly positive? Do you get strokes from your family? from work? from friends? Are you able to ask for the strokes you want, or are you limited in the amount of positive stroking you can tolerate?

8. Do you really believe that most people are able to change the early decisions that they made about themselves, others, and life? What forces operate against a person in his or her attempt to change and make new decisions? How can a person make and retain new decisions?

9. Are games to some extent necessary for survival? If they are not, why do you suppose that so many of us cling to our manipulative game-playing strategies? What do you suppose would happen if a person gave up all his or her manipulative games and became completely straight and honest in all transactions with others?

10. According to Harris (1967), the essence of a cure in TA therapy is as follows: "If a patient can put into words why he does what he does and how he has stopped doing it, then he is cured, in that he knows

what the cure is and can use it again and again" (p. 238). Do you agree? Is this enough? If so, why? If you don't agree, what else do you think is necessary?

References and Suggested Readings

Berne, E. *Transactional Analysis in psychotherapy.* New York: Grove Press, 1961.

Berne, E. *Games people play.* New York: Grove Press, 1964.

Berne, E. *Principles of group treatment.* New York: Oxford University Press, 1966.

Berne, E. *Sex in human loving.* New York: Simon & Schuster, 1970.

Berne, E. *What do you say after you say hello?* New York: Grove Press, 1972.

Goulding, R., & Goulding, M. Injunctions, decisions, and redecisions. *Transactional Analysis Journal,* 1976, 6:1.

Harper, R. *The new psychotherapies.* Englewood Cliffs, N.J.: Prentice-Hall, 1975.

*Harris, T. *I'm OK—You're OK.* New York: Avon, 1967.

Holland, G. Transactional Analysis. In R. Corsini (Ed.), *Current psychotherapies.* Itasca, Ill.: Peacock, 1973.

*James, M., & Jongeward, D. *Born to win: Transactional Analysis with Gestalt experiments.* Reading, Mass.: Addison-Wesley, 1971.

McNeel, J. The parent interview. *Transactional Analysis Journal,* 1976, 6:1.

Schiff, J. L., with Day, B. *All my children.* New York: Evans, 1970.

*Steiner, C. *Scripts people live: Transactional Analysis of life scripts.* New York: Grove Press, 1974.

CHAPTER SEVEN

BEHAVIOR

THERAPY

Introduction

Behavior therapy has come to mean the application of a diversity of techniques and procedures that are rooted in a variety of theories of learning. It involves the systematic application of principles of learning to change behavior toward more adaptive ways. This approach has made significant contributions to both clinical and educational settings.

Grounded in learning theory, behavior modification and behavior therapy are approaches to counseling and psychotherapy that are concerned with behavior change. It is important to understand that no single learning theory undergirds the practice of behavior therapy; rather, a number of diverse theories of learning contribute to this general therapeutic approach. Instead of considering behavior therapy as a unified and singular approach to therapy, it is more accurate to think in terms of the behavior therapies, which include a variety of principles and methods that are not yet integrated into a unified system.

The development of the behavior therapies is marked by a phenomenal growth since the late 1950s. In the early 1960s infrequent reports of the use of behavior-therapy techniques appeared in the professional literature. Now behavior therapy and behavior modification occupy a place of prominence in the field of psychotherapy and in many areas of education. The professional literature, both journals and books, attest to the increase of popularity of this approach. The increased influence of behavior therapy is also manifested in the number of psychology departments that are geared to training clinical and counseling psychology students in behavioral methods. Many training programs today clearly emphasize a behavioral orientation. This trend becomes more impressive when we consider that during the late 1950s and early 1960s few departments of psychology and psychiatry, as well as few related mental-health training programs, were involved in any substantial way with behavior therapy. Behavior modification has had an enormous impact in the field of education, particularly in the area of special education of children with learning and behavior problems.

One of the most important aspects of the behavior-modification movement is its emphasis on operationally defined, observable, and measurable behavior. Behavior, not unmeasurable constructs that are vitally related to psychodynamic approaches, is the focus of therapeutic attention. To their credit, the proponents of behavior therapies have provided themselves with an objective indication of their activities. Behavioral change as the specific criterion lends itself to an immediate evaluation of the efficacy of their work and the rate at which they progress toward clearly specified therapeutic goals. That much of the growth of the behavior therapies is due to the large body of research is also characteristic of the movement. The procedures are continually being refined because of the commitment to subject these procedures to rigorous testing to determine how well they actually work. Because behavior therapy rests on the experimental results of its theoretical claims, the basic concepts continue to be strengthened and developed.

Key Concepts

View of Human Nature

Behaviorism is a scientific view of human behavior. Its basic proposition is that behavior is orderly and that carefully controlled experiments will reveal the laws that control behavior. The position includes restricting methods and procedures to observable data.

The behavioristic approach does not spell out any philosophical assumptions directly regarding human nature. The individual is seen as having an equal potential for positive and negative tendencies. Human beings are essentially shaped and determined by their sociocultural environments. All human behavior is learned. Although behaviorists believe that ultimately all behavior is the result of environmental forces and the individual's genetic endowment, they do include decision making as one kind of behavior. The behaviorist's view of human nature is frequently distorted by the oversimplified explanation of the individual as a helpless pawn of fate who is solely determined by environmental and genetic influences and reduced to merely a responding organism. Contemporary behavior therapy is not strictly a deterministic and mechanistic approach that rules out any possibility of choice potential of clients. Only the "radical behaviorists" exclude the possibility of self-determinism.

Nye (1975), in his discussion of B. F. Skinner's "radical behaviorism," makes it clear that the radical behaviorists stress that humans are controlled by environmental conditions. Their strong deterministic stand is linked to a firm commitment to the search for observable behavior patterns. They describe in specific detail the various observable factors that influence learning and make the argument that humans are controlled by external circumstances.

The view of "radical behaviorism" allows no room for the assumption that human behavior is governed by choice and freedom. The radical behavioristic philosophy rejects the concept of the person as a free agent who shapes his or her own destiny. Past and present situations in the objective world determine behavior. The environment is the primary shaper of human existence.

John Watson, the founder of the behavioristic approach to psychological science, was a radical behaviorist who asserted that he could take any healthy infant and make the infant into anything he desired—doctor, lawyer, artist, beggar, thief—through environmental shaping. Thus Watson excluded from psychology concepts such as consciousness, self-determinism, and any other subjective phenomena. He constructed a psychology of the observable conditions of behavior. Marquis (1974) contended that behavior therapy is like engineering in that it applies scientific information to discover technical solutions to human problems. Thus the focus is on how people learn and what conditions determine their behavior.

Unique Characteristics of Behavior Therapy

Behavior therapy, in contrast to most other therapy approaches, is characterized by (a) a focus on overt and specific behavior, (b) a precision and spelling out of treatment goals, (c) a formulation of a specific treatment procedure appropriate to a particular problem, and (d) an objective assessment of the outcomes of therapy.

Behavior therapy is not based on a systematic set of concepts, nor is it rooted in a well-developed theory. Although it has many techniques, it has few concepts. It is an inductive approach based on experiments, and it applies the experimental method to the therapeutic process. The therapist's question might be "What is the specific behavior that this individual wants to change, and what new behavior does he or she desire to learn?" This specificity necessitates a careful observation of the client's behavior. Vague and general descriptions are not acceptable: the behavior that a client wishes to change is specified. It is important also that the specific conditions that determine the problem behavior be identified, so that new conditions can be created to modify the behavior. The main therapeutic concern is to isolate the problem behavior and then create the means of changing it.

Basically, behavior therapy is aimed at goals of acquiring new behavior, eliminating maladaptive behavior, and strengthening and maintaining desirable behavior. A precise statement of goals of treatment is specified. A general statement of a goal is unacceptable; instead, the client attempts to state in concrete ways the kinds of problematic behavior he or she wishes to change. After developing precise treatment goals, the therapist must choose the most appropriate procedure(s) for accomplishing these goals. Available is a variety of techniques, which vary in their effectiveness in the treatment of particular problems. For example, aversion techniques appear useful as an aid to establishing impulse control; those who are timid in self-expression and in personal relationships might benefit from assertive training; behavior rehearsal can be useful in strengthening newly acquired behaviors; desensitization seems most useful in treating phobias; modeling combined with positive reinforcement appears appropriate for the acquisition of complex social behavior.

Since the target behavior is clearly specified, treatment goals detailed, and therapeutic methods delineated, it follows that the outcomes of therapy can be evaluated. Behavior therapy incorporates well-defined criteria for improvement or cure. Because behavior therapy emphasizes evaluation of the effectiveness of the techniques employed, a continual evolution and refinement of treatment procedures marks the therapeutic process.

Classical Conditioning versus Operant Conditioning

Two major streams form the essence of the methods and techniques of learning-based approaches to counseling and psychotherapy: classical conditioning and operant conditioning. Classical conditioning, or respondent conditioning, derives from the work of Pavlov. Basically, it involves the presence of an unconditioned stimulus (UCS) that automatically evokes a conditioned response (CR), which is similar to the unconditioned response (UCR) when it is associated with the unconditioned stimulus. If the UCS is paired with a conditioned stimulus (CS), then gradually the CS leads to the CR. In the example shown in Figure 7-1, the UCS (cat food) evokes a UCR, the cat's salivating. Opening a can of cat food with an electric can opener becomes a CS because it is paired with the food and evokes the CR, the salivating of the expectant cat.

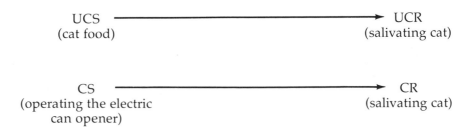

UCS ——————————————————————→ UCR
(cat food)   (salivating cat)

CS ——————————————————————→ CR
(operating the electric   (salivating cat)
can opener)

Figure 7-1 Design for Classical Conditioning

The work both of Salter and of Wolpe derives largely from the classical-conditioning model. Specific techniques such as systematic desensitization and aversion therapy are based on the principles of classical conditioning. These techniques will be described below in the section on the application of behavioral techniques and procedures.

Operant conditioning, which is the other major stream of learning-based therapy approaches, involves rewarding the individual for a desired behavior at the time the behavior occurs. This approach is also known as "instrumental" conditioning, because certain instrumental behavior by an active organism has to occur before reinforcement of the behavior occurs. Skinner, who is associated primarily with operant conditioning, has developed principles of reinforcement that account for the acquisition of certain learned patterns of behavior. In operant conditioning, the use of positive reinforcement strengthens behavior, and the use of punishment weakens it. The conditioned behavior operates on the environment and is instrumental in gaining a reward.

Many behavior-modification techniques and procedures derive from the operant-conditioning model. Some specific examples of procedures that are associated with operant conditioning include positive reinforcement, extinction, punishment, modeling, and the use of token economies. These therapeutic techniques will be described later in this chapter.

The Therapeutic Process

Therapeutic Goals

Goals of counseling and psychotherapy occupy a place of central importance in behavior therapy. The client selects the counseling goals, which are specifically defined at the outset of the therapeutic process. Continual assessment throughout therapy determines the degree to which these goals are being effectively met.

The general goal of behavior therapy is to create new conditions for learning. The rationale is that all behavior is learned, including maladaptive behavior. If neurosis is learned, it can be unlearned, and more effective behaviors can be acquired. Behavior therapy consists essentially of a process that eliminates unadaptive learning and furnishes learning experiences wherein appropriate responses have not been learned.

There are several misconceptions regarding the issue of goals in behavior therapy. One common misconception is that the goal is simply to remove symptoms of a disturbance and that once these symptoms are eliminated new symptoms appear because the underlying causes were not treated. Most behavior therapists would not accept the notion that their approach is merely symptomatic treatment, for they see the therapist's task as eliminating maladaptive behavior and assisting the client to replace it with more adjustive behavior (Ullman & Krasner, 1965).

Another common misconception is that client goals are determined and imposed by the behavior therapist. There appears to be some truth in this statement, particularly as it pertains to some in situations such as mental hospitals. A clear trend in modern behavior therapy, however, moves toward involving the client in the selection of goals, and a good working relationship between the therapist and the client is seen as necessary (though not sufficient) in order to clarify therapeutic goals and cooperatively work toward the means to accomplish them.

Whereas the early proponents of this approach seem to have emphasized the expert role of the therapist in deciding goals and behavior, more recent practitioners give weight to the importance of the client's active stance in choosing goals and the client's active involvement in the therapy process. They make it clear that therapy cannot be imposed on an unwilling client and that the therapist and the client need to work together for common objectives. In discussing this issue related to the current practice of behavior therapy, Goldstein (1973) commented as follows:

> Obviously the process of behavior therapy is not one of straightforward reconditioning of the patient. The therapist cannot *impose* conditioning or relearning on anyone, for the most potent of techniques is useless without the cooperation and motivation of the patient. The therapeutic techniques to be used, whatever they may be for a given person, must be embedded in the context of a "working relationship" between the therapist and the patient. A working relationship is one in which the therapist and patient are working together toward a commonly agreed upon goal. If this is not accomplished then, in the vast majority of cases, therapy will be ineffective [p. 220].

Broad, general goals are not acceptable to the behavior therapist. Assume that a client seeks therapy aimed at self-actualization. Such a general goal needs to be translated into specific behavioral changes that the client wishes to make and analyzed into specific actions that the client desires so that both the therapist and the client are able to more concretely appraise where they are going and how to get there. For example, the broad goal of self-actualization could be broken down into some of the following, more concrete subgoals: (1) to assist the client in being more assertive and expressing his or her thoughts and desires in situations calling for assertive behavior; (2) to help the client eliminate unrealistic fears that prevent him or her from engaging in social events; and (3) to resolve an inner conflict that is keeping the client from making an important life decision.

Krumboltz and Thoresen (cited in Huber & Millman, 1972) have developed a set of three criteria for formulating an acceptable goal in behavioral counseling: "(1) It must be a goal desired by the client; (2) the counselor must be willing to help the client achieve this goal; (3) it must be possible to assess the extent to which the client achieves this goal" (p. 347). But what if the client is unclear in the definition of his or her problem and presents only fuzzy goals? Krumboltz and Thoresen agree that most clients do not describe their problems in simple and clear language. The therapist's task is to actively and empathetically listen to the client's concerns. The therapist reflects back what he or she understands to determine whether his or her perception of the client's thoughts and feelings is correct. Most of all, the therapist helps the client describe how he or she would like to act instead of the way he or she currently acts. By focusing on the specific behaviors in a client's present life, the therapist helps the client translate the client's confusion into a concrete goal that is possible to attain.

The Function and Role of the Therapist

The behavior therapist must assume an active, directive role in treatment, for the therapist applies scientific knowledge to discovering solutions to human problems. The behavior therapist typically functions as a teacher, director, and expert in diagnosing maladaptive behavior and in prescribing curative procedures that, it is hoped, lead to new and improved behavior.

As a result of his thorough review of psychotherapy literature, Krasner (1967) argued that the role of any psychotherapist, regardless of his or her theoretical alliance, is really that of a "reinforcement machine." Whatever the therapist might think he or she is doing, he or she is basically involved in doling out both positive and negative social reinforcements. Even though the therapist perceives himself or herself as being neutral regarding value judgments, the therapist shapes the client's behavior in both direct and indirect ways. Krasner (1967) stated that "the therapist or influencer is a 'reinforcement machine,' which by its very presence is supplying generalized reinforcement at all times in the therapy situation, irrespective of the particular technique or personality involved" (p. 202). He contended that the client's behavior is subject to subtle manipulation by the therapist's reinforcing behavior. This frequently occurs without the awareness of either client or therapist. Krasner (1967), in citing the literature, demonstrated that the role of the therapist is to manipulate and control psychotherapy by his or her knowledge and skills in employing learning techniques in a social-reinforcement situation. Krasner further contended that, although most therapists are uncomfortable in the role of "controller" or "manipulator" of behavior, these terms accurately describe what the therapist's role actually is. He cited evidence showing that, by virtue of the therapist's role, the therapist has "the power to influence and control the behavior and values of other human beings. For the therapist not to accept this situation and to be continually unaware of influencing effects of his behavior on his patients would itself be 'unethical' " (p. 204).

Goodstein (1972) also pointed to the role of the therapist as a reinforcer. According to Goodstein, "the role of the counselor is to facilitate the development of such socially appropriate behavior by systematically reinforcing this kind of client behavior" (p. 274). A therapist's interest, attention, and approval (or disinterest and disapproval) are powerful reinforcers of client behavior. These reinforcers are mainly of an interpersonal nature, and they involve both verbal and nonverbal language, frequently without the therapist's full awareness. Goodstein points out that the therapist's role of controlling the client's behavior through reinforcement goes beyond the counseling situation and is carried into the client's behavior in the real world as well: "The counselor rewards certain responses that the client reports performing in real-life situations and punishes others. These rewards are approval, interest, and concern . . . such reinforcement would be especially important during the period when the client is trying out new responses or behavior that is as yet not regularly reinforced by others in the client's life" (p. 275). One reason for unsuccessful results is that the therapist insufficiently reinforces the newly developing client behavior.

Another important function is the therapist's role modeling for the client. Bandura (1969) indicated that most of the learning that occurs through direct experience can also be acquired through observation of others' behavior. He developed the point that one of the fundamental processes by which clients can learn new behavior is through imitation, or the social modeling provided by the therapist. The therapist, as a person, becomes a significant role model for the client. Since the client often views the therapist as worthy of emulation, the client often patterns attitudes, values, beliefs, and behavior after the therapist. Thus the therapist should be aware of the crucial role that he or she plays in the process of identification. For the therapist to be unaware of the power he or she has in actually influencing and shaping the client's way of thinking and behaving is for the therapist to deny the central importance of his or her own personhood in the therapeutic process.

The Client's Experience in Therapy

One of the unique contributions of behavior therapy is that it provides the therapist with a system of well-defined procedures to employ within the context of a well-defined role. It also provides the client with a well-defined role, and it stresses the importance of client awareness and participation in the therapeutic process. Carkhuff and Berenson (1967) indicated that, even though the client might often be in the role of a "passive recipient of techniques," the client is kept well informed about the therapeutic techniques employed. They asserted that, "while the therapist has principal responsibility, the client is the major focus of attention, with little regard for social values, parental influence, and unconscious processes. To their credit, the behavior modification therapists are the first to share with their patients a detailed explanation of what is, and what will be done, at each stage of the treatment process" (p. 92).

The client's involvement in the therapeutic process should thus be thought of as being more active than a passive recipient of techniques, as Carkhuff and Berenson implied. To be sure, the client must be actively involved in the selection and determination of goals, he or she must possess the motivation to change, and he or she must be willing to cooperate in carrying out therapeutic activities, both during the therapeutic sessions and outside therapy in real-life situations. If the client is not actively involved in this way in the therapeutic process, the chances are that the outcomes of therapy will not be successful.

Marquis (1974), utilizing the principles of the behavioral approach to foster effective personality change, viewed the client's role as active in the therapy process. Within the behavior-therapy model, Marquis described a three-phase program that involves the full and active participation of the client. First, the client's present behavior is analyzed and "a clear understanding is reached of the terminal behaviors which are to be sought with the client's full participation in every part of the process of setting goals" (p. 368). Second, alternative paths the client might take to reach his or her goals are explored. Third, a treatment program is planned, which is usually based on small, incremental steps from the client's present behavior toward behavior that is likely to help the client reach his or her goal.

An important aspect of the client's role in behavior therapy is that he or she is encouraged to experiment with new behavior for the purpose of enlarging his or her repertoire of adaptive behaviors. In therapy, the client is helped to generalize and transfer the learning acquired within the therapeutic situation to situations outside therapy. Again, this approach underscores the importance of the active involvement and willingness of the client to extend and apply his or her emerging behavior to real-life situations.

This therapy is not complete unless actions follow verbalizations. The client must do far more than merely gather insights, for in behavior therapy the client must be willing to take risks. That real-life problems must be solved with new behavior outside therapy means that an action phase is essential. Successes and failures of the attempts to implement new behavior are a vital part of the therapeutic adventure.

The Relationship between Therapist and Client

There appears to be a tendency on the part of some critics to characterize the relationship between the therapist and the client in behavior therapy as mechanically manipulative and highly impersonal. Most writers in this area, however, especially Wolpe (1958, 1969), assert that establishing a good personal relationship is an essential aspect of the therapeutic process. As was discussed earlier, an essential role for the therapist is that of a reinforcing agent, a role that is contingent on establishing a therapeutic relationship. Behavior therapists do not have to be cast in the cold and impersonal role that reduces them to programmed machines that impose a set of techniques on robot-like clients.

It does appear, however, that most behavior therapies do not assign an all-important role to the relationship variables. Nonetheless, most of them do assert that factors such as warmth, empathy, authenticity, permissiveness, and acceptance are considered necessary, but not sufficient, conditions for behavior change to occur within the therapeutic process. On this issue, Goldstein (1973) maintained that establishing a working relationship sets the stage for therapy to occur. He noted that "such a relationship in and of itself is not sufficient as a maximally effective therapy" (p. 220). Before any therapeutic intervention can occur with any degree of effectiveness, the therapist must establish an atmosphere of trust by showing that "(1) he understands and accepts the patient, (2) that the two of them are working *together,* and (3) that the therapist has at his disposal the means to be of help in the direction desired by the patient" (p. 221).

Application: Therapeutic Techniques and Procedures

One of the contributions of behavior therapy is the development of specific therapeutic procedures that lend themselves to refinement through the scientific method. Behavioral techniques must be shown to be effective through objective means, and there is a constant effort to improve techniques. Krumboltz and Thoresen (cited in Huber & Millman, 1972) maintained that "behavioral counseling is a self-correcting system" (p. 350). Although behavior therapists may make mistakes in diagnosis or in applying techniques, the results of their mistakes are obvious to them. They receive direct feedback from the client. Either the client improves or he or she does not. As Krumboltz and Thoresen put it, "Techniques that do not work can always be eliminated and new techniques can be tried" (p. 350). They emphasize that techniques must be tailored to the individual needs of the client and that no technique should ever be employed routinely with every client without considering alternative methods of accomplishing the client's goals. Further, they call for evaluation of therapeutic procedures and improvement of the procedures on the basis of relevant evidence.

Krumboltz and Thoresen (cited in Huber & Millman, 1972) encourage experimenting with therapeutic procedures: "There are no restrictions on the possible techniques behavioral counselors can try except, of course, ethical ones. Experimentation is an essential part of the counselor's job" (p. 349). Thus there is no list of approved techniques that a behavioral counselor can employ. Instead, "the door must be kept open to all procedures that might be helpful to the extent of encouraging those who may be trying some novel or 'far-out' technique even if it does not fit the existing pattern of techniques" (p. 349). Apparently Krasner (1967) agreed with that point of view: "The therapist has a broad spectrum of behavioral techniques available to him, limited only by his ingenuity in varying his behavior and the setting" (p. 206).

In behavior therapy a variety of specific techniques can be systematically employed, and their results can be evaluated. These techniques can be used when they are appropriate, and many of them can be incorporated into the practice of psychotherapy based on other models. The specific methods described below have applicability to both individual and group counseling and therapy.

Key Techniques in Behavior Therapy

Systematic Desensitization

Systematic desensitization is one of the most widely used techniques in behavior therapy. It is used for extinguishing negatively reinforced behavior, and it involves eliciting an antagonistic response. Desensitization aims at teaching the client to emit a response that is inconsistent with anxiety.

Wolpe (1958, 1969), the developer of the technique, argued that all neurotic behavior is an expression of anxiety and that the response of anxiety can be eliminated by finding responses inherently antagonistic to it. By classical conditioning, the anxiety-producing power of the stimulus can be weakened and the symptom of anxiety can be controlled and eliminated through the stimulus substitution of the positive incompatible response.

Systematic desensitization also involves relaxation techniques. The client is taught to relax and to associate the state of relaxation with imagined or visualized anxiety-provoking experiences. Situations are presented in a series that moves from the least to the most threatening. The hierarchy of anxiety-producing stimuli is repeatedly paired with relaxing stimuli until the connection between those stimuli and the response of anxiety is eliminated. In this technique, Wolpe has developed a response—that is, relaxation, which is physiologically incompatible with anxiety—that is systematically associated with aspects of the threatening situation. The procedure of this counterconditioning model works as follows:

1. Systematic desensitization begins with a behavioral analysis of the stimuli that elicit anxiety in a particular area, such as rejection, jealousy, criticism, disapproval, or any phobia. Time is devoted to constructing a hierarchy of the client's anxieties in a particular area. The therapist constructs a ranked list of situations that elicit increasing degrees of anxiety or avoidance. The hierarchy is arranged in order from the worst situation that the client can imagine down to the situation that evokes the least anxiety. For example, if it has been determined that the client has anxiety related to fear of rejection, it would be possible to arrange rejection situations from the most disturbing to the least disturbing. The highest anxiety-producing situation might be rejection by the spouse, next by a close friend, and then by a co-worker. The least-disturbing situation might be a stranger's indifference toward the client at a party.

2. During the first few sessions the client is given relaxation training, which consists of contracting and then gradually relaxing different muscles until a state of complete relaxation is achieved. Before relaxation training begins, the client is told how relaxation is to be used in desensitization, how to use it daily, and how to relax certain parts of the body. Relaxation training is based on the technique outlined by Jacobsen (1938) and described in detail by Wolpe (1969). Suggesting thoughts and creating imagery of previously relaxing situations such as sitting by a lake or wandering through a beautiful field are often employed. It is important that the client reach a state of calm and peacefulness. The client is taught how to relax all the muscles and is taken through the various parts of the body, with emphasis on the facial muscles. The arm muscles are relaxed first, followed by the head, then the neck and shoulders, the back, abdomen and thorax, and then the lower limbs. The client is instructed to practice relaxation outside the session for about 30 minutes each day. When the client has learned to relax quickly, the desensitization procedure begins.

3. The desensitization process involves the client's being completely relaxed with eyes closed. The therapist describes a series of scenes to the client and asks the client to imagine himself or herself in each of the scenes.

A neutral scene is presented, and the client is asked to imagine it. If the client remains relaxed, he or she is asked to imagine the least anxiety-arousing scene. The therapist moves progressively up the hierarchy until the client signals that he or she is experiencing anxiety, at which time the scene is terminated. Relaxation is then induced again, and the client continues through all the scenes in the hierarchy. Treatment ends when the client is able to remain in a relaxed state while imagining the scene that was formerly the most disturbing and anxiety producing.

Systematic desensitization is an appropriate technique for treating phobias, but it is a misconception that it can be applied only to the treatment of fears. It can be effectively applied to a large variety of anxiety-producing situations, including interpersonal ones, and to examination fears, generalized fears, neurotic anxieties, and sexual dysfunctions of impotence and frigidity.

When is the desensitization procedure contraindicated? Wolpe (1969) cited three reasons for failures in desensitization: (1) difficulties in relaxation, which may be due to difficulties in communication between the therapist and the client or to a client who is extremely inhibited; (2) misleading or irrelevant hierarchies, which might involve dealing with the wrong hierarchy; and (3) inadequacies in imagery.

How can systematic desensitization be applied to group therapy? Shaffer and Galinsky (1974), in a discussion of the development of behavior-therapy groups, indicated that as yet no articulated group model has emerged. Behavior-therapy group approaches typically introduce individually oriented behavioral procedures into a group setting. For groups using systematic-desensitization procedures, individual techniques are applied directly to the group. Shaffer and Galinsky credit Lazarus as one of the first to use desensitization procedures with groups.

The group procedure is advocated also for clients who are anxious in specific situations. The group is usually composed of participants with similar fears and anxieties. The group climate is seen as a supportive and reinforcing agent. Thus the members of the group support each other in their risk-taking activities, both inside and outside the group, and reinforcement is given for successes.

Implosive Therapy and Flooding

Flooding techniques are based on the paradigm of experimental extinction. The technique consists of the repeated presentation of the conditioned stimulus without reinforcement. It differs from systematic desensitization in that no counterconditioning agent is used, nor is a hierarchy of anxieties constructed. The therapist presents the anxiety-producing stimuli, the client imagines the situation, and the therapist attempts to maintain the client's anxiety.

Stampfl (1975) developed a related technique called "implosive therapy." As does systematic desensitization, implosive therapy assumes that neurotic behavior involves the conditioned avoidance of anxiety-producing stimuli. The technique differs from systematic desensitization in the attempt of the therapist to elicit a massive flood of anxiety. The rationale of the technique is that, if a person is repeatedly exposed to some anxiety-ridden situation and if no dire consequences occur, the anxiety is reduced or eliminated. The client is directed to imagine threatening scenes. With repeated exposure in the therapeutic setting, where the expected, feared consequences do not occur, the threatening stimuli lose the effect of producing anxiety, and the neurotic avoidance is extinguished.

Stampfl (1975) cited several examples of how implosive therapy works. He described a client who complained of obsessive tendencies related to dirt. The client washed his hands up to 100 times a day and had exaggerated fears of germs. The procedures for treating the client included (1) discovering what stimuli trigger what symptoms, (2) assessing how the symptoms are related and how they shape the patient's behavior, (3) asking the client to close his eyes and imagine as vividly as possible what is being described without reflecting on its appropriateness to his situation, (4) moving closer and closer to the client's greatest fears and attempting to have him imagine what he most wants to avoid, and (5) repeating each theme until it no longer arouses anxiety in the client.

Stampfl (1975) cited several studies that attest to the efficacy of implosive therapy with hospitalized mental patients, with neurotics, with psychotics, and with people suffering phobic symptoms. Stampfl asserted that this approach differs from conventional therapies in its deemphasis of insight as a therapeutic agent. It is a direct method of challenging the patient to "stare down his nightmares."

Assertive Training

A behavioral approach that is rapidly gaining popularity is assertive training, which is particularly applicable for interpersonal situations in which an individual has difficulties in feeling that it is appropriate or right to assert himself or herself. Assertive training can be helpful for the following people: (1) those who cannot express anger or irritation; (2) those who are overly polite and who allow others to take advantage of them; (3) those who have difficulty in saying "no"; (4) those who find it difficult to express affection and other positive responses; (5) those who feel they don't have a right to have their own feelings or thoughts.

How does the approach work? Assertive training uses role-playing procedures. A typical problem could be the difficulty a client experiences in holding his or her ground with superiors at work. For example, a client might complain that he or she frequently feels pressured by his or her boss to do things that he or she judges to be unfair impositions and that he or she generally has trouble in behaving in an assertive fashion with the boss. First, the client plays the role of the boss, modeling it for the therapist, while the therapist models the way he or she thinks the client could handle the boss. Then they switch roles, with the client trying the new behavior and the therapist playing the role of boss. The client might coach the therapist on how to play the boss more realistically as the therapist coaches the client in ways of being more assertive with the boss. A shaping process occurs as the new behavior is reached by approximations. Also, some deconditioning of anxiety over confronting the boss occurs, and the client's more assertive stance toward the boss becomes polished.

Assertive behavior is first practiced in the role-playing situation, and then there is an attempt to practice it in real-life situations. The therapist provides guidance by showing how and when the client might regress into old, unassertive behavior and might offer guidelines to reinforce newly acquired assertive behavior.

Shaffer and Galinsky (1974) described how assertive-training, or "expressive-training," groups are structured and how they function. The group is made up of eight to ten members with similar backgrounds, and the sessions last for two hours. The therapist serves the functions of initiating and directing role-playing, coaching, reinforcing, and acting as a role model. In the group discussions the therapist functions as an expert, lending guidance in the role-playing situations and giving feedback to the members.

As with most behavior-therapy groups, the assertive-training group is characterized by a high degree of leader-provided structure. The sessions are typically structured as follows: The first session, which begins with a didactic presentation on unrealistic social anxiety, focuses on unlearning ineffective internal responses that lead to a lack of assertiveness and on learning a repertoire of new assertive behaviors. The second session might introduce some relaxation training, and each member describes specific behaviors in interpersonal situations that he or she feels are problems for him or her. Members then make contracts to carry out previously avoided assertive behavior before the next session. During the third session members describe the assertive behaviors that they tried in real-life situations. Their attempts are evaluated, and, if they have not been fully successful, the group may be directed in role-playing. The later sessions consist of additional relaxation training, more contracts for out-of-group assertion experiences, followed by evaluation of new behavior and by more role-playing. The later sessions can also be geared to the individual needs of the members. Some groups tend to focus on additional role-playing, evaluation, and coaching; others tend to focus on a discussion of attitudes and feelings that make assertive behavior difficult.

Assertive-training group therapy basically consists of behavioral rehearsal applied to groups, and the aim is to help individuals develop more direct ways of relating in interpersonal situations. The focus is on practicing, through role-playing, newly emerging relationship skills so that individuals might be able to overcome their inadequacies and learn how to express their feelings and thoughts more openly, as though they had a right to "own" these reactions.

For those readers who desire a more detailed discussion of the procedures involved in assertive training, I suggest Alberti and Emmons' *Stand*

Up, Speak Out, Talk Back, Wolpe's *The Practice of Behavior Therapy,* and Smith's *When I Say No I Feel Guilty.*

Aversion Therapy

Aversion-conditioning techniques, which have been widely used to gain relief from specific behavioral disturbances, involve the association of the symptomatic behavior with a painful stimulus until the unwanted behavior is inhibited. The aversion stimuli typically include punishment with an electric shock or emetic mixtures. Aversion control can involve either the removal of a positive reinforcer or the employment of various kinds of punishment. An example of removing positive reinforcers might be the elimination of a child's temper-tantrum behavior by ignoring the child's temper tantrum. If the social reinforcement of gaining attention is removed, the unwanted behavior tends to diminish in frequency. An example of the use of punishment as a means of control might involve inhibiting the maladaptive behavior of an autistic child by applying an electric shock to the child when specific undesirable behavior occurs.

Aversion control can also involve a combination of positive and negative reinforcements. In general, the results of the research seem to indicate that aversion therapy is most successful when it is used in conjunction with positive control. It appears that the effects of negative reinforcers are most enduring and have few ill side-effects when they are combined with other procedures and when alternatives for reward exist. For example, if the aim is to reduce competitive behavior and increase cooperative behavior in children, the competitive behavior could be punished while the cooperative behavior could be positively reinforced.

Aversion techniques are the most controversial of the behavioral methods, although they are widely used methods for getting people to behave in desired ways. Conditions are created so that people do what is expected of them in order to avoid aversive consequences. Most social institutions use these aversive procedures to control the members' behavior and to shape the individual's behavior along expected lines: churches use excommunication; schools use failure and expulsion; industries use unemployment and pay-docking; and governments use fines and prison sentences.

Aversion control is frequently characteristic of parent-child relationships. Controls can operate directly and with consciousness, but often they operate in subtle and indirect ways. Both children and parents can be controlled by what happens in certain situations, but the situations might not be obvious. Thus children are given certain privileges (or denied them) if they conform to certain expected behavior (or if they do not behave appropriately). The child also learns to use aversive control on his or her parents. The child learns that his or her parents have a tolerance level for his or her crying, shouting, pleading, and pouting and learns when they will finally submit to his or her demands.

In more formal and therapeutic settings, aversive techniques are frequently used in the treatment of a wide range of maladaptive behaviors, including excessive drinking, drug addiction, smoking, obesity, obsessions, compulsions, fetishes, gambling, homosexuality, and sexual deviations such as pedophilia. The technique has been most prominently used in the treatment of alcoholism. Instead of being forced to refrain from liquor, the alcoholic is required to drink. Each drink is accompanied by a strong emetic, the effect of which is illness followed by retching and vomiting. The alcoholic will eventually become somewhat ill by even looking at a bottle of liquor and will find alcoholic fumes discomforting. Knowledge of the effects created tends to inhibit the drinking behavior, although it is possible that the alcoholic might revert to the old drinking patterns after a short period of abstinence. In addition to treating alcoholism, aversion procedures have been used with some success in treating sexual deviations by associating a painful stimulus with the inappropriate sexual object or act.

That the purpose of aversive procedures is to provide ways of curbing maladaptive responses for a period of time so that there is an opportunity to acquire alternative behaviors that are adaptive and that will prove reinforcing in themselves is an important point. A popular misconception is that behavior-therapy techniques based on punishment are the therapist's most important tools. Punishment should be used infrequently, even though clients may seek to eliminate unwanted behavior through punishment. When alternative measures to punishment are available, punishment should not be used. Positive measures that lead to new and more appropriate behavior should be attempted before employing negative reinforcers. Often behavior can be changed through positive reinforcement alone, which reduces the chances of creating any disturbing side-effects of punishment. Further, if punishment is to be used, it is crucial that alternative forms of adaptive behavior be clearly and specifically delineated and that the punishment be administered in such a manner as not to result in the client's feeling rejected as a person. It is important that the client be helped to see that the aversive consequences are associated only with the specific maladaptive behavior.

Skinner (1948, 1971) is an outspoken opponent of the use of punishment as a means of controlling human relations or of serving the purposes of society's institutions. According to Skinner, positive reinforcement is far more effective in controlling behavior, for the outcomes are more predictable and the chance that undesirable behaviors will be generated is lower. Skinner (1948) argued that punishment is an evil that, although intended to suppress unwanted behavior, does not weaken the tendency to respond even if for a time it suppresses certain behavior. Undesirable outcomes, according to Skinner, are associated with the use of both aversive control and punishment.

Whenever punishment is used, there is a chance of creating additional, emotional side-effects such as the following undesirable outcomes: (1) the punished person's unwanted behavior might be suppressed only when the punisher is present; (2) if no alternatives to punished behavior exist, the person might become excessively withdrawn; and (3) the effect of punishment may be generalized to related behaviors. Thus a student who fails a subject in school might come to hate all subjects, school, all teachers, and perhaps even learning in general.

Operant Conditioning

Operant behavior is emitted behavior that is characteristic of an active organism. It is behavior that operates on the environment to produce consequences. Operant behavior constitutes the most significant behavior in daily living, including reading, speaking, dressing, eating with utensils, and playing, to mention just a few. According to Skinner (1971), if behavior is rewarded the probability increases that the behavior will be repeated in the future. The principle of reinforcement is the core of operant conditioning, for it accounts for behavior patterns that are established, maintained, or extinguished. The following operant-conditioning methods are briefly described below: positive reinforcement, response shaping, intermittent reinforcement, extinction, modeling, and token economies.

Positive Reinforcement. Establishing a behavior pattern by arranging for a reward, or reinforcement, to immediately follow most or many of the performances of the desired behavior is a powerful way to change behavior. Reinforcers, which can be primary or secondary, account for a wide range of behaviors. Primary reinforcers satisfy basic physiological needs. For example, food and sleep are primary reinforcers. Secondary reinforcers, which satisfy psychological and social needs, come to be valued because of their prior association with primary reinforcers. For example, smiles, nods of approval, praise, gold stars, tokens, money, gifts, and so on are powerful means of shaping desired behavior. Applied to psychotherapy, positive reinforcement necessitates specification of desired behavior, discovery of what is a reinforcing agent for a given individual, and the systematic use of the positive reinforcement to increase the desired behavior.

Response Shaping. In response shaping, current behaviors are gradually modified by reinforcing small elements of the desired new behavior, thereby successively approximating the end behavior. Response shaping consists of establishing a response that is not initially in an individual's behavior repertoire. Positive reinforcement is frequently used in this process. Response shaping is used extensively in schools and in working with the behavior problems of children. Thus, if a teacher wishes to shape cooperative as opposed to competitive behavior, the teacher can give attention and approval to the desired behavior. With autistic children who lack adaptive motor, verbal, emotional, and social behavior, more adaptive behavior in these areas can be shaped by giving either or both primary and secondary reinforcers.

Intermittent Reinforcement. Besides merely shaping behavior, reinforcements also maintain established behavior. In order to maximize the value of reinforcers, one must understand the prevailing conditions under which reinforcements occur. Further, the schedules of reinforcement are important. Continuous reinforcement rewards behavior every time it is emitted. Intermittent reinforcement varies the rate at which a reward is given for emitting specific behavior. Behavior that is conditioned by intermittent means is generally more resistant to extinction than is behavior conditioned by continuous reinforcements.

In applying reinforcement to situations involving behavioral change, one must during initial stages reward each instance of the desired behavior. If possible, reinforcements should immediately follow the performance of the desired behavior. In this way, the recipient learns what specific behavior is rewarded. As the behavior increases in frequency, however, reinforcements can decrease in frequency. For example, if a child is given praise each time he or she successfully completes a math problem, the child is more likely to give up when he or she encounters a failure than if he or she were praised occasionally. The principle of intermittent reinforcement explains why people persist in playing slot machines or betting on horse races. They are rewarded enough to keep going, even though they may lose more than they gain.

Extinction. When a response is made continuously without reinforcement, that response tends to drop out. Therefore, since learned behavior patterns tend to weaken and become eliminated over a period of time if they are not reinforced, one way of eliminating maladaptive behavior is to remove the reinforcement for it. Extinction in these cases may be slow because the behavior has been maintained by long periods of intermittent reinforcement. Wolpe (1969) believes that the cessation of reinforcement should be both abrupt and complete. For example, if a child displays show-off behavior at home and at school, one way of diminishing that behavior would be for both the parents and the teacher to avoid giving attention to the undesired behavior as much as possible. Positive reinforcement can at the same time be applied to acquiring desired behavior as well as to simply extinguishing the child's attention-getting behavior.

A therapist, teacher, or parent who introduces extinction as the main technique to eliminate undesirable behavior should note that the behavior may initially get worse before it is extinguished or reduced. For example, if a child has learned that by nagging he or she usually gets what he or she wants, the child may intensify his or her nagging when his or her demands are not immediately met. Thus a toleration for a transition period is essential.

Modeling. In the behavioral technique of modeling, a person observes a model and then is reinforced for imitating the model's behavior. Bandura (1969) contended that all the learning that can be acquired through direct experience can also be acquired indirectly by observing others' behavior and the consequences for it. Thus certain social skills can be acquired by observing and imitating the behavior of appropriate models. Also, disturbing emotional reactions can be extinguished by observing others approach feared objects or situations without experiencing dire consequences for their behavior. Self-control can be learned through the observation of others who are punished. The status and prestige of models are significant, for people are generally influenced by the behavior of models who occupy high status and prestige in the eyes of the observer.

Token Economies. Token economies can be applied to shape behavior when approval and other intangible reinforcers do not work. Under this system, appropriate behavior may be reinforced with tangible reinforcements (tokens) that can later be exchanged for desired objects or privileges. Tokens can be used to obtain cigarettes, candy, and toys, to participate in certain programs, and so on. The token system is much like the real-life situation in which workers are paid for their production. Thus the use of tokens as reinforcers for appropriate behavior has several advantages: (1) tokens do not lose their incentive value; (2) tokens can reduce the delay that exists between appropriate behavior and its reward; (3) tokens can be used as a concrete measure of motivation of a person to change certain behaviors; (4) tokens are a form of positive reinforcement; (5) the person has an opportunity to decide how to use earned tokens; and (6) tokens tend to serve the purpose of bridging the gap that often exists between an institution and outside life.

Token economies are an example of extrinsic reinforcement; that is, a person does something for the "carrot on the end of the stick." The goal of this procedure is to convert extrinsic motivation into intrinsic motivation. It is hoped that the person's acquisition of the desired behavior will in itself eventually become rewarding enough to maintain the new behavior.

Summary and Evaluation

An important contribution of the behavior-therapy approach is the systematic way that its therapeutic methods and techniques have been subjected to experimental verification. Thus the procedures are in a continual process of refinement and development, and the criterion of producing desirable results is supreme. Clinical results on behavioral methods generally have been encouraging in terms of both success rate and efficiency (Sherman, 1973). To their credit, behavior therapists have based their approach upon several variables: precise identification of maladaptive behavior, the treatment procedures, and the behavior changes. Proponents of the approach contend that research and comparative studies are necessary if the strengths and weaknesses of each therapy approach are to be identified (Sherman, 1973). In this way, improved psychotherapeutic methods can be developed.

The remainder of this section focuses on some common criticisms and on some misconceptions of the approach. I will briefly explore a number of myths regarding behavior modification, discuss some of the major objections that are raised against behavior therapy, and mention some of its limitations and contributions.

Criticism 1: Behavior therapy does not treat causes but superficially deals with symptoms. The psychodynamic model in the medical tradition sees psychopathology as rooted in unconscious and underlying processes and asserts that removal of symptoms does not remove the underlying cause of these symptoms. Hence, if one group of symptoms is removed, another group of symptoms will take its place. The psychodynamic view charges that behavior therapy leaves the basic causes of neurosis untouched and that at best the behavioristic approach is designed to bring temporary relief of symptoms and that at worst a client's condition might become aggravated.

Behavior therapists argue that the above objections are not supported by the research. For example, Wolpe (1969) has done follow-ups up to a year after desensitization and found little of the expected substitution of symptoms. Rachman (1967, pp. 252–255) argued that behavior therapy is not "superficial," if that term implies "incomplete treatment" or if the term implies that this type of therapy can be used successfully with "certain minor types of behavior disorders." He contended that considerable clinical and experimental evidence demonstrates that behavior therapy is "both complete and capable of being applied in many types of disorders." Rachman cites examples of therapeutic successes with phobic states and anxiety neuroses of long-standing duration and with other disorders such as stuttering, enuresis, drug addiction, alcoholism, homosexuality, and tension states. He makes the point clear that complete or near-complete recovery has been reported without either the therapist's or client's knowledge of the "basic cause" of the disorder.

Criticism 2: Behavior therapy does not apply to people who are functioning at relatively high levels. One limitation of this approach frequently mentioned is that behavior therapy is interested only in a tolerable level of functioning. It is sometimes proposed that those who are in search of meaning and self-actualization are not helped much by behavior-therapy techniques. Patterson (1973), in his evaluation of behavior therapy raised the concern that "One might ask the behavior therapist how he might decondition the pain or suffering of the client who suffers from a realization that he is not functioning up to his potential or up to his aspiration level, who has a concept of himself as a failure, or who experiences a lack of meaning in his life" (p. 154).* Carkhuff and Berenson (1967, p. 97) contended that the basic and only aim of behavior modification is rehabilitative. Although they agreed that conditioning techniques might "alleviate some degree of suffering," they argued that a rich awareness and a full life do not result from these techniques. In fact, they assert that "the behavior-modification approach drains the therapy experience of all creativity for the client." It does not provide a person with "the experience and conditions for self-fulfillment or self-actualization."

In my judgment, those criticisms are, to a large extent, accurate. It does appear that behavior therapy does not have much to offer for the client who does not have specific maladaptive problems. For a person seeking increased self-actualization, this approach seems limited. However, in some

*From *Theories of Counseling and Psychotherapy*, 2nd ed., by C. H. Patterson. Copyright 1973 by Harper & Row, Publishers, Inc. This and all other quotations from this source are reprinted by permission.

ways behavior therapy might be able to help a person who wants to become more assertive and independent. Assertive training can be useful for people with this kind of desire.

Criticism 3: Behavior modification is applicable only to specific anxieties, phobias, and circumscribed problems. A major criticism directed against this approach is that it focuses almost exclusively on treating well-defined, overt symptoms such as phobias, tension states, speech disorders, enuresis, addiction to drugs or alcohol, and sexual problems. Broader problems of personal and social adjustment, which practitioners most often encounter in psychotherapy, are not dealt with in this modality.

That point of contention does carry some validity. More diffuse complaints are difficult to deal with by using behavior-therapy techniques. However, the assertion is not entirely true. The criticism is often made by those who have not accepted the laborious task of delineating specifically and behaviorally the nature of the problems. Heine (1971) answered this objection when he wrote: "The behaviorists' retort is that traditional therapists have simply ignored data such as when, where, with whom, and under what circumstances clients actually experience the complex problems of which they complain. Behaviorists assert that seemingly complicated sets of symptoms could, in fact, be broken down into discrete behavioral units manageable through use of one of the techniques based on learning theory" (p. 123).

Criticism 4: Behavior modification does not work. This assertion does not seem justified in light of empirical evidence. Considerable evidence indicates that behavior-modification techniques do work, particularly with patients with specific problems in daily functioning. Some of this evidence indicates (1) that schizophrenics show marked improvement in response to operant-conditioning techniques; (2) that autistic children can be trained to function at higher levels through the use of operant conditioning; (3) that alcoholics show improvement after aversive conditioning; (4) that assertive training can help the timid, the sexually inhibited, and the withdrawn; (5) that enuresis can successfully be stopped; and (6) that sexual responses can be rearranged to increase the functioning of individuals who complain of impotence or frigidity. Rachman (1967) described studies that demonstrate that behavior therapy does work in successfully treating a wide range of neurotic conditions, including phobias, hysteria, enuresis, sexual disorders, tics, tension states, and children's disorders. Carkhuff and Berenson (1967, p. 100) assert that the clinical and research evidence implies that behavior modification techniques are well suited for (1) use in experimental settings, (2) efforts in human engineering, and (3) situations where there is an acute shortage of time.

Criticism 5: Behavior modification works too well. Some critics are concerned that conditioning techniques will be too effective and might be used to manipulate clients. They fear that freedom and individual responsibility will be reduced by the therapist who perceives his or her role as a human engineer. They fear that the therapist will impose a regime upon a helpless client and, ultimately, that an elite core of behaviorists can design and control what they might consider a utopian state.

In discussing the problem of behavioral control versus free will, Marquis (1974) cited Krasner's contention that "behavioral control is nothing new, and that parents, teachers, clergymen, policemen, and judges have exercised powerful control over human behavior since the dawn of time" (p. 367). The point is that behavior control can be used for good or evil. If behavioral technology is effective, it can be used for good by improving the quality of human living.

Criticism 6: Behavior therapy may change behaviors, but it does not change feelings. Some critics argue that feelings must change before behavior can change. The behaviorist's point of view is that, if one changes another's behavior, one effectively has been an agent in changing the feelings also. Empirical evidence has not borne out the criticism that feelings must be changed first before behavior change takes place.

Criticism 7: Behavior therapy ignores the important relational factors in therapy. The charge is often made that the importance of the relationship between the client and the therapist is discounted in behavior therapy. Although it appears to be true that behavior therapists do not place primary weight on the relationship variable, this does not mean that the approach is condemned to a mechanical and nonhumanistic level of functioning. As was discussed above in the section dealing specifically with the relationship between therapist and client, behavior therapy is most effective when there is cooperation and a working relationship—that is, when both the client and the therapist are working toward the same goal, namely, the client's goal. It is undoubtedly true that some therapists are attracted to behavior therapy because they can be directive, or they can play the role of expert, or they can avoid the anxieties and ambiguities of establishing a personal relationship. This is not an intrinsic characteristic of the approach, however, and many behavior therapists are more humanistic in practice than some of the therapists are who profess to practice existentially oriented humanistic therapy. A review of the case studies of persons like Wolpe and Lazarus makes it apparent that there is considerably more to the therapeutic relationship than is implied in the theoretical orientation.

Criticism 8: Behavior therapy does not provide insight. If this assertion is indeed true, the behavior-modification theorist would probably respond that insight isn't necessary. Behavior is changed directly. If the goal of insight is eventual change of behavior, then behavior modification, which has proven results, has the same effect as insight. If the goals are the same, then the efficacy of the two techniques should be an empirical one. On the other hand, many people want not just to change their behavior but also to gain an understanding of why they behave the way that they do. The answers are often buried deep in past learning and in historical events. Although it is possible for behavior-modification therapists to give explanations in this realm, in fact they usually do not.

Criticism 9: Behavior therapy ignores historical causes of present behavior. This is in opposition to the historical approach or traditional psychoanalytic approach of Freud and others. The Freudian assumption is that early traumatic events are the root of present dysfunction. Discover the original causes, induce insight in the client, and then the present behavior will change. The behavior modifiers may acknowledge that the deviant responses have historical origins, but they would maintain that the responses are still in effect because they are still being maintained by reinforcing stimuli. Relearning of new responses or changing environmental stimuli is what is necessary for behavior change.

Although it is true that there are some limitations to the practice of counseling and therapy with the behavior-therapy approach, I hope that the reader will come to realize that the approach does offer some unique contributions. The specificity of the approach helps the practitioner to keep clearly in focus the client's goals and to define ways of checking on the therapist's and the client's mutual progress in reaching those goals. I emphasize again that a therapist need not subscribe totally to behavior therapy in order to derive practical benefits from the specific behavioral techniques. Most therapists, often without their awareness, do in fact employ in an unsystematic fashion many behavioral techniques. Their behavior does reinforce and shape client behavior, much the same way that the behavior therapist systematically and consciously applies reinforcement to shape client behavior. Moreover, a therapist can systematically use many behavioral techniques and incorporate them into his or her own repertoire of therapeutic procedures, even though he or she does not consider himself or herself a behavior therapist. Therapists, knowingly or unknowingly, shape the responses of their clients by means of a wide range of social reinforcers or by the absence of reinforcement. Many behavioral procedures can be incorporated into a more eclectic framework and even into an existential-humanistic theory. Some of the techniques and methods are tools that a therapist can use with the client and for the client as they both work toward clear goals determined by the client. I hope that the reader can see that it may even be possible to be a humanistically oriented behavior therapist!

Questions for Evaluation

1. Do you agree with the view of human nature implied by the behavioral approach? What are the implications for both the client and the therapist of the philosophical assumptions underlying the approach?
2. Behavior therapy is based on a functional analysis of the problem behavior by which clear objectives are formulated and during which treatment is continually evaluated and adapted to suit the unique needs and requirements of each client. What is the most effective way of conducting this analysis of problem behavior? How can the therapist help the client clarify behavioral objectives? In what ways can the treatment be evaluated? How are the appropriate procedures selected for a particular client with specific problems? How can the therapeutic gains in the treatment setting be translated into new and more effective behavior in everyday life? What are the factors that can facilitate the transfer of learning from therapy to outside life? What are the possible dangers or adverse side-effects of some of the behavioral methods, and how might they be minimized?

3. Skinner (1948, 1971) called for a society that is based on the prediction and control of individuals. In his utopian novel, *Walden II*, he described the possible use of positive-reinforcement contingencies to control all behavior within a society. The purpose of the control would be to maximize the good for all members. Do you see this as a desirable possibility? What would your utopian society look like? Who would make the decisions concerning what kinds of behavior would be "desirable"? What dangers can you see?

4. What are the problems you can see in applying behavioral procedures to involuntary subjects? What are the practical problems? What are the ethical issues? Do you think that it is ethical that some institutions have the power to impose conditioning techniques upon unwilling subjects? Consider populations such as severely retarded children in institutions, convicted criminals who habitually pose a threat to society, sexual offenders such as child molesters, and institutionalized alcoholics, drug addicts, and mental patients.

5. Do you think that behavior-therapy procedures are applicable to persons seeking increased personal growth rather than the removal of their maladaptive behavior? If so, which therapy techniques do you think are best suited for clients desiring self-actualization as opposed to treatment?

6. How do you imagine a behavior therapist might proceed with a client whose complaint is a lack of meaning and purpose in life?

7. What is your reaction to those critics who assert that behavior therapy works too well in that the conditioning techniques could be used to manipulate clients and thus reduce their freedom? Are you concerned that behavior modifiers might design and control a program for ends that are not in the best interests of the clients?

8. Behavior therapists suggest that an individual's attitudes can be changed by changing the behavior first. In other words, behavior change precedes attitude change. Many traditional therapies assume that insight and awareness are requisites for behavior change and that only if a person changes his or her attitudes first can behavior change occur. What is your opinion? Do you think that attitude change can lead to behavior change? Do you think that behavior change can lead to attitude change? Can both occur?

9. Compare and contrast behavior therapy with the other therapeutic approaches you have studied thus far. In what ways do you think behavior therapy is unique? What are some of its distinct advantages and disadvantages?

10. What aspects of behavior therapy could you apply to yourself in order to increase your self-understanding? Does this approach offer you specific means by which to change some of your behavior? What kinds of specific behavioral changes might you desire, and how do you think behavioral methods might be useful to you?

References and Suggested Readings

Alberti, R. E., & Emmons, M. L. *Your perfect right: A guide to assertive behavior.* San Luis Obispo: Impact, 1970.

*Alberti, R. E., & Emmons, M. L. *Stand up, speak out, talk back.* New York: Pocket Books, 1975.

Ayllon, T., & Azrin, N. H. *The token economy.* New York: Appleton-Century-Crofts, 1968.

Azrin, N. H., & Holz, W. C. Punishment. In W. K. Honig (Ed.), *Operant behavior.* New York: Appleton-Century-Crofts, 1966.

Bandura, A. *Principles of behavior modification.* New York: Holt, Rinehart and Winston, 1969.

Bandura, A., & Walters, R. H. *Social learning and personality development.* New York: Holt, Rinehart and Winston, 1963.

Carkhuff, R., & Berenson, B. *Beyond counseling and therapy.* New York: Holt, Rinehart and Winston, 1967.

Feldman, M. P., & MacCulloch, M. J. *Homosexual behavior: Therapy and assessment.* Oxford: Pergamon Press, 1971.

Goldstein, A. Behavior therapy. In R. Corsini (Ed.), *Current psychotherapies.* Itasca, Ill.: Peacock, 1973.

Goodstein, L. Behavioral views of counseling. In B. Stefflre and W. H. Grant (Eds.), *Theories of counseling* (2nd ed.). New York: McGraw Hill, 1972.

Heine, R. *Psychotherapy.* Englewood Cliffs, N.J.: Prentice-Hall, 1971.

Huber, J., & Millman, H. (Eds.). *Goals and behavior in psychotherapy and counseling.* Columbus, Ohio: Merrill, 1972.

Jacobsen, E. *Progressive relaxation.* Chicago: University of Chicago Press, 1938.

Krasner, L. The reinforcement machine. In B. Berenson & R. Carkhuff (Eds.), *Sources of gain in counseling and psychotherapy.* New York: Holt, Rinehart and Winston, 1967.

Marquis, J. Behavior modification theory: B. F. Skinner and others. In A. Burton (Ed.), *Operational theories of personality.* New York: Brunner/Mazel, 1974.

Martin, D. *Introduction to psychotherapy.* Monterey, Cal.: Brooks/Cole, 1971.

*Nye, R. *Three views of man.* Monterey, Cal.: Brooks/Cole, 1975.

Patterson, C. H. *Theories of counseling and psychotherapy* (2nd ed.). New York: Harper & Row, 1973.

Rachman, S. Behavior therapy. In B. Berenson & R. Carkhuff (Eds.), *Sources of gain in counseling and psychotherapy.* New York: Holt, Rinehart and Winston, 1967.

Salter, A. *Conditioned reflex therapy.* New York: Creative Age Press, 1949.

Shaffer, J., & Galinsky, M. D. *Models of group therapy and sensitivity training.* Englewood Cliffs, N.J.: Prentice-Hall, 1974.

*Sherman, A. R. *Behavior modification: Theory and practice.* Monterey, Cal.: Brooks/Cole, 1973.

*Skinner, B. F. *Walden II.* New York: Macmillan, 1948.

*Skinner, B. F. *Beyond freedom and dignity.* New York: Knopf, 1971.

*Smith, M. *When I say no I feel guilty.* New York: Bantam, 1975.

Stampfl, T. Implosive therapy: Staring down your nightmares. *Psychology Today,* February 1975.

Ullman, L., & Krasner, L. (Eds.). *Case studies in behavior modification.* New York: Holt, Rinehart and Winston, 1965.

*Wenrich, W. W. *A primer of behavior modification.* Monterey, Cal.: Brooks/Cole, 1970.

*Williams, R., & Long, J. *Toward a self-managed life-style.* Boston: Houghton-Mifflin, 1975.

Wolpe, J. *Psychotherapy by reciprocal inhibition.* Stanford, Cal.: Stanford University Press, 1958.

*Wolpe, J. *The practice of behavior therapy.* New York: Pergamon Press, 1969.

Wolpe, J., & Lazarus, A. *Behavior therapy techniques.* New York: Pergamon Press, 1966.

Yates, A. J. *Behavior therapy.* New York: Wiley, 1970.

CHAPTER EIGHT

RATIONAL-
EMOTIVE
THERAPY

Introduction

I selected Albert Ellis's rational-emotive therapy (RET) for inclusion because I think that it can challenge the student to think through some basic issues underlying counseling and psychotherapy. RET departs radically from several of the other systems presented in this book—namely, the psychoanalytic, existential-humanistic, client-centered, and Gestalt approaches. RET has more in common with the therapies that are cognitive/behavior/action oriented in that it stresses thinking, judging, deciding, analyzing, and doing. RET is highly didactic, very directive, and concerned more with the dimensions of thinking than with those of feeling.

The concepts of rational-emotive therapy raise several thorny questions that it would be well to keep in mind as you read this chapter: Is psychotherapy essentially a process of reeducation? Should the therapist function mainly as a teacher? Is it appropriate for therapists to use propaganda, persuasion, and highly directive suggestions? How effective is it to attempt to rid clients of their "irrational beliefs" by using logic, advice, information, and interpretations?

Finally, Ellis and Carl Rogers are in sharp contrast in regard to the value and necessity of a personal relationship between the client and the therapist. As you read, try to clarify and define your position on the central issue of whether the client-therapist relationship is the core variable that determines client change or whether other variables, such as the therapist's skill, insightfulness, knowledge, and ability to help the client cut through self-defeating attitudes, are even more important.

Key Concepts

View of Human Nature

Rational-emotive therapy is a school of psychotherapy that is based on the assumption that human beings are born with a potential for both rational, straight thinking and irrational, crooked thinking. People have predispositions for self-preservation, happiness, thinking and verbalizing, loving, communion with others, and growth and self-actualization. They also have propensities for self-destruction, avoidance of thought, procrastination, endless repetition of mistakes, superstition, intolerance, perfectionism and self-blame, and avoidance of actualization of growth potentials. They have the tendencies within both to stick with old, dysfunctional behavior patterns and to discover a variety of ways to engage in self-sabotage.

Humans do not have to be resigned to being victims of early conditioning. Rational-emotive theory asserts that people have vast untapped resources for actualizing their potentials and that they can change their personal and social destinies. However, according to rational-emotive psychology, people are born with the tendency to insist that all their wants, demands, wishes, and needs be met in life; if they do not immediately get what they want, they condemn both themselves and others (Ellis, 1973a, pp. 175–176).

RET stresses that humans think, emote, and behave simultaneously. Rarely do they emote without thinking, for feelings are usually excited by the perception of a specific situation. As Ellis (1974) put it, "When they emote, they *also* think and act. When they act, they *also* think and emote. When they think, they *also* emote and act" (p. 313). In order to understand self-defeating behavior, one must understand how a person emotes, thinks, perceives, and acts. To modify dysfunctional patterns, one ideally should employ a variety of perceptual-cognitive, emotive-evocative, and behavioristic-reeducative methods (Ellis, 1973a, p. 171).

Regarding human nature, Ellis (1967, pp. 79–80) contends that both the Freudian psychoanalytic approach and the existential approach are mistaken and that the methodologies founded on those psychotherapeutic systems are ineffective and inadequate. Ellis charges that the Freudian view of human nature is false because the existential-humanistic view of human nature is partly correct. Ellis asserts that the individual is not completely a biologically determined animal driven by instincts. He sees the individual as unique and as having the power to understand limitations, to change basic views and values that the individual uncritically introjected as a child, and to challenge self-defeating tendencies. People have the capacity to confront their value systems and reindoctrinate themselves with different beliefs, ideas, and values. As a result, they will behave quite differently from how they behaved in the past. Thus, because they can think and work until they actually make themselves different, they are not passive victims of past conditioning.

Ellis does not fully accept the existential view of the self-actualizing tendency, because of the fact that humans are biological animals with strong instinctoid tendencies to behave in certain ways. Thus Ellis contends that, once people are conditioned to think or feel in a certain way, they tend to continue behaving in that manner even though they might realize that their behavior is self-defeating. Ellis thinks it is incorrect to assume that an existential encounter with an accepting, permissive, authentic therapist will usually root out an individual's deeply ingrained patterns of self-defeating behavior.

RET and the Theory of Personality

The theoretical view of certain characteristics of personality and behavior, and its disturbances, separates the rational-emotive approach in significant respects from the theory underlying most other approaches to psychotherapy. A summary of the RET view of human nature follows.

Neurosis, defined as "irrational thinking and behaving," is a natural human state that afflicts all of us to some degree. This state is deeply rooted merely because we are human beings and live with other human beings in society.

Psychopathology is originally learned and aggravated by the inculcation of irrational beliefs from significant others during childhood. However, we actively reinstill false beliefs by the processes of autosuggestion and self-repetition. Hence, it is largely our own repetition of early-indoctrinated irrational thoughts, rather than a parent's repetition, that keeps dysfunctional attitudes alive and operative within us.

Emotions are the products of human thinking. When we *think* something is bad, then we *feel* bad about that thing. Ellis (1967) maintained that "emotional disturbance, therefore, essentially consists of mistaken, illogical, unvalidatable sentences or meanings which the disturbed individual dogmatically and unchallengingly *believes*, and upon which he therefore emotes or acts to his own defeat" (p. 82).

RET insists that blame is the core of most emotional disturbances. Therefore, if we are to cure a neurosis or psychosis, we'd better stop blaming ourselves and others. We'd better learn to accept ourselves in spite of our imperfections. Anxiety stems from internal repetition of the sentence "I don't like my behavior and would like to change" and the self-blaming sentence "Because of my wrong behavior and my mistakes, I am a rotten person and I am to blame, and I deserve to suffer." According to RET, this anxiety is unnecessary. A person can be helped to see that precise, irrational sentences are false, self-blaming traps that he or she has acquired.

RET contends that people do not need to be accepted and loved, even though it might be desirable. The therapist teaches clients how to feel unhurt even when they are unaccepted and unloved by significant others. Although RET allows people to experience sadness over being unaccepted, it attempts to help them find ways of overcoming all deep-seated manifestations of depression, hurt, loss of self-worth, and hatred.

RET hypothesizes that, because we are raised in society, we tend to be victims of fallacious ideas, that we tend to keep reindoctrinating ourselves over and over with those ideas in an unthinking and autosuggestive manner, and that consequently we keep the ideas operant in our overt behavior. Some of the main irrational ideas that we continually internalize and that inevitably lead to self-defeat are, according to Ellis (1967), the following:

1. the idea that it is a dire necessity for an adult human being to be loved or approved by virtually every significant other person in his community;
2. the idea that one should be thoroughly competent, adequate, and achieving in all possible respects if one is to consider oneself worthwhile;
3. the idea that certain people are bad, wicked, or villainous and that they should be severely blamed and punished for their villainy;
4. the idea that it is easier to avoid than to face certain life difficulties and self-responsibilities;
5. the idea that it is awful and catastrophic when things are not the way one would very much like them to be;
6. the idea that human unhappiness is externally caused and that people have little or no ability to control their sorrows and disturbances; and
7. the idea that one's past history is an all-important determiner of one's present behavior and that, because something once strongly affected one's life, it should indefinitely have a similar effect [p. 84].

The A-B-C Theory of Personality

The A-B-C theory of personality is central to RET theory and practice. A is the existence of a fact, an event, or the behavior or attitude of an individual. C is the emotional consequence or reaction of the individual; the reaction can be either appropriate or inappropriate. A (the activating event) does not cause C (the emotional consequence). Instead, B, which is the person's belief about A, causes C, the emotional reaction. For example, if a person experiences depression after a divorce, it may not be the divorce itself that causes the depressive reaction but the person's *beliefs* about being a failure, being rejected, or losing a mate. Ellis would maintain that the beliefs about the rejection and failure (at point B) is what causes the depression (at point C), not the actual event of the divorce (at point A). Thus human beings are largely responsible for creating their own emotional reactions and disturbances.

How is an emotional disturbance fostered? It is fed by the illogical sentences that the person continually repeats to himself or herself such as "I am totally to blame for the divorce," "I am a miserable failure, and everything I did was wrong," "I am a worthless person," "I feel lonely and rejected, and that is a terrible catastrophe." Ellis (1974) makes the point that "you feel the way you think" (p. 312). Disturbed emotional reactions such as depression and anxiety are initiated and perpetuated by the self-defeating Belief System, which is based on irrational ideas that one has incorporated. Although Ellis (1974) contended that emotional disturbances can be eliminated or modified by directly working with the feelings (depression, anxiety, hostility, fear, and so on), he stated that "the quickest, most deep-seated, most elegant, and longest-lasting technique of helping people to change their dysfunctional emotional responses is probably through enabling them to see clearly what they are strongly telling themselves—at B, their Belief System—about the stimuli that are impinging on them at A (their Activating Experiences) and teaching them how to actively and vigorously Dispute (at D) their irrational Beliefs" (pp. 312–313).

Elsewhere Ellis (1973a, pp. 179–180) emphasized that, because humans have the capacity for thinking, they are able to "train themselves to change or eliminate their self-sabotaging beliefs." It takes self-discipline, thinking, and work to learn to understand and confront irrational Belief Systems. Both curative and preventive changes in disturbance-creating tendencies are possible if people are assisted in gaining focus on "crooked thinking" and "inappropriate emoting and behaving." How can people be helped in zeroing in on their "magical Belief Systems"? Ellis (1973a) replies that, "by a highly active-directive, didactic, philosophic, homework-assigning therapist (who may or may not have a warm, personal relationship with them), they are much more likely to radically change their symptom-creating Beliefs than they are if they mainly work with a dynamically oriented, client-centered, conventional existentialist, or classical behavior modification-centered therapist" (pp. 179–180).

RET assumes that, since people's irrational beliefs and values are causally linked to their emotional and behavioral disturbances, the most efficient way of helping them to make basic personality changes is to confront them directly with their philosophies of life, to explain to them how their ideas make them disturbed, to attack their irrational ideas on logical grounds, and to teach them how to think logically, thereby enabling them to change or eliminate their irrational ideas. RET thus confronts clients with their irrational Beliefs and attacks, challenges, questions, and disputes those Beliefs.

After the A-B-C comes D, Disputing. Essentially, D is the application of the scientific method to help clients challenge their irrational Beliefs that lead to disturbances in their emotions and behavior. Since the principles of logic can be taught, these principles can be used to destroy any unrealistic, unverifiable hypothesis. This logicoempirical method can help clients give up self-destructive ideologies.

The Therapeutic Process

Therapeutic Goals

Ellis (1973a) indicated that many roads taken in RET are aimed at one major goal: "the minimization of the client's central self-defeating outlook and his acquiring a more realistic, tolerant philosophy of life" (p. 184). According to Ellis, the psychotherapist's main goal had better be that of demonstrating to clients that their self-verbalizations have been and still are the prime source of their emotional disturbances.

RET strives for a thorough philosophical and ideological reevaluation based on the assumption that human problems are philosophically rooted. Thus RET is not aimed primarily at symptom removal (Ellis, 1967, p. 85; 1973a, p. 172); rather, it is designed to encourage the client to critically examine his or her most basic values. If a client's presenting problem is a fear of failing in his or her marriage, the aim is not merely to reduce that specific fear; instead, the therapist attempts to work with the client's exaggerated fears of failing in general. RET goes beyond symptom removal in that the main goal of the therapy process is to help the client free himself or herself of nonreported and reported symptoms.

In summary, the therapeutic process consists of curing irrationality with rationality. Since the individual is essentially a rational being and since the source of his or her unhappiness is based on unreason, it follows that the individual can attain happiness by learning to think rationally. The therapy process is thus largely, although not entirely, a teaching/learning process.

The Function and Role of the Therapist

The main therapeutic activities of RET are carried out with one central purpose: to help the client get free of illogical ideas and learn to substitute logical ideas in their place. The aim is to get the client to internalize a rational philosophy of life, just as he or she internalized a set of dogmatic, irrational, and superstitious beliefs from both parents and culture.

To achieve this aim, the therapist has specific tasks. The first step is to show clients that their problems are related to irrational beliefs and to show them how they developed their values and attitudes by attempting cognitively to show them that they have incorporated many "shoulds," "oughts," and "musts." Clients must learn to separate their rational beliefs from their irrational beliefs. To achieve this client awareness, the therapist serves the function of a counterpropagandist who challenges the self-defeating propaganda that the client originally accepted without question as truth. The therapist encourages, persuades, and at times even commands the client to engage in activities that will act as counterpropaganda agents.

A second step in the therapeutic process takes clients beyond the stage of awareness by demonstrating that they presently keep their emotional disturbances active by continuing to think illogically and by repeating self-defeating sentences that keep the influence of earlier years functional. In other words, because clients keep reindoctrinating themselves, they are responsible for their own problems. That the therapist merely shows clients that they have illogical processes is not enough, for a client is apt to say "Now I understand that I have fears of failing and that these fears are exaggerated and unrealistic. Nevertheless, I *still feel* fearful of failing!"

To get beyond clients' mere recognition of irrational thoughts and feelings, the therapist takes a third step of attempting to get clients to modify their thinking and abandon their irrational ideas. Rational-emotive psychology assumes that their illogical beliefs are so deeply ingrained that clients won't normally change them by themselves. The therapist must assist clients to come to the understanding of the relationship between their self-defeating ideas and their unrealistic philosophies that leads to the vicious cycle of the self-blaming process.

Thus the final step in the therapeutic process is to challenge clients to develop rational philosophies of life so that they can avoid becoming the victims of other irrational beliefs. Tackling only specific problems or symptoms can give no assurance that other illogical fears will not emerge. What is desirable, then, is for the therapist to attack the core of the irrational thinking and to teach clients how to substitute rational beliefs and attitudes for the irrational ones.

The therapist who works within the RET framework functions differently from most of the other more conventional therapists. Because RET is essentially a cognitive and active-directive behavioral therapeutic process, it often minimizes the intense relationship between the therapist and the client. RET is an educative process, and the therapist's central task is to teach the client ways of self-understanding and changing. The therapist mainly employs a rapid-fire, highly directive, persuasive methodology that emphasizes cognitive aspects. Ellis (1973a, p. 185) gives a picture of what the rational-emotive practitioner does:

1. pins the client down to a few basic irrational ideas that motivate much disturbed behavior;
2. challenges clients to validate their ideas;
3. demonstrates to clients the illogical nature of their thinking;
4. uses a logical analysis to minimize clients' irrational beliefs;
5. shows how these beliefs are inoperative and how they will lead to future emotional and behavioral disturbances;
6. uses absurdity and humor to confront the irrationality of clients' thinking;
7. explains how these ideas can be replaced with more rational ideas that are empirically grounded; and
8. teaches clients how to apply the scientific approach to thinking so that they can observe and minimize present or future irrational ideas and illogical deductions that foster self-destructive ways of feeling and behaving.

The Client's Experience in Therapy

To a large measure, the client's role in RET is like that of a student, or learner. Psychotherapy is viewed as a reeducative process whereby the client learns how to apply logical thought to problem solving.

The therapeutic process focuses on the client's experience in the present. Like the client-centered and existentially oriented approaches to therapy, RET mainly emphasizes here-and-now experiences and the client's present ability to change his or her patterns of thinking and emoting that he or she acquired earlier. The therapist does not devote time to exploring the client's early history and making connections between the client's past and his or her present behavior. Nor does the therapist explore in depth the client's relationships with his or her parents or siblings. Instead, the therapeutic process stresses that, regardless of clients' basic, irrational philosophies of life, they are presently disturbed because they still believe in their self-defeating views of themselves and their worlds. Questions of when, why, or how they acquired their irrational philosophies are of secondary importance. The central issue is how clients can become aware of their self-defeating messages and challenge them. Ellis (1974) asserts that clients will often improve even if they never understand the origin or development of their problems.

A central experience of the client in RET is gaining insight. RET assumes that the client's acquisition of emotional insight into the sources of his or her disturbances is a crucial part of the therapeutic process. Ellis (1967) defined emotional insight as "the patient's knowing or seeing the causes of his problems and *working*, in a determined and energetic manner, to apply this knowledge to the solution of these problems" (p. 87). Thus RET emphasizes interpretation as a therapeutic tool.

RET postulates three levels of insight. For an illustration of these levels, let's assume that a male client is working on his fear of women. He feels threatened by attractive women, and he is afraid of how he might react to a powerful woman and what she might do to him. Using this example we can distinguish the three levels of insight. In the first, the client becomes aware that there is some antecedent cause of his fear of women. This cause would not be that his mother tried, for example, to dominate him but his irrational beliefs that she should not have tried to dominate him and that it was, and still is, awful that she did try.

On the second level of insight, the client recognizes that he is still threatened by women and feels uncomfortable in their presence because he still believes in, and keeps repeating endlessly to himself, the irrational beliefs that he once accepted. He sees that he keeps himself in a state of panic with women because he continues to tell himself "Women can castrate me!" or "They'll expect me to be a superman!" or some other irrational notion.

The third level of insight consists of the client's acceptance that he will not improve, nor will he change in any significant way, unless he works diligently and practices changing his irrational beliefs by actually doing things of a counterpropaganda nature. Thus his "homework assignment" might be to approach an attractive female and ask her for a date. While on this date, he needs to challenge his irrational notions and his catastrophic expectations and beliefs of what might happen. Merely talking about his fears will not do much to change his behavior. What is important is that he engage in activity that will torpedo the underpinnings of his irrational fears.

RET stresses particularly the second and third levels of insight, namely, the client's acknowledgment that it is himself that now keeps the originally disturbing ideas and feelings alive and that he had better rationally-emotively face them, think about them, and work to eliminate them.

The Relationship between Therapist and Client

The issue of the *personal* relationship between the therapist and the client takes in RET a meaning that is different from that in most other forms of therapy. According to Ellis, personal warmth and affection and a personal relationship between therapist and client, an intense relating, is of secondary importance. Ellis (1973a, p. 172) does not believe that a deep or warm personal relationship is either a necessary or a sufficient condition for psychotherapy. He believes, however, that a good rapport between the client and the therapist is highly desirable.

According to Ellis (1973a, p. 196) rational-emotive practitioners tend to be informal and to be themselves. They are highly active and directive and often give their own views without hesitation. They may be objective, cool, and barely warm to most of their clients. They may do good work with clients that they do not personally like, since their main interest is not in relating personally but in helping their clients deal with emotional disturbances.

Note that, although the personal relationship or warmth and affection between the therapist and the client is not viewed as primarily important in RET, this does not mean that transference is not viewed as significant. Ellis (1967, p. 87) believes that the relationship between the therapist and the client plays a significant part in the therapeutic process but in a way different from that in most psychotherapies. Ellis contended that RET emphasizes the importance of therapists as models for their clients. During the course of therapy, they model that they are not highly emotionally disturbed and that they are living rationally. They also model courage for their clients in that they directly present the clients' irrational belief systems to them without being worried that they will lose the clients' love and approval.

RET thus stresses the help a client can get from a highly trained and rational therapist. Further, RET stresses the therapist's full tolerance and unconditional positive regard for the personhood of the client in that the therapist avoids blaming the client. The therapist continues to accept the client as a worthwhile human being because the client exists and not because of the client's accomplishments.

Application: Therapeutic Techniques and Procedures

Key RET Techniques and Procedures

RET allows for considerable leeway for a practitioner to be eclectic. Most systems of psychotherapy assume a single, crucial requisite for effective personality change to occur. Ellis (1967, p. 89), however, hypothesizes that there is probably no single condition or necessary and sufficient set of conditions that is essential for change to occur. RET contends that people can experience personality change through many diverse avenues such as having significant life experiences; learning vicariously by reading about others' experiences; entering into a relationship with a therapist; viewing movies; listening to tape recordings; practicing specific homework assignments; carrying on mail correspondence along RET lines; spending time alone for thinking and meditating; and in many other ways deciding to make lasting personality change.

The essential technique of RET is active-directive teaching. Very soon after therapy is initiated, the therapist assumes an active teaching role to reeducate the client. The therapist demonstrates the illogical origin of the client's disturbances and the self-verbalizations that perpetuate the disturbances in the life of the client.

Above all, RET is a didactic process and hence stresses cognitive methods. Ellis (1974) indicated that the use of behavioral methods such as homework assignments, desensitization, operant conditioning, hypnotherapy, and assertion training "tend to be employed in an active-directive manner that has the therapist playing the role of a teacher more than that of an intensely relating partner" (p. 231).

Therapists are typically active in an RET session and do considerable talking rather than passive listening to clients. Even during initial sessions they might confront clients with evidence of irrational thinking and behaving. They use interpretation freely and are not too concerned about clients' resistances. They attack self-defeating philosophies; they explain, persuade, and lecture clients. Ellis (1967) noted that "to the usual psychotherapeutic techniques of exploration, ventilation, excavation, and interpretation, the rational therapist adds the more direct techniques of confrontation, confutation, deindoctrination, and reeducation. He thereby frankly faces and resolutely tackles the most deep-seated and recalcitrant patterns of emotional disturbance" (p. 85). In speaking about the variety of therapeutic procedures used by the rational therapist, Ellis (1973a) made the point that "such wide-ranging methods are most effectively employed when done with the intent of helping the client to achieve a deep-seated cognitive change" (p. 172).

In keeping with its didactic spirit, the use of activity "homework assignments" has been incorporated as an integral part of the practice of RET (Ellis, 1973a, pp. 192–195; 1974, pp. 322-325). Homework assignments are means to help the client practice in attacking irrational fears. The homework methodology is based on the desensitization process, and it is often done on a hierarchy of graded assignments that slowly increase in difficulty.

The theory behind RET homework assignments is that, because people practice telling themselves irrational sentences that create their disturbed feelings, they are self-conditioned by their own thinking and imagining processes. Thus they often create a negative, self-fulfilling prophesy and actually fail because they told themselves in advance that they would. Additionally, Ellis (1974) sees most clients as "short-range hedonists with high degress of low frustration tolerance" (p. 324). He contended that most people tend to avoid the momentary discomfort of anxiety even at the expense of foregoing longer-ranging satisfactions. The homework procedure is designed to help clients experience the anxiety that they can work through for personal growth. As Ellis (1974) put it "RET homework assignments usually are ways of encouraging them to become longer-range hedonists: to stick with their present pains . . . and even temporarily exacerbate them in order to ultimately diminish or eradicate these self-defeating behaviors" (pp. 324–325). According to Ellis, clients have practiced self-verbalizations that result in disturbances in emotions and in behavior, and the homework assignments allow them to practice counterconditioning with a rational set of beliefs.

Before concluding this section on the therapeutic techniques and procedures, I should like to explore the issue of the kind of client population that can most effectively be helped by RET methods. Ellis does not assert that all clients can effectively be helped through logical analysis and reconstruction. Some are not bright enough to follow a rigorous rational analysis, some are too detached from reality, some are too old and inflexible, and some are too philosophically prejudiced against logic to accept rational analysis.

What kinds of individuals are most effectively treated with RET? Ellis (1973a, p. 191) stressed the point that a client's willingness to engage in hard work in practicing the homework assignments is a crucial variable in the success of therapy. Also, the rational-emotive approach is more effective with clients who are not seriously disturbed or with those who have a single major symptom. Some types of clients treated with RET procedures include those with moderate anxiety or marital problems, those with sexual difficulties, those with neurotic personality disorders, those with character disorders, juvenile delinquents and adult criminals, borderline psychotics, psychotics who have some contact with reality, and clients with psychosomatic problems.

Application to Individual Therapy

RET, as applied to one-to-one work, is generally designed for relatively brief therapy. Ellis (1973a, p. 193) contended that it is preferable that individuals with severe emotional disturbances continue both individual and group therapy for a period of six months to a year so that they have a chance to practice what they are learning. As for individuals with a specific problem or those who are going to stay in therapy only for a short time, RET can teach clients many of the basics of how to attack the underlying sources of their problems in from one to ten sessions. These sessions consist basically of explaining the A-B-C method of understanding any emotional disturbance, pointing out the irrational premises undergirding the problem, and teaching how to start working and practicing at converting irrational ideas into rational philosophies.

Ellis (1973a, p. 192) stated that most clients who are seen individually have one session weekly for anywhere between 5 and 50 sessions. The clients begin by discussing their most pressing problems and describing their most upsetting feelings. Then the therapist discovers the precipitating events that lead to the upsetting feelings. He or she also gets the clients to see the irrational beliefs that they associated with the events and gets them to dispute their irrational beliefs by assigning them homework activities that will help them directly work on undoing their irrational ideas and assist them in practicing more rational ways of being. Each week the therapist checks their progress, and the clients continually learn how to dispute their irrational system until they do more than merely lose their symptoms—that is, until they learn a more tolerant and rational way of living.

Application to Group Therapy

RET is very suitable for group therapy, for all the members are taught to apply RET principles to each other in the group setting. They get an opportunity to practice new behaviors that involve taking risks and they get abundant opportunities to exercise homework assignments. In the group setting members also have an opportunity to experience assertive training, role-playing, and a variety of risk-taking activities. They can learn social skills and practice interacting with others in after-group sessions. Both other group members and the leader can observe their behavior and give feedback on their behavior. In individual therapy a client usually gives after-the-fact reports, but in a group setting clients are able to engage in ongoing group contacts designed to foster a radical philosophical change. Ellis recommends that most RET clients experience group as well as individual therapy at some point in their therapy.

Ellis (1969) has developed a special form of group therapy, known as "A Weekend of Rational Encounter," that utilizes RET methods and principles. The weekend marathon is divided into two main parts. The first part consists of 14 hours of continuous rational-encounter therapy, followed by 8 hours of rest; the second part includes about another 10 hours of therapy. During the initial stages of the weekend encounter, members experience a series of directed activities, both verbal and nonverbal, designed to get them to know each other. Participants are asked to share their most shameful experiences and are encouraged to engage in risk-taking.

In the beginning stages emotive-evocative procedures are used, and neither problem solving nor decision making is attempted. As the marathon progresses, the same logical principles of rational thinking that are used in one-to-one therapy are applied to the group. Thus the marathon, which consists of a heavy dose of rational-cognitive and behavior-action methods, is more than an experiential session during which feelings are explored and shared. At the later stages of the marathon, some of the deepest personal problems of the group members are explored with cognitive procedures. Ellis (1969) indicated that, during the closing hours of the rational-encounter weekend marathon, "the group and the leader usually tend to smoke out anyone who has not as yet brought up a problem for detailed discussion. Such individuals are directly asked why they have not said too much about themselves previously and are induced to look for a major problem and to discuss it openly" (p. 121). Also toward the end of the session, specific homework assignments are given to each of the group members. A postsession is held six to eight weeks later to check the progress they have made with their assignments as well as to evaluate their current status. Although Ellis (1969) believes that a rational-encounter weekend is most likely not the last word in marathon group therapy, he does see it as an intensive experience that serves as a good introduction to RET. He asserted that this format is "specifically designed to show group members what their fundamental self-defeating philosophies are and to indicate how they can work at changing these philosophies, in the here and now and thereafter. It is consequently a therapeutic experience that is oriented toward experiencing and behavior modification toward self-expression and the specific teaching of new personality skills" (pp. 126–127).

Summary and Evaluation

There are aspects of RET that I find to be very valuable as I work with clients, either individually or in groups. I believe that significant others in our pasts have contributed to the shaping of our current life-styles and philosophies of life. Yet, in strong agreement with Ellis, I contend that we are the ones who are responsible for maintaining certain self-destructive ideas and attitudes that influence our daily transactions. We may have learned that we should be perfect and that it is essential to be loved and approved of by everyone; the problem, however, is that we originally uncritically accepted some of those notions, and now we still apply them relentlessly to ourselves. I see value in confronting clients with questions such as What are your assumptions and basic beliefs? Have you really scrutinized some of the core ideas that you live by to determine if they are your own values or merely introjects? In addition, I value thinking as well as feeling and experiencing in psychotherapy. I am critical of many group approaches, particularly encounter and sensitivity groups, where thinking, judging, and evaluating is looked upon with scorn and where experiencing here-and-now feelings and "gut reactions" is seen as equivalent to psychological health. After a person has experienced a cathartic or highly intensive emotional experience related to earlier traumas, it seems that some attempt at conceptualization and putting meaning to the experience is essential if it is to have any lasting effect on client change. RET does offer the cognitive dimension and does challenge the client to examine the rationality of many of his or her decisions and values.

Another contribution of RET is its emphasis on putting newly acquired insights into action. The homework-assignment method is well suited to enabling clients to practice new behaviors and assisting them in the process of their reconditioning. Reality therapy, behavior therapy, and Transactional Analysis share with RET this action orientation. Clients can gain a multitude of insights and can become very aware of the nature of their problems, but I question the value of self-understanding unless specific plans that lead to behavioral changes desired by the client are implemented. RET insists on this action phase as a crucial part of the therapy process.

RET has some definite limitations, many of which Ellis, as cited earlier in this chapter, has pointed out. Since the approach is highly didactic, I believe that it is essential for the therapist to know himself or herself well and to take care not to merely impose his or her own philosophy of life on his or her clients. The issue of what constitutes rational behavior is central here. The fact that the rational therapist assumes such a confrontive and directive position creates certain dangers. The therapist's level of training, knowledge and skill, perceptiveness, and accuracy of judgment are particularly important in RET. Because the therapist has a large degree of power by virtue of persuasion and directiveness, psychological harm is more possible in RET than in the less directive client-centered approach. The RET therapist must be aware of when to "push" clients and when not to. There is the danger that an untrained therapist who uses RET might view therapy as "beating down" clients with persuasion, indoctrination, logic, and advice. Thus a practitioner can misuse RET by reducing it to dispensing quick-cure methods—that is, by telling clients what is wrong with them and how they should change.

Questions for Evaluation

Below is a series of questions designed to stimulate your own critical evaluation of the advantages and disadvantages of RET.

1. Do you believe that it is desirable for one to "think" one's way through "irrational" aspects of life such as joy, ecstasy, craziness, sadness, despair, abandonment and loneliness, rage, fear, and hatred? Should one be "cured" of those feelings? What would life be like if one were almost exclusively rational?

2. RET views anxiety as the result of self-blame. Ellis maintains that blaming ourselves or others is pernicious. Do you agree? Is it desirable to remove all guilt? If one gets to a point where one never experiences guilt, does this mean that one is an accomplished psychopath? What kind of guilt is healthy? What kind is unhealthy?

3. Do you agree with the contention that one does not need love and acceptance from other significant people? Is it realistic to teach a client ways of enjoying life while feeling unloved? Is this a persuasive form of denial?

4. Can you apply to your own life the concept that one tends to keep irrational ideas alive by repeating these ideas to oneself? What are some examples in your own life?

5. Review Ellis's list of common irrational ideas that many of us have learned in society. What is your evaluation of these ideas? What other irrational ideas could you add to the list? What ideas can you relate to personally? In what ways do you still cling to some irrational premises? Have you tried to eradicate them?

6. The rational-emotive therapist teaches a client a philosophy of life. Whose philosophy is taught? Is teaching a philosophy of life appro-

priate in counseling? Does this approach assume that the therapist is the one with the "correct" beliefs? Do you consider indoctrination as therapy?

7. Do you think that RET is too simplistic? Is it really teaching a client how to successfully suppress basic feelings? Take for example a client who says "I know I feel guilty over an abortion, and I've been through the experience 98 times in my therapy. I know it's dumb, but I still feel guilty, though I wish I didn't. So, what can I do about it?" Ellis appears to believe that intellectual persuasion will eventually convince the client that she no longer need blame herself, nor will she need to cling to the "irrational belief" of her guilt. Could this form of therapeutic intervention aid her in suppressing her feelings? Would she have merely persuaded herself that she should not feel the way she actually does?

8. What criteria do you employ to determine whether or not a person's philosophy of life is rational?

9. Would a constant repetition of corrective sentences make one more of a robot than a spontaneous creator?

10. Do you believe that, with its emphasis on thinking, RET gives enough attention to the emotional aspects of therapy?

References and Suggested Readings

*Ellis, A. *Reason and emotion in psychotherapy.* New York: Lyle Stuart, 1962.

Ellis, A. Rational-emotive psychotherapy. In D. Arbuckle (Ed.), *Counseling and psychotherapy.* New York: McGraw-Hill, 1967.

Ellis, A. A weekend of rational encounter. In A. Burton (Ed.), *Encounter: The theory and practice of encounter groups.* San Francisco: Jossey-Bass, 1969.

Ellis, A. Rational-emotive therapy. In R. Corsini (Ed.), *Current psychotherapies.* Itasca, Ill.: Peacock, 1973. (a)

*Ellis, A. *Humanistic psychotherapy: The rational-emotive approach.* New York: Julian Press, 1973. (b)

Ellis, A. Rational-emotive theory: Albert Ellis. In A. Burton (Ed.), *Operational theories of personality.* New York: Brunner/Mazel, 1974.

*Ellis, A., & Harper, R. *A new guide to rational living* (Rev. ed.). Hollywood: Wilshire Books, 1975.

Patterson, C. H. *Theories of counseling and psychotherapy* (Rev. ed.). New York: Harper & Row, 1973.

CHAPTER NINE

REALITY

THERAPY

Introduction

I selected William Glasser's reality therapy for inclusion in this book for several reasons. First, this approach (as does Ellis's rational-emotive therapy) provides a good contrast to most of the other counseling approaches explored in this book. Second, reality therapy has gained popularity among school counselors, elementary and secondary teachers and principals, and rehabilitation workers. Third, it presents many of the basic issues in counseling that underlie such questions as What is reality? Should a therapist teach his or her patients? What should be taught? What model should the therapist provide? Whose philosophy should be taught? What is the role of values in counseling? As you read this chapter keep these questions in mind and compare reality therapy with the other therapeutic approaches you have studied.

Reality therapy is a system that focuses on present behavior. The therapist functions as a teacher and a model and confronts the client in ways that help the client face reality and fulfill basic needs without harming himself or herself or others. The heart of reality therapy is acceptance of personal responsibility, which is equated with mental health. Glasser developed this therapy from his conviction that conventional psychiatry is based largely on mistaken assumptions. Reality therapy, which describes principles and procedures designed to help people achieve a "success identity," is applicable to psychotherapy, counseling, teaching, group work, marriage counseling, institutional management, and community development. Reality therapy is a form of behavior modification, for, particularly in its institutional applications, it is essentially a type of nonrigorous operant conditioning. In my opinion, one reason for Glasser's popularity is that he has succeeded in translating some concepts of behavior modification into a relatively simple and straightforward model of practice.

Key Concepts

View of Human Nature

Reality therapy is based on the premise that there is a single psychological need that is present throughout life: the need for identity, which includes a need to feel a sense of uniqueness, separateness, and distinctiveness. The need for identity, which accounts for the dynamics of behavior, is seen as universal among all cultures.

According to reality therapy, it is most useful to consider identity in terms of a "success identity" versus a "failure identity." In the formation of identity, each of us develops from involvements with others and with the self-image by which we feel relatively successful or unsuccessful. Others play a significant role in helping us clarify and understand our identities. Love and acceptance are directly related to identity formation. According to Glasser (1965), the basis of reality therapy is to help clients fulfill the basic psychological needs, which include "the need to love and to be loved and the need to feel that we are worthwhile to ourselves and to others" (p. 9).

The view of human nature includes a contention that a "growth force" impels us to strive for a success identity. As Glasser and Zunin (1973) stated, "We believe that each individual has a health or growth force. Basically people want to be content and enjoy a success identity, to show responsible behavior and to have meaningful interpersonal relationships" (p. 297). Personal suffering can be changed only with a change in identity. This viewpoint asserts that, because individuals can change how they live, feel, and behave, they can thus change their destinies. Identity change is contingent on behavioral change.

It is clear, then, that reality therapy does not rest on a deterministic philosophy of human nature but is built on the assumption that the person is ultimately self-determining. This principle implies each person's responsibility to accept the consequences of his or her behavior. Apparently, the person becomes what he or she decides to become.

Characteristics of Reality Therapy

There are at least eight characteristics that define reality therapy:
1. Reality therapy rejects the concept of mental illness. It assumes that specific forms of behavior disorders are the result of irresponsibility. This

approach does not deal with psychological diagnoses. It equates mental ill-ness with irresponsible behavior, and it equates mental health with respon-sible behavior.

2. Reality therapy focuses on present behavior rather than on feelings and attitudes. Although it does not assert that feelings and attitudes are unimportant, it does stress becoming aware of present behavior. Also, the reality therapist does not depend on insight to change attitudes but main-tains that attitude change follows behavior change.

3. Reality therapy focuses on the present, not on the past. Since a person's past is fixed and cannot be changed, all that can be changed is the present and the future. If the past is discussed in therapy, it is always re-lated to the client's current behavior. The therapist is open to exploring all aspects of the client's present life, including his or her hopes, fears, and values. Therapy stresses the client's strengths, potentials, successes, and positive qualities, not merely his or her misery and symptoms. Glasser (1965) urged that the client be seen as a "person with wide potential, not just as a patient with problems" (p. 31). He discouraged devoting therapy time to rehashing problems and failures and suggested that the therapist look for a client's strengths and emphasize them in the conversations. He does not advocate recounting history and exploring the past, for he sees this as an unproductive venture. Further, it is a "waste of time to discuss past mistakes with the therapist" (p. 32). He raises the question "Why become involved with the irresponsible person he was? We want to become involved with the responsible person we know he can be" (p. 32).

4. Reality therapy emphasizes value judgments. It places central impor-tance on the client's role in judging the quality of his or her own behavior in order to determine what is contributing to his or her failure in life. It deems that change is unlikely without looking at behavior and making some de-termination of its constructiveness or destructiveness. If clients come to realize that they are not getting what they want and that their behavior is self-destructive, there is a real possibility for positive change to occur, sim-ply because they decide that alternatives might be preferable to their present unrealistic style.

5. Reality therapy does not emphasize transference. It does not view the traditional concept of transference as important. It sees transference as a way for the therapist to remain hidden as a person. Reality therapy calls for a genuine way of being for therapists—that is, that they be themselves, not play the role of the client's mother or father. Glasser (1965) contended that clients do not look for a repeat of unsuccessful involvements in their past but that they seek a satisfying human involvement with a person in their present existence. The therapist can be the person who helps them fulfill their needs in the present by establishing a personal and genuine relationship.

6. Reality therapy stresses the conscious, not the unconscious, aspects. Psychoanalytic theory, which assumes that insight and awareness of uncon-scious processes is a requisite for personality change, emphasizes ways of tapping unconscious conflicts through techniques such as analysis of trans-ference, dream analysis, free associations, and analysis of resistance. By

contrast, reality therapy emphasizes what clients are doing wrong, how their present behavior is not getting them what they want, and how they might engage in a plan for successful behavior based on responsible and realistic behavior. The reality therapist examines the client's present life in detail and assumes that the client will discover the conscious behavior that does not lead to the fulfillment of his or her needs. Thus reality therapy contends that to emphasize the unconscious is to sidetrack the central issue of the client's irresponsibility and give him or her an excuse for avoiding reality. Also, whereas insight might be interesting, reality therapy does not see it as essential to producing change.

7. Reality therapy eliminates punishment. Glasser maintains that punishment aimed at changing behavior is ineffective and that punishment for failing to implement plans results both in reinforcing the client's failure identity and in harming the therapeutic relationship. He cautions against the therapist's use of deprecating statements, for this is punishment. Instead of using punishment, Glasser advocates allowing the client to experience the natural consequences of his or her behavior.

In his book *Schools without Failure*, Glasser (1969) explored in detail the problem of failure as a way of punishing students in the school situation. He contended that "the major problem of the schools is a problem of failure" (p. 7).* He called for an educational system that is rooted in an educational philosophy whereby successful learning experiences are possible. He asked that educators "examine the deficiencies in education itself that lead to school failure, then set a course which will correct them" (p. 11). He outlined specific proposals for programs that will prevent failure and increase the chances of successful learning experiences for school children.

8. Reality therapy emphasizes the concept of responsibility, which Glasser (1965) defined as "the ability to fulfill one's needs, and to do so *in a way that does not deprive others of the ability to fulfill their needs*" (p. 13). Learning responsibility is a lifelong process. Even though all of us possess the need to love and be loved and the need to feel a sense of worthiness, we are not naturally endowed with the ability to fulfill these needs. Responsibility consists of learning how to meet these needs in reality. Glasser contended that "we must learn to correct ourselves when we do wrong and credit ourselves when we do right" (p. 10). In order to improve our conduct when it is below our standards, we need to evaluate our own behavior or have it evaluated. Thus an essential part of reality therapy involves morals, standards, value judgments, and right and wrong behavior, for they are all intimately related to the fulfillment of the need for self-worth. According to Glasser, a responsible person does that which gives him or her a feeling of self-worth and a feeling that he or she is worthwhile to others.

Glasser (1965) contends that teaching responsibility is a core concept in reality therapy. Whereas most animals are driven by instinct, humans have developed the capacity to learn and to teach responsibility. Reality therapy thus stresses the therapist's teaching function. The therapist teaches clients

*From *Schools Without Failure*, by W. Glasser. Copyright 1969 by Harper & Row, Publishers, Inc. This and all other quotations from this source are reprinted by permission.

better ways to fulfill their needs by exploring the specifics of their daily lives and then making directive statements and suggestions of ways to solve problems more effectively. Therapy becomes a special kind of education wherein definite plans are made and realistic and responsible means of meeting personal needs are examined.

The Therapeutic Process

Therapeutic Goals

As is true of most systems of psychotherapy, the overall goal of reality therapy is to help the individual achieve autonomy. Essentially, autonomy is the state of maturity that accounts for the person's ability to relinquish environmental support and substitute internal support. This maturity implies that people are able to take responsibility for who they are and what they want to become and to develop responsible and realistic plans to fulfill their goals. Reality therapy assists people in defining and clarifying their life goals. Further, it assists them in clarifying the ways they frustrate their progress toward their self-defined goals. The therapist helps the client discover alternatives in reaching goals, but it is the client who decides his or her own goals of therapy.

Glasser and Zunin (1973) agree that the therapist should have some goals in mind for the client but that they should be expressed in terms of concepts of individual responsibility rather than in terms of behavioral goals, as the client must determine those for himself or herself. They state that the criteria for successful psychotherapy depend largely on the client-determined goals. Although there are no rigid criteria the attainment of which marks the termination of therapy, the general criteria of attaining responsible behavior and fulfilling the client's goals indicate that the client is able to follow through with his or her plans independently and that there is no longer a need for treatment.

The Function and Role of the Therapist

The basic job of the reality therapist is to become involved with the client and then get him or her to face reality. Glasser (1965) feels that, when the therapist confronts clients, he or she forces them to decide whether or not they will take the "responsible path." The therapist does not make value judgments and decisions for clients, for to do so would take away the responsibility that belongs to them. The therapist's task is to serve as a guide to help clients realistically appraise their own behavior.

Some who have read Glasser have developed a distorted notion that the therapist should function as a moralist. Glasser (1972), asserting that his principle of evaluation behavior has been frequently misunderstood, has disavowed the role of the moralist:

Some people accept and others reject Reality Therapy because they misunderstand this principle. Both groups believe the Reality Therapist acts as a moralist, which he does not; he never tells anyone that what he is doing is wrong and that he must change. The therapist does not judge the behavior; he leads the patient to evaluate his own behavior through his involvement and by bringing the actual behavior out in the open [p. 119].

The reality therapist is expected to give praise when clients act in a responsible way and to show disapproval when they do not. Clients demand this type of judgment, according to Glasser (1965, p. 28). The therapist must be willing to function as a teacher in the relationship with the client. He or she must teach the client that the aim of therapy is not directed toward happiness. The reality therapist assumes that the client can create his or her own happiness and that the key to finding happiness is through accepting responsibility. Therefore, the therapist does not accept any excuses or ignore reality, nor does he or she accept the client's blaming anything or anybody external for his or her own present unhappiness. To do so would be to engage the client in "psychiatric kicks" that will soon fade away and lead to resentment.

Another important function of the reality therapist is to set limits, including those in the therapeutic situation and those that life places on the individual. Glasser and Zunin (1973) pointed to the contractual arrangement as a type of limit-setting. Contracts, which are often a part of the therapy process, might include having the client reporting on his or her successes as well as failures in work outside the therapy situation. Frequently a contract determines a specific time limit for the duration of therapy. At the end of this time, therapy might terminate, and the client is allowed to fend for himself or herself. Some clients function more effectively when they are aware that the therapy sessions are limited to a certain number.

Apart from those functions and tasks, the therapist's ability to get involved with the client and to get the client involved in the therapeutic process is considered to be paramount. This is often a difficult function, especially when the client is not seeking counseling or when he or she is coming for "help" solely out of provision of his or her probation. Glasser (1965) indicates that the way involvement between two strangers occurs has a lot to do with necessary qualities of the therapist. The greater degree to which the therapist has these qualities, the more able he or she is to create the type of involvement with the client that will promote successful outcomes. According to Glasser (1965), some of these personal attributes, or qualities, include the therapist's ability and willingness to be demanding, yet sensitive; fulfill his or her own needs in reality; openly share his or her own struggles; be personal and not maintain an aloof stance; allow his or her own values to be challenged by the client; not accept excuses for evasion of responsible action; demonstrate courage by continually confronting clients, regardless of the opposition from clients, when they are not living realistically; understand and emphathize with the client; and establish a genuine involvement with the client.

The Client's Experience in Therapy

Clients in reality therapy are not those who have learned to lead responsible lives but those who are described as irresponsible. Even though their behavior is inadequate, unrealistic, and irresponsible, it is still an attempt to fulfill their basic needs of being loved and loving and of feeling a sense of self-worth. Their behavior is an attempt to gain a sense of identity, even though it might well be a "failure identity." The therapeutic concern is with those who have not learned, or have lost their ability, to live responsible lives.

Clients are expected to focus on their present behavior instead of their feelings and attitudes. The therapist challenges them to take a critical look at what they are doing with their lives and then make value judgments regarding the effectiveness of their behavior in attaining their life goals. Since clients can control their behavior more easily than they can their feeling and thinking, their behavior is the focus of therapy. If a client complains of feeling anxious, the therapist might ask "What are you doing to make yourself anxious?" The focus is not on the anxious feeling but on helping the client gain awareness of what he or she is now doing to make himself or herself anxious. Constant examination and evaluation of what the client is doing continues throughout therapy.

Once clients make certain judgments about their behavior and decide how they want to change, they are expected to develop specific plans to change failure behavior into success behavior. Clients must make a commitment to carry out these plans; action becomes a must. They cannot escape their commitment by blaming, explaining, or giving excuses. They must be actively involved in implementing their therapeutic contracts in responsible ways if any progress is to occur.

The Relationship between Therapist and Client

Before effective therapy can occur, an involvement between the client and the counselor must develop. Clients need to know that the helping person—that is, the therapist—cares enough about them to both accept them and help them fulfill their needs in the real world. Specific principles or concepts that provide the framework for the process of learning that occurs as a result of the relationship between the therapist and the client or between the teacher and student, which Glasser (1965, 1969) and Glasser and Zunin (1973) developed throughout their writings, are briefly reviewed below.

1. Reality therapy is based on the personal relationship and involvement of the therapist with the client. The therapist, by warmth, understanding, acceptance, and belief in the capacity of a person to develop a success identity, must communicate that he or she cares. Through the personal involvement with the therapist the client learns that there is more to life than focusing on failures, misery, and irresponsible behavior. The therapist also demonstrates his or her caring by refusing to accept blaming or excuses from the client. The therapist cares enough to view the client in terms of what the

client might become if he or she decides to live by facing reality. While a warm relationship is being established, entanglements are to be avoided. It is the therapist's job to define the therapeutic situation so that the client understands the nature, purpose, and direction of the relationship.

Glasser (1969) believes that involvement, as applied to schools, is vital to a child's attaining a success identity. He charged that there is too much aloofness and attempts to motivate by external means in the classroom. Just as he calls for a personal relationship between therapist and client, Glasser (1969) sees involvement as crucial in teacher/student relationships.

2. Planning is essential in reality therapy. The therapeutic situation is not limited merely to discussions between the therapist and the client. They must develop plans that, once established, must be carried out; action is an essential part of reality therapy. Much of the most significant work of the therapeutic process, then, consists in helping the client identify specific ways to change failure behavior into success behavior. Plans should be realistic and within the limits of the motivation and capacities of each client. Plans are not absolute but are mainly alternative ways a person can solve problems and expand successful life experiences. Plans for action must be specific, concrete, and measurable. Plans need not be rigid; an endless number of plans can be applied to problem solving. If one plan does not work, it should be reevaluated, and other alternatives can then be considered. Glasser and Zunin (1973, p. 302) see it as valuable to put the plan in writing, in the form of a contract. Then the client can be accountable for his or her subsequent actions in carrying out the plans.

In *Schools Without Failure*, Glasser (1969) has developed the concept of involving students in planning for relevant and successful learning experiences. He charges that schools often lack relevance for the learner: "Schools usually *do not teach* a relevant curriculum; when they do, *they fail to teach the child how he can relate this learning to his life outside of school*" (p. 50). If schools become involved in relevance, then planning real-life learning experiences that lead to a success identity becomes feasible. Glasser discusses the details of the nature, structure, and functioning of "class meetings." He provides specific ways of getting these meetings started, and gives numerous concrete suggestions of how to keep class meetings going. In this way, teachers and students together can develop plans for a meaningful curriculum.

3. Commitment is the keystone of reality therapy. After individuals make value judgments about their behavior and decide on plans for action, the therapist assists them in making a commitment to implement their plans in their daily life. Resolutions and plans become meaningless unless there is a decision to carry out the plans. Glasser and Zunin (1973) pointed out that "a primary characteristic of individuals who have failure identities is that they have a strong unwillingness to commit themselves" (p. 302). Hence it is in following through with plans that clients acquire a sense of self-worth.

Applied to the school situation, the same principle holds true. Glasser (1969) emphasized that *"we must teach children commitment"* but that it is "not enough, however, for a child to make a value judgment; he must choose a better way and commit himself to his choice. It is from commitment that we gain maturity and worthwhileness. It is from commitment that we gain understanding of real love" (p. 22).

4. Reality therapy accepts no excuses. It is clear that not all the client's commitments will be actualized. Plans do fail, but when they do the reality therapist accepts no excuses. The therapist is not interested in listening to the client's excuses, blaming, and explanations of why his or her plan failed. Glasser stresses that the therapist should not blame or deprecate the client for failing, nor should the therapist "play detective" and search for the reasons for the failure. Glasser thinks that people know why things went wrong; thus instead of focusing on why, the therapist focuses on what the client intends to do to accomplish what he or she decided to do. Glasser (1965, p. 27) contended that it is essential that the therapist "insist that the patient face the reality of his behavior." The therapist's task is to care enough for the client that he or she makes the client "face a truth that he has spent his life trying to avoid; *he is responsible for his behavior.*" The therapist never condones or excuses any of the client's irresponsible behavior.

The principle of not accepting excuses is also essential in schools. Glasser (1969) pointed out that "teachers who care accept no excuses" (p. 23). He asserted that, when children make value judgments and commitments to change their behavior, no excuse for not meeting their commitments should be accepted. Hence the teacher or the therapist should not belabor the reasons why a plan failed, for this serves only to reinforce the failure identity.

Application: Therapeutic Techniques and Procedures

Major Techniques and Procedures

Reality therapy can be characterized as verbally active. Its procedures focus on the client's strengths and potentials as related to his or her current behavior as he or she attempts to succeed in life. In assisting the client to create a success identity, the therapist might use a range of techniques such as the following:

1. engage in role-playing with the client;
2. use humor;
3. confront the client and not allow any excuses;
4. help the client to formulate specific plans for action;
5. serve as a role model and teacher;
6. set definite limits and structure the therapy situation;
7. use "verbal shock therapy" or appropriate sarcasm to confront the client with his or her unrealistic behavior; and
8. get involved with the patient in his or her search for more effective living.

Reality therapy does not include some commonly accepted therapeutic approaches. Psychiatrists who practice reality therapy apply drugs and medications conservatively, for medication tends to remove personal responsibility for behavior. Further, the practitioner of reality therapy does not devote time to acting as a "detective" in search of reasons but attempts to convey an attitude of working together with clients to help them achieve their stated goals. Diagnostic techniques are not a part of reality therapy, for diagnosis is seen as a waste of time at best and, at worst, damaging to a client by pinning a label (such as "schizophrenic") on the client that tends to perpetuate irresponsible and unsuccessful behavior. Other techniques not used are interpretation, insight, nondirective interviews, prolonged silences, free association, analysis of transference and resistance, and dream analysis.

Applications to Counseling Situations

Glasser and Zunin (1973) believe that the techniques of reality therapy are applicable to a wide range of behavior and emotional problems. They assert that the procedures of reality therapy have been successful in treating "specific individual problems such as problems of anxiety, maladjustment, marital conflicts, perversions, and psychoses" (p. 307).

An area in which reality therapy has been used extensively and with great success is the treatment of youthful law offenders. Results of Glasser's work at the Ventura School for Girls indicates that reality therapy procedures in the program significantly reduced the recidivism rates (Glasser & Zunin, 1973).

Reality therapy is well suited to individual therapy, group therapy, and marriage counseling. In individual therapy, therapists generally see their clients once a week for a 45-minute session. Matching the therapist and the client bears no particular importance. At the outset, therapists might in consultation with the client decide the duration of therapy.

Group psychotherapy is an effective vehicle by which to apply the procedures of reality therapy. The group process can be a powerful agent in helping clients implement their plans and follow through with their commitments. The members are encouraged to write down specific contracts and read them to the group. Involvement with other group members in a meaningful way is an inducement to stick by the commitments made. The use of co-therapists is frequent and has been found to be a valuable adjunct in reality-therapy groups (Glasser & Zunin, 1973).

Marriage counseling or conjoint marital therapy is often practiced by the reality therapist, according to Glasser and Zunin (1973). They view this type of counseling as a time-limited series of sessions, usually from 5 to 15 visits. At the end of this time an evaluation is made to determine what if any progress has been made and whether continued sessions are in order. It is important to establish at the outset whether the couples are (a) deciding to terminate the relationship; (b) wanting to explore the pros and cons of continuing the relationship; or (c) quite sure they wish to remain married but are seeking help in improving their relationship. The therapist is encouraged to be active and should raise questions leading to understanding the general marriage dynamics and style as the partners relate to each other.

Some questions that are likely to be posed are "What are you doing that makes you feel good (or bad) about yourself?" "What is your spouse doing that makes you feel good (or bad) about yourself?" "What specific changes would each of you most like to make in your marriage?"

Application to Schools

Reality therapy has direct implications for school situations. Glasser first became concerned about children's learning and behavior problems while he was working with delinquent girls at the Ventura School for Girls of the California Youth Authority. He noted the almost universal history of school failure among these girls, and this finding led him to the public schools as a consultant. Glasser (1965) developed the concepts for helping children in problem solving that he described in his book *Reality Therapy*.

As he continued his work in the public elementary schools, he became convinced that the stigma of failure permeated the atmosphere in most schools and had a damaging effect on most children in schools. The elimination of failure in the school system and the prevention, rather than merely the treatment, of delinquency became two of his goals.

Glasser (1969) believes that education can be the key to effective human relating, and, in his book *Schools without Failure*, he proposed a program to eliminate failure, emphasize thinking instead of memory work, introduce relevance into the curriculum, substitute discipline for punishment, create a learning environment where children can maximize successful experiences that will lead to a success identity, create motivation and involvement, help students develop responsible behavior, and establish ways of involving the parents and the community in the school. In 1970 the William Glasser Center was established at LaVerne College for the purpose of implementing in the schools the philosophy and procedures described in *Schools without Failure*. The purpose was met largely through in-service seminars that enabled schools to build their own Schools without Failure. LaVerne College in California now offers a master's-degree program in Schools without Failure. The courses offered through the LaVerne College program emphasize involvement, relevance, thinking, and ways to reduce failure and increase success. They give attention also to attitude change, communication skills, group processes, and problem solving.

Summary and Evaluation

Reality therapy seems well suited to brief interventions in crisis-counseling situations and to working with youths or adults who are in institutions for criminal behavior. Realistically, in those situations and with that type of population, long-term psychotherapy that explores unconscious dynamics and explores one's past may be extremely limited. Glasser developed his approach because of his contention that psychoanalytic procedures did not work for that population.

The advantages of the approach appear to be that it is relatively short-term therapy, and it deals with conscious behavioral problems. The client is confronted with the necessity of evaluating his or her behavior and making a value judgment. Insight and awareness are not seen as enough; a plan of action and a commitment to following through are seen as the core of the therapeutic process. Clients might want to manufacture excuses, play blaming games, and make others responsible for their current problems. Since reality therapy accepts no excuses, and insists on acceptance of responsibility for the way he or she is, the client must look inward and search for alternatives. Assume that a youth is in a correctional facility and is a product of a miserable environment where his parents hated him and abused him physically and psychologically. Regardless of the reasons for his conflicts with the law, he now needs to decide whether his behavior is getting him what he wants. In this respect, reality therapy encourages clients to exercise freedom and responsibility.

In my estimation, a shortcoming of reality therapy is that it does not give enough emphasis to the place of unconscious psychodynamics and the person's past as a determinant of present behavior. Whereas Glasser apparently accepts the role of the past and the unconscious as causal factors of present behavior, he rejects the value of those factors in modifying present behavior. As Glasser (1965) put it, "certainly patients, like everyone else, have reasons of which they may be unaware for behaving the way they do . . . But we are doing therapy, and not research into the causes of human behavior, and we have found that knowledge of cause has nothing to do with therapy" (p. 53). He discounts the contributions of the psychoanalytic approach and gives little credit to Freud's discoveries.

My major concern is that reality therapy can become a superficial type of intervention because it utilizes an overly simplistic framework for therapeutic practice. As is rational-emotive therapy, reality therapy is vulnerable to the type of practitioner that could assume the role of expert in deciding for others questions such as how life should be lived, what is realistic or unrealistic, what is right or wrong behavior, and what constitutes responsible behavior. Thus the therapist who is unaware of his or her own needs to "straighten people out" can stunt clients' growth and autonomy by becoming overly moralistic and by strongly influencing clients to accept the therapist's view of reality instead of searching within for their own answers. Further, this approach reduces solutions of all problems to a few common denominators: acceptance of personal responsibility, commitment to realistic values, conscious decision making. There are other dimensions stressed by the various therapies that are not seriously considered within the framework of reality therapy.

Finally, Glasser's view of mental illness as "irresponsibility" is controversial. I find the viewpoint both overly simplistic and invalid. It neglects to acknowledge that many mental patients were highly responsible citizens prior to the onset of their symptoms. Further, patients may remain responsible in many areas of their lives while exhibiting psychotic or bizarre behavior. I raise the following questions: Is extreme stress a causal factor of emotional and behavioral disorders? Are physiological factors related to mental illness? Can all forms of behavioral problems be reduced simply to irresponsible behavior?

Questions for Evaluation

The following questions are directly related to the theory and practice of reality therapy. I suggest that you review them as a basis for integrating certain aspects of reality therapy into your counseling philosophy.

1. How can a therapist judge acceptable, realistic behavior? Whose creeds and values should be used to judge the acceptability of behavior?
2. Wrestle with the problem of defining "reality." Is the therapist's view of reality more real than the client's view of reality? What about the problem that exists when the therapist and the client live in different experiential worlds? Can a white, middle-class therapist who has experienced little divergence in life-styles effectively guide a black or brown youngster who lives in the ghetto or in the barrio? Can the therapist enter the world of reality of the client? Can he or she understand values and behavior that are sharply divergent from his or her own?
3. Do you see a contradiction in the idea that a therapist must reject irresponsible behavior yet accept the client and maintain involvement with the client? Is rejection of a person's behavior a subtle rejection of that person?
4. How realistic is it to assume that real involvement between a therapist and a client can occur when the client makes it frankly known that he or she wants no part of "head-shrinking"? Assume that your client is a "delinquent" in a youth authority camp and that he has to see you for therapy. He comes for several sessions, remains closed, and tells you each time that he does not want to be there and that he wants to quit. How would you handle this? What are your own values in regard to "mandatory counseling"? What if your views conflict with the agency that employs you?
5. Glasser's approach suggests that the therapist be a model for the client to emulate. Should the therapist be so? How can a therapist decide whether or not he or she is a model worth emulating? Should the therapist seek to have the client pattern himself or herself according to all the counselor's values? Which values should be emulated?
6. Glasser maintains that the client needs to know that the therapist cares for him or her and that one way of evidencing caring is to reject behavior that does not help the client fulfill his or her needs in a responsible way. Do you agree? How can you determine whether your client feels that you care? What does caring imply to you? What if the truth of the matter is that you don't care for your client? What would you do if you had a strong aversion to the client?
7. Where do you stand on Glasser's idea that a therapist should give

praise when the client acts responsibly and show disapproval when the client acts irresponsibly? Do you think that these responses might encourage the client to adopt your values so that he or she is liked and accepted by you? Is this type of value judgment conducive to developing inner direction? Is it appropriate to therapy? Can it really be avoided? Do all therapists make value judgments in some form or another?

8. What advantages do you see in the insistence on focusing exclusively on the present? How does it avoid digging for useless artifacts in a person's history? How does it eliminate the blaming game?

9. What limitations do you see in insisting that your client not explore past experience? Can one really understand or change one's present if one refuses to become aware of one's past? Are you not a victim now unless you understand your past?

10. Do you agree with Glasser's concept that mental illness is the result of irresponsibility? Can you think of any other causes of mental illness besides irresponsibility?

References and Suggested Readings

*Glasser, W. *Reality therapy.* New York: Harper & Row, 1965.

Glasser, W. *Schools without failure.* New York: Harper & Row, 1969.

Glasser, W. *The identity society.* New York: Harper & Row, 1972.

Glasser, W., & Zunin, L. Reality therapy. In R. Corsini (Ed.), *Current psychotherapies.* Itasca, Ill.: Peacock, 1973.

CHAPTER TEN

CASE ILLUSTRATION: CONTRASTS AND COMPARISONS OF APPROACHES

Introduction

The purpose of this chapter is to illustrate how the various therapies might approach the understanding of the same client. One client, Stan, will be viewed in the light of each therapeutic approach in regard to questions such as What particular dimensions of Stan's life and behavior would be given focus? What are the psychodynamics or concepts that explain the existence of his problems? What are the general goals? What possible techniques and methods would implement these goals? What might be some characteristics of the relationship between Stan and the therapist? How might the therapist proceed, and what would be the therapist's function?

Presenting a single case is of particular value in pointing out the contrasts among the approaches and the parallels among therapies that emphasize similar or compatible concepts and practices. The case illustration of Stan exposes you to the approaches of eight different models in the attempt to provide some basis for integration among the approaches and to help you gain more understanding of the practical applications of these models with the same person. This concrete illustration may be helpful in understanding how therapists with divergent orientations operate. I hope that you will be able to sharpen your focus on certain attributes of each approach that can be incorporated into a personalized style of counseling. To make this chapter more personally meaningful, I suggest that you put yourself in the situation of seeking psychological counseling. Provide your own background informa-

171

tion and develop your own goals for what you hope to accomplish. Then, *as a client*, work through each of these therapies.

The Case of Stan

The setting is a college counseling center, where both individual and group counseling by a qualified staff are available. The client, Stan, comes in for an intake counseling interview and gives the counselor these facts. Stan says: "I'm a 25-year-old junior in college, a psychology major, and I've recently decided to eventually work toward a master's degree in counseling psychology. I took a course, "Psychology of Personal Adjustment," last semester that was group-oriented with a self-understanding and personal-growth slant. We were asked to write an autobiographical paper, and as a result of that I became aware that there are certain areas in my life that I want to change, or at least understand better. In this class we were told about the services offered in the counseling center, and I decided that, if I hope to work with people as a counselor someday, I'd better take a closer look at myself. I'd like to have weekly, individual counseling sessions and would like to join a counseling group, because I need experience in relating to others and could gain from their feedback. My hope is that I can continue counseling for at least a semester, and maybe for a year."

That is the essence of Stan's introduction. Before leaving this initial session, he gives the counselor his autobiography so that the counselor will have a better understanding of where he has been, where he is now, where he would like to go, and what he wants for himself.

Stan's Life Sketch

Stan's autobiography reads as follows:
Where am I *currently* in my life? At 25 years of age, I feel I've wasted most of my life. By now I should be finished with college and into a good job, but instead I'm only a junior. I realize that I can't do that much with a B.S. in psychology, so I hope to get a master's degree in counseling and eventually work as a counselor with kids who are in trouble. I feel I was helped by someone who cared about me, and I'd like to have a similar influence on young people. At this time I live alone, have very few friends, and feel very scared and inferior with people my own age or older. I feel good when I'm with kids, because they are so honest. I worry a lot whether I'm smart enough to get through all the studies I'll need to do before I can become a counselor. One of my problems is that I drink heavily and frequently get drunk. This happens mostly when I feel all alone and scared that I'll always feel as lonely and isolated as I do now. In the past I used drugs heavily, and once in a while I still get loaded. I'm scared of people in general but of strong and attractive women in particular. I feel all cold, sweaty, and

terribly uptight when I'm with a woman. Maybe I think they are judging me and I know they'll find out that I'm not much of a man. I'm afraid I just can't measure up to what they expect of a man—you *always* have to be so strong, and tough, and perfect. And I'm not all this, so I often wonder if I'm adequate as a man.

I feel a terrible anxiety much of the time, particularly at night. Sometimes I feel so terrified that I feel like running, but I just can't move. It's awful because I often feel like I'm dying at times like this. And then I fantasize about committing suicide and wonder who would care. Sometimes I see my family coming to my funeral feeling very sorry that they didn't treat me better. Much of the time I feel guilty—like I haven't worked up to my potential, that I've been a failure, that I've wasted much of my time, and that I let people down a lot. I can really get down on myself and wallow in my guilt, and I feel very *depressed.* At times like this I tell myself how rotten I am, how I'll never be able to change, and how I'd be better off dead. Then I would not have to hurt anymore, and I wouldn't have to want either. It is very difficult for me to get close to anyone—and I can't say that I have ever loved a person and I surely know that I have never felt fully loved or wanted.

Everything isn't so bleak, because I did have enough guts to leave a lot of my shady past behind me and did struggle to get into college. And I like my determination—I *want* to change, and I have sought out counseling because I know I need someone to help me keep honest. I'm seeking a woman therapist because I feel more afraid of women than men. I like about myself that I feel scared a lot but that I also can feel my feelings and that I am willing to take risks even though I'm scared. That's why I chose to work with a woman.

What was my past like? Where have I been and what are some significant events and turning points in my life? A major turning point was the confidence my supervisor had in me at the summer youth camp where I worked during the past few summers. He encouraged me to go to college and said he saw a lot of potential in me for becoming a fine counselor with young people. That was hard for me to *really* believe, but his faith inspired me to begin to believe in myself. My marriage and divorce was another turning point. This "relationship" didn't last long before my wife left me. That was a severe blow to my manhood. She was a strong and dominant woman who took delight in telling me how worthless I was and how she couldn't stand to get near me. We had sex only a few times, and most of the time I was impotent. That was another blow to my ego. I'm so afraid to get close to a woman for fear that she will swallow me up. My parents never got a divorce, but I wish they had. They fought most of the time. I should say, she did most of the fighting. She was dominant and continually bitching at my father, whom I always saw as weak, passive, and mousey next to her. He'd *never* stand up to her. My folks always compared me unfavorably to my older sister and older brother—they were "perfect" children, successful, and honor students. My younger brother and I fought a lot, and he was the one who was spoiled rotten by them. I really don't know what happened to me and how I turned out to be the failure of all the four children.

In high school I took to the drug scene and got involved with the wrong crowd and got thrown into a youth rehabilitation facility for stealing. Later I was expelled from regular school for fighting, and I landed in a continuation high school, where I'd go to school in the mornings and have afternoons for on-the-job training. I got into auto mechanics and was fairly successful and even managed to keep myself employed for three years as a mechanic.

Back to my parents. I remember my father telling me: "You are really dumb. Why can't you be like your sister and brother? You'll never amount to a hill of beans! Why can't you ever do anything right?" And my mother treated me much like she treated my father. She would say: "Why do you do so many things to hurt me? Why can't you grow up and be a man? You were a mistake—I wish I didn't have you! Things are so much better around here when you are gone!" I recall crying myself to sleep many nights— feeling so terribly alone and filled with anger and hate. And feeling so disgusted with myself. There was no talk of religion in my house, nor was there any talk about sex. In fact, I always find it hard to imagine my folks ever having sex.

Where would I like to be five years from now? What kind of person do I want to become, and what kinds of changes do I most want in my life? Most of all, I'd just like to start feeling better about myself. I really have an inferiority complex, and I really know how to put myself down. I want to like myself much more than I do now. I hope I can learn to love at least a few other people and, most of all, women. I want to lose my fear that women can destroy me. I'd like to feel equal with others and not always have to feel apologetic for my existence. I don't want to suffer from this anxiety and guilt. And I hope that I can begin to think of myself as an OK person. I really want to become a good counselor with kids, and to do this I know I'm going to have to change. I'm not certain how I'll change, or even what are all the changes I hope for. I do know that I want to get free of my self-destructive tendencies and learn to trust people more. Maybe when I begin to like myself more, then I'll be able to trust that others might find something about me that is worth liking.

The Various Approaches

Psychoanalytic Therapy

The psychoanalytic approach would focus on the unconscious psychodynamics of Stan's behavior. Considerable attention might be given to material that he repressed such as his anxiety related to the threatened breakthrough of his sexual and aggressive impulses. In his past he had to rigidly control both these impulses, and when he didn't he got into trouble. He also developed a strong superego by introjecting parental values and standards and making them his own. These aspirations were unrealistic, for they were perfectionistic goals. He could be loved only if he became perfect; yet no matter what he attempted it never seemed adequate. He internalized his guilt, which became depression. At the extreme, Stan demonstrated a self-destructive tendency, which is a way of inflicting punishment on himself. His depression could be explained as the hostility he felt toward his parents and siblings, but, instead of directing these feelings toward them, he turned them inward toward himself. Stan's preoccupation with drinking could be hypothesized as evidence of an "oral fixation." Because during his early childhood he never received love and acceptance, he is still suffering from this deprivation and still desperately searching for approval and acceptance from others. Stan's sex-role identification was fraught with difficulties. He learned the basis of female-male relationships through his early experiences with his parents. What he saw was fighting, bickering, and discounting. His father was the weak one who always lost, and his mother was the strong, domineering force that could and did hurt men. Stan identified with his weak and impotent father; he generalized his fear of his mother to all women. It could be further hypothesized that he married a woman who was similar to his mother and who stimulated Stan's feelings of impotence in her presence.

Since Stan selected a woman therapist, the opportunity to develop a transference relationship and work through it would be the core of the therapy process. An assumption is that Stan would eventually relate to his therapist as he did to his mother and that the process would be a valuable means of gaining insight into the origin of his difficulties with women. The analytic process would stress an intensive exploration of Stan's past. The goal would be to make the unconscious conscious so that he would no longer be determined by unconscious forces. Stan would devote much therapy time to reliving and exploring his early past. As he would talk he would gain increased understanding of the dynamics of his behavior. He would begin to see connections between his present problems and early past experiences in childhood. Thus he would explore memories of relationships with his siblings and with his mother and father and also explore how he generalizes his view of women and men from his view of these family members. It could be expected that he would reexperience old feelings and would uncover buried feelings related to traumatic events. Some questions for Stan could include: What did you do when you felt unloved? What did you have to do as a child with your negative feelings? Could you express your rage, hostility, hurt, and fears? What effects did your relationship with your mother have upon you? and What did this teach you about all women?

The analytic process would focus on key influences in Stan's developmental years. As Stan came to understand how he had been shaped by these past experiences, he would become increasingly able to exert control over his present functioning. Many of his fears would become conscious, and then his energy would not have to remain fixed upon defending himself from unconscious feelings. Instead, he could make new decisions about his current life. He could do this only if he worked through the transference relationship, however, for the depth of his therapy endeavors would largely determine the depth and extent of his personality changes.

Existential-Humanistic Therapy

The counselor or therapist with an existential-humanistic orientation would approach Stan with the view that he has the capacity to expand his consciousness and decide for himself the future direction of his life. The therapist would want Stan to realize more than anything else that he does not have to be the victim of his past conditioning but that he can be the architect in redesigning his future. He can free himself of his deterministic shackles and accept the responsibility that comes with the freedom of directing his own life. This approach would not stress techniques but would emphasize the importance of the therapist's understanding of Stan's world primarily by establishing an authentic relationship as a means to a fuller degree of self-understanding.

What would be some possible dimensions that might be explored with Stan? He could be confronted with the ways he is attempting to escape from his freedom—through alcohol and drugs. His anxiety would not be seen as something that needs to be "cured"; rather, Stan would need to learn that realistic anxiety is a vital part of living with uncertainty and freedom. Since there are no guarantees and since the individual is ultimately alone, Stan could expect to experience some degree of healthy anxiety, aloneness, guilt, and even despair. These conditions are not neurotic in themselves, but the way Stan orients himself to these conditions and how he copes with his anxiety would be seen as critical.

Stan talks about feeling so low at times that he imagines suicide. The existential therapist might view this as symbolic. Could it be that Stan is feeling that he is dying as a person? Is he using his human potential? Is he choosing a dead way of merely existing instead of affirming life? The existentially oriented therapist would confront Stan with the issue of the meaning and purpose in his life. Is there any reason for Stan to want to continue living? What are some of Stan's projects that enrich his life? What can he do to find a sense of purpose that will make him feel more significant and more alive?

Guilt is a dominating force in Stan's life. However, much of his guilt is neurotic guilt, for it is based on his view of letting others down and not meeting their expectations. He must learn that guilt can serve a valuable function if it is based on his awareness of not utilizing his own potentials. Stan also needs to accept the reality that he may at times feel alone, for choosing for oneself and living from one's own center accentuates the experience of aloneness. He is not, however, condemned to a life of isolation, alienation from others, and loneliness. The existential therapist would see Stan's hope in his learning to discover his own centeredness and in living by the values he chooses and creates for himself. By doing so, Stan could become more of a substantial person and could learn to appreciate himself more. When he does, the chances are lessened that he will have a clinging need to secure approval from others, particularly his parents and parental substitutes. Instead of forming a dependent relationship, he could relate to others out of his strength. Only then would there be the possibility of overcoming his feelings of separateness and isolation.

Client-Centered Therapy

Stan's autobiography indicates that he has a fairly clear idea of what he wants for his life. He has stated goals that are meaningful for him. He is motivated to change and seems to have sufficient anxiety to work toward these desired changes. The client-centered counselor would thus have faith in Stan's ability to find his own way and would trust that he has within himself the necessary resources for personal growth. Thus this orientation would not emphasize diagnosis or probe for information from Stan's past. Instead, Stan would be encouraged to speak freely about his feelings of being a failure, of being inadequate, or feeling unmanly, of his hopelessness at times, and of his fears and uncertainties. The therapist would allow Stan the freedom and security to explore threatening aspects of himself and would refrain from judging and criticizing Stan for his feelings. To do this the counselor would have to do much more than merely reflect the content of Stan's verbalizations. The client-centered practitioner would attempt to fully experience in the present moment what it must be like to live in Stan's world. As more than a mechanical technique, the therapist's authentic relationship with Stan would be based on a concern, a deep understanding and appreciation of his feelings, a nonpossessive warmth and acceptance, and a willingness to allow him to explore any and all of his feelings during the therapeutic hour. The therapist would convey to Stan the basic attitudes of understanding and accepting, and, through the therapist's positive regard Stan, it is hoped, would be able to drop his pretenses and more fully and freely explore his personal concerns.

Basically, Stan would grow personally in the relationship with his therapist, who would be willing to be genuine. Stan could use the relationship to learn to be more accepting of himself, with both his strengths and limitations. He would have the opportunity to openly express his fears of women, of not being able to effectively work with people, and of feeling inadequate and stupid. He could explore how he feels judged by his parents and by authorities. He would have an opportunity to express his guilt—that is, the ways he feels he has not lived up to his parents' expectations and how he has let them and himself down. He could also relate his feelings of hurt over not having ever felt loved and wanted. He could express the loneliness and isolation, as well as the need to blunt these painful feelings with alcohol or drugs, that he so often feels.

In relating his feelings Stan would no longer be totally alone, for he would take the risk of letting his therapist into his private world. In doing so, how would Stan be helped? Through the relationship with the therapist he would gradually get a sharper focus of his experiencing and would be able to clarify his own feelings and attitudes. Stan would be seen as having the capacity to muster his own strengths and make his own decisions. In short, the therapeutic relationship would tend to free Stan from his self-defeating ways. Because of the caring and faith he would experience from his therapist, he would be able to increase his own faith and confidence in his ability to resolve his difficulties and discover a new way of being.

Gestalt Therapy

The Gestalt-oriented therapist would surely want to focus on Stan's unfinished business that he has with his parents, siblings, and ex-wife. It would appear that his unfinished business is mainly feelings of resentment that he has toward them; yet he turns this resentment inward toward himself. His present life situation would be spotlighted, but he may also need to reexperience past feelings that could be interfering in his present attempts to develop intimacy with others. In Gestalt therapy Stan would not merely talk about past experiences; rather, he would be asked to imagine himself in earlier scenes with his wife as though the painful situation were occurring in the here-and-now. He would relive and reexperience the situation, perhaps by talking directly to his wife. He could tell her of his resentments and hurts and eventually complete his unfinished business with her. It would be important also that he speak with his older brother and sister, toward whom he feels resentment because they were always seen as the "perfect" children in the family. He would need symbolically to talk with his mother and father, as though he were the child again. It is not necessarily a part of the Gestalt approach that in real life he actually speak with these significant people, but it is essential that he deal with them in his therapy sessions. He would be encouraged to say to them (in the therapeutic sessions) what he had never told them before. The therapist might ask "What are your resentments toward each of these people?" "What did you want from them that you never received?" "How would you have liked to have been treated by them?" "What do you need to tell them now so that you can keep from being destroyed by your resentments?"

Essentially, the Gestalt approach is geared toward clearing up Stan's earlier unfinished business that obstructs his present functioning. Through awareness of what he is now doing and how he keeps himself locked into his past, Stan can increasingly assume personal responsibility for his own life. In working toward this end, some of the following techniques might be used: Stan could engage in a "game of dialogue" in which his "top dog" side could talk with his underdog side. For Stan, both of these dimensions within himself are struggling for control. Stan would play both parts for himself, and the empty-chair technique could be used. Through this procedure, it is hoped, Stan could realize the self-torture game he continues to play with himself. Stan also maintains that he has difficulty in feeling like a man, especially in relationships with strong women. He might become the little boy in exaggerated fashion and talk to a powerful woman (in the empty chair), and then he could become the threatening woman and talk back to his little-boy side. The main point is that he would face his fears and engage in a dialogue with the polarities that exist within him. The aim is not to extract his feelings but to learn to live with his polarities. Why must he be either a "little boy" or a "powerful superman"? Cannot he learn to be a man who at times feels threatened and weak?

Most of the techniques and Gestalt exercises would serve one main function for Stan: to assist him in gaining a fuller sense of what he is doing in the present to keep significant figures alive and powerful within himself. As he gained more complete awareness of how dependent he allows himself to be upon them, he would have the opportunity to find a center within himself and live for his own purposes rather than remain controlled by them.

Transactional Analysis

Since Transactional Analysis (TA) is a contractual form of therapy, Stan would begin his therapy by developing with the therapist a contract that would specify areas of his life he desires to change. A general area that Stan indicates that he would like to modify is learning how to feel "okay," for now he feels "not okay" much of the time. How might his therapy proceed with a TA orientation? Whereas the focus would be on present behavior and transactions with others as well as on his attitudes toward himself, exploration of the past, to the extent that early decisions could be identified, would also be important. Essentially, Stan would need to learn that his decision of the way he had to be in order to survive when he was a child may no longer be appropriate and that he can modify his early decision. For Stan, the decision was "I am stupid, and it is best that I am not here, and I am a loser."

In addition to making this early decision, Stan accepted a list of injunctions and messages that he still lives by, including "Don't be"; "Be a man, which means be strong always"; "Be perfect"; "Don't trust women"; "You'll never become anything"; and "You can't do anything right." Perhaps the basic injunction, and the most dangerous one, is the message "Don't be." In many ways Stan was programmed with the message "You were an accident, and the best way for you to be is to become invisible." He received many negative strokes, and he was discounted as a person of worth. Now he finds it difficult to maintain intimate relationships and to accept positive strokes. He has invested considerable energy in collecting "bad feelings"—including his feelings of anxiety, guilt, self-deprecation, and his suicidal thoughts— which would be explored as a part of the therapeutic process.

The TA therapist most likely would confront Stan with the games that he is playing such as "Poor Me," "Victim," "Martyr," and "Helpless One." Stan's "racket," the collection of feelings that he uses to justify his life script and his early decision, is at once both a "guilt racket" and a "depression racket." Stan appears to be saving up his feelings of guilt and depression, and the games he plays with others often have depression and guilt as a pay-off. In his case, when he finally gathers up enough self-condemnation

and depression, he could feel justified in taking his life, which is the concluding action that his life script calls for. His accepting the message "don't
be" is a particular problem that would be essential to explore in therapy.

Throughout the course of his therapy, Stan would be taught how to
analyze his life scripts. He would be shown that he bases his lifetime plan
on a series of decisions and adaptations. Through script analysis he would
identify the life pattern he appears to be following, and, as he became more
aware of his life script, he would be able actively to do something about
changing his programming. It is through increased awareness that he could
break free of his early scripting.

Stan's autobiography indicates that he has introjected a "Critical Parent" who punishes him and drives him to feel that whatever he does is not
quite enough. If Stan hopes to learn how to love others more fully, it will be
important for him to learn how to be kinder to and less demanding of himself. He would need to be able to nourish himself, accept his successes, and
open himself to others.

Behavior Therapy

The initial task of a therapist with a behavioral orientation would be to
help Stan translate some of his general goals into concrete and measurable
ones. Thus, if Stan said "I want to feel better about myself," the therapist
might ask "What do you mean?" "When do you feel good?" "What can you
do to narrow down your broad goal?" If Stan said "I want to get rid of my
inferiority complex," the therapist might counter with "What behaviors lead
to your feelings of inferiority?" In Stan's case, some concrete aims would
include his desire to function without drugs or alcohol. Most likely aversion
conditioning would not be used, but he might be asked to keep a record of
when he drinks and what events lead up to his drinking.

Stan indicated that he doesn't want to feel apologetic for his existence.
He might then be asked to engage in some assertive-training exercises with
his therapist. If Stan has trouble in talking with his professors, the therapist
could demonstrate to Stan ways in which he could approach his professors
more directly and confidently. This procedure would include modeling,
role-playing, and behavior rehearsal. Stan could then try new behaviors
with his therapist, who would play the role of his professors and then give
feedback on how strong or apologetic Stan seemed.

Stan's anxiety in relation to women also could be explored by be-
havior-rehearsal methods. The therapist could play the role of a woman
whom Stan wants to date. Stan could practice being the way he would like
to be with his date and could say the things to his therapist that he might be
afraid to say to his date. He could thus explore his fears, get feedback on the
effects of his behavior, and experiment with more assertive behavior.

Systematic desensitization may be appropriate to working with Stan's
fear of failing. First, Stan would learn relaxation procedures. Then he would
list his specific fears relating to failure. At the top of his list might be sexual
impotence with a woman. At the bottom of the list might be talking to a

female student whom he does not feel threatened by. He would then imagine a pleasant scene and begin a desensitization process beginning with his lesser fears and working up to the anxiety associated with his greatest fear.

Therapy would focus on modifying the behavior that results in Stan's feelings of guilt and anxiety. This approach would not place importance on his past except to the extent necessary to modify his faulty learning. The therapist would not explore Stan's childhood experiences but would work directly with Stan's present behaviors that are causing his difficulties. Insight would not be seen as important, nor would having Stan experience or re-experience his feelings. The assumption would be that, if he can learn more appropriate coping behaviors, if he can eliminate unrealistic anxiety and guilt, and if he can acquire more adaptive responses, then his presenting symptoms will decrease and he will report a greater degree of satisfaction.

Rational-Emotive Therapy

The rational therapist would have as broad objectives minimizing Stan's self-defeating attitudes and helping him to acquire a more realistic outlook on life. To begin with, Stan would be taught that he is the one who is keeping alive some of his irrational ideas by reindoctrinating himself in an unthinking manner and that he can learn to challenge the source of his difficulties. If he learned how to think more rationally, then he might begin to feel better. What are some of the steps that a rationally oriented therapist might employ to assist Stan in ridding himself of irrational beliefs and in internalizing a rational philosophy of life?

First, the therapist would challenge Stan to examine the many "shoulds," "oughts," and "musts" that he had blindly accepted. He or she would confront Stan on the issue of his continued repetition of specific, illogical sentences and irrational beliefs, which in Stan's case are "I always have to be strong, tough, and perfect"; "I'm not a man if I show any signs of weakness"; "If everyone didn't love me and approve of me, then things would be catastrophic"; "If a woman rejected me, then I really would be diminished to a 'nothing' "; "If I fail, then I am a rotten person"; and "I feel apologetic for my existence because I don't feel equal to others."

Second, the therapist would ask Stan to evaluate the ways he now keeps reindoctrinating himself with those self-defeating sentences. The therapist would not only attack specific problems, but he would also attack the core of Stan's irrational thinking by confronting him with ideas such as the following: "You are not your father, and you do not need to continue telling yourself that you are just like him"; "What your parents told you about yourself you have bought fully, but you no longer need to accept without question their value judgments about your worth"; "You say that you are such a failure and that you feel inferior. Do your present activities support this? Why do you continue to be so hard on yourself?" "Does having been the scapegoat in your family mean that you need to continue making yourself the scapegoat?"

Third, once Stan has understood the nature of his irrational beliefs and become aware of how he maintains faulty notions about himself, the therapist would urge him to work diligently at attacking them by engaging in counterpropaganda. He or she would give Stan specific "homework assignments" that would help him deal with his fears. For instance, at some point the therapist would probably ask Stan to explore his fears of attractive and powerful women and his reasons for continuing to tell himself "They can castrate me"; "They expect me to be strong and perfect"; and "If I am not careful, they will dominate me." His homework could include approaching a woman for a date. If he succeeded in getting the date, he could challenge his catastrophic expectations of what might happen. What would be so terrible if she did not like him or if she refused the date? Why does he have to get all his confirmation from one woman?

In addition to using "homework assignments," the therapist might use many other behavioral techniques such as role-playing, humor, sarcasm, modeling, behavior rehearsal, and desensitization. Basically, the therapist would work in an active-directive manner and would focus on cognitive and behavioral aspects. The therapist would give little attention to Stan's past but would highlight Stan's present, illogical thinking by bringing it to his attention, by demonstrating the illogical links, and by teaching him to rethink and reverbalize in a more logical and constructive way. Thus Stan could learn how to be different by telling himself a new set of statements that might include "I can be lovable"; "I am able to succeed as well as fail at times"; "I need not make all women into my mother"; and "I don't have to punish myself by making myself feel guilty over past failures because it is not essential to always be perfect."

Reality Therapy

Reality therapy would not dwell on Stan's past experiences with failure but would focus on what he can do in the present to achieve a "success identity." Stan has already indicated what he considers "success" for himself, and he has indicated some specific changes that he desires. Therapy would emphasize Stan's desired behavioral changes, not his feelings and attitudes about himself. The assumption would be that, if Stan can begin to increase his self-esteem and come to recognize his strengths, his negative feelings about himself will change.

How might the therapist with a reality-therapy orientation proceed with Stan? Some possible strategies and ways of approaching Stan would include, first, a specific contract that would set a time limit for the duration of the sessions and for the goals of therapy as well. The goals would have to be specific and concrete, and the therapist would help Stan determine how realistic his goals are by asking, for example, "Are your needs now being met?" and "Are you satisfied with your current behavior?" Since Stan would respond negatively to both those questions, the therapist would challenge Stan to make a value judgment concerning his present life by asking "How do you want to change?" "What can you do now to change?" "Are

you willing to make a commitment to changing certain self-destructive behaviors? For instance, your drinking interferes with your studies and with
forming close relationships, and it contributes to low self-esteem." The
therapist could ask Stan to judge whether his drinking patterns are worth
the price he pays for these immediate pleasures. If Stan agreed that his
drinking is not conducive to getting what he wants in terms of long-range.
satisfaction, he could make specific plans to eliminate his drinking. There
would be no excavation into his past to explore the reasons for his drinking,
nor would Stan be allowed to offer excuses or engage in blaming others.
Regardless of how or why he began doing things that contributed to his
"failure identity," the point is that Stan would be able to do something to
change his behavior so that he can enjoy successes.

Some specific suggestions that the therapist could make to Stan to help
him change his behavior might include the following: "Next time you are
lonely and want to get drunk, make a decision to call a friend and talk with
him or her about your loneliness. Decide to do something with your feelings
besides blunting them with alcohol"; "You mention that you are uncomfortable when meeting people. Even though you may experience uneasiness,
put yourself into situations where you can make new acquaintances. Write
down your feelings, and observe and make a note of what you do when you
are in these situations, and bring a report to your next therapy session"; and
"Instead of exploring why you feel inferior, focus on what you do when you
feel this way and on situations that accentuate your feelings of inferiority."

Reality therapy might give considerable emphasis to Stan's strong
points. A few years ago, Stan saw himself as a "loser," and today he has
made significant progress toward utilizing his talents. He is doing well in
college, he is involved in volunteer work, and he relates well with young
people. Therapy could help Stan formulate plans to help him continue in
the direction of his successes. In short, Stan would receive credit for the
gains he has made and encouragement to face the fact that he is responsible
for the kind of life he is currently leading. He would see that he can do more
than he once believed to be possible.

CHAPTER ELEVEN

BASIC
ISSUES IN
COUNSELING AND
PSYCHOTHERAPY

Introduction

This chapter deals with certain basic issues that cut across all the theoretical approaches to therapeutic practice. The discussion reviews key concepts related to human nature and their implications for counseling and psychotherapy. By comparing and contrasting views of the nature of the therapeutic process, I attempt to show that some integration, with respect to goals and procedures, of the various approaches is possible. The issues of the role and function of the therapist, the experience of the client, and the client-therapist relationship are highlighted. The central purpose of this chapter is to put into perspective some of the basic issues that are dealt with by every counseling theory. A further aim is to summarize the key ideas of all of the current therapies and to unify some concepts, Six tables are presented to help you see more clearly areas of convergence and divergence among the eight therapy approaches with respect to these basic issues.

Key Concepts and Philosophy

In a survey of the current approaches to counseling and psychotherapy, it becomes evident that there is not a common philosophy that unifies all the models. Concepts regarding human nature, the goals of therapy that are rooted in the view of human nature, and the techniques subscribed to tend to be different for each approach. Differences are especially noticeable among the philosophical assumptions underlying three very different models: the psychoanalytic approach, the behavioral approach, and the existential-humanistic approach. It is my conviction that our views of human nature and the basic assumptions that undergird our views of the therapeutic process have significant implications for the way we develop our therapeutic practices. I am also persuaded that, because they do not pay sufficient attention to their philosophical assumptions, many practitioners operate as though they had no set of assumptions regarding their clients. In my opinion, a central task is to make our assumptions explicit and conscious, so that we can establish some consistency between our beliefs about human nature and the way we implement our procedures in counseling or therapy. Our philosophical assumptions are important because they specify how much reality we are able to perceive, and they direct our attention to the variables that we are "set" to see. Thus a Freudian analyst and a client-centered therapist work in ways that vary considerably from each other, and they have very different concepts of human nature. Let us now review some of the contrasting viewpoints.

The Freudian psychoanalytic approach views human nature through deterministic spectacles. It assumes that human beings are determined largely by the unconscious, by drives and irrational forces, by psychic energy, by seeking a homeostatic balance, and by early childhood experiences. In practice this approach stresses an impersonal and anonymous role of the therapist and puts the therapist in the expert role of diagnosing, formulating a conceptualization of the client's history, determining a treatment plan, and using interpretation techniques to gradually uncover unconscious material. It stresses insight and understanding of the past, which is achieved by skillful interpretation. It is definitely a long-term approach to psychotherapy that is aimed at major personality change. Psychoanalysis does, however, view the client as able to change and able to reshape his or her future; the client is not hopelessly determined by childhood experiences and unconscious repressed dynamics. The goal of making the unconscious conscious places the person in a position of change. Change is possible as a result of insight into the causes of emotional disturbances.

The behavior therapist, on the other hand, is not much concerned with abstract concepts like the basic human nature but focuses instead on observable, specific behaviors. The client determines the goals, but the therapist must be expert enough to develop a specific treatment plan to help the client realize the specific, concrete changes desired. The approach emphasizes objective assessment of the efficacy of the treatment procedures. Although it does not spell out philosophical concerns, it does assume that human behavior is the product of learning; that is, one is conditioned by external influences, and one's learned behavior is shaped by reinforcement or the lack of it. But, as does psychoanalysis, the behavioral approach assumes that one is able to change by rearranging external contingencies. What has been learned can be unlearned, and new patterns of effective behavior can replace ineffective, learned behaviors. This therapeutic approach has several charac-

Table 11-1   The Basic Philosophies

Psychoanalytic Therapy	Human beings are basically determined by psychic energy and by early experiences. Unconscious motives and conflicts are central in present behavior. Irrational forces are strong; the person is driven by sexual and aggressive impulses. Early development is of critical importance, for later personality problems have roots in repressed childhood conflicts.
Existential-Humanistic Therapy	The central focus is on the nature of the human condition, which includes capacity for self-awareness, freedom of choice to decide one's fate, responsibility and freedom, anxiety as a basic element, the search for a unique meaning in a meaningless world, being alone and being in relation with others, finiteness and death, and a self-actualization tendency.
Client-Centered Therapy	The view of humans is positive; humans have an inclination toward becoming fully functioning. In the context of the therapeutic relationship the client experiences feelings that were previously denied to awareness. The client actualizes potential and moves toward increased awareness, spontaneity, trust in self, and inner directedness.
Gestalt Therapy	The person strives for wholeness and integration of thinking, feeling, and behaving. The view is antideterministic, in that the person is seen to have the capacity to recognize how earlier influences are related to present difficulties.
Transactional Analysis (TA)	The person has potential for choice. What was once decided can be redecided. Although the person may be a victim of early decisions and past scripting, self-defeating aspects can be changed with awareness.
Behavior Therapy	Humans are shaped and determined by sociocultural conditioning. The view is basically deterministic, in that behavior is seen as the product of learning and conditioning.
Rational-Emotive Therapy (RET)	Humans are born with potentials for rational thinking but with tendencies toward crooked thinking. They tend to fall victim to irrational beliefs and to reindoctrinate themselves with these beliefs. Therapy is cognitive/behavior/action oriented and stresses thinking, judging, analyzing, doing, and redeciding. This model is didactic-directive. Therapy is a process of reeducation.
Reality Therapy	The person has a need for identity and can develop either a "success identity" or a "failure identity." The approach is based on growth motivation and is antideterministic.

teristics: it is objective in its orientation and does not stress the subjective dimensions of human experiencing, which cannot be directly observed. It is a specific approach that utilizes specific treatment procedures based on specific goals, not on global orientation. It is an action-oriented therapy. Instead of being concerned with verbalizations, belief and attitude systems, awareness of cause-effect dynamics, or awareness of past influences, it focuses on behavior and actions. Generally, the behavior model is a short-term approach to therapy, as opposed to the long-term, depth-probing psychoanalytic approach.

A third major force is the existential approach. The existential view assigns willing, choosing, and deciding a central place in therapy. It views the human as a being that possesses awareness and freedom to make fundamental choices that shape his or her life. The practice of existential therapy is based on an ongoing encounter between the client and the therapist in which the client is a partner in his or her search for self. Based also on understanding the subjective aspects of experiencing, it tends to stress the affective dimension. It is an approach that is geared to helping the client reclaim his or her responsibility for choosing the quality of his or her life. It tends to be a future-oriented therapy. Both Frankl and May stress that the person can best be understood by observing what the person is becoming, not by delving into the past. The existential approach also stresses insight and awareness, which the client gains through direct experience rather than through the therapist's interpretations. The client is expected to talk, and the client decides what will be explored during the therapy hour.

The fact that a therapist's view of human nature is vitally related to the view of the nature of the therapeutic process has definite implications for the application of therapeutic techniques. A point I want to emphasize is that each of the counseling approaches provides a different dimension of understanding the person, and each can provide the framework for increasing understanding of behavior and for examining reality. Although there are among the various models some points of divergence in philosophy, concepts, and practice, there are also some points of convergence. The models are not necessarily incompatible and mutually exclusive. Thus one's existential orientation does not necessarily preclude one's use of techniques drawn from behavior therapy or from some of the more objective, rationally oriented cognitive theories. That all these theories represent different vantage points for understanding human behavior doesn't mean that one theorist has "the truth" while the others are in error. Each point of view can offer the counselor a perspective for helping clients in their searches for self. My plea is that we study all the theories, that we not allow ourselves to be converted to any single doctrine, and that, in taking something from every .viewpoint, we integrate their perspectives into our own style—that is, incorporate and develop a way of working with clients that is our own. I call for an integration of these values and caution against rigidly adhering to any one mode as the one with all the truth.

What effect does our theoretical preference have on our behavior in our relationships with clients? My position is that our views of human nature dictate our goals and our manners of working with clients. We need to be

Table 11-2   Key Concepts

Psychoanalytic Therapy	Normal personality development is based on successful resolution and integration of psychosexual stages of development. Faulty personality development is the result of inadequate resolution of some specific stage of psychosexual development. Id, ego, and superego constitute the basis of personality structure. Anxiety is a result of repression of basic conflicts. Ego defenses are developed to control anxiety. Unconscious processes are centrally related to current behavior.
Existential-Humanistic Therapy	Essentially an approach to counseling and therapy rather than a firm theoretical model, it stresses core human conditions. Normally personality development is based on the uniqueness of each individual. Sense of self develops from infancy. Self-determination and tendency toward growth are central ideas. Psychopathology is the result of failure to actualize human potential. Distinctions are made between "existential guilt" and "neurotic guilt" and between "existential anxiety" and "neurotic anxiety." Focus is on the present and on what one is becoming; that is, the approach has a future orientation. It stresses self-awareness before action. It is an experiential therapy.
Client-Centered Therapy	The client has the potential for becoming aware of problems and the means to resolve them. Faith is placed in the client's capacity for self-direction. Mental health is a congruence of ideal self and real self. Maladjustment is the result of a discrepancy between what one wants to be and what one is. Focus is on the present moment and on the experiencing and expressing of feelings.
Gestalt Therapy	Focus is on the what and how of experiencing in the here-and-now to help the client accept his or her polarities. Key concepts include personal responsibility, unfinished business, avoiding, experiencing, and awareness of the now. It is an experiential therapy that stresses feelings and the influence of unfinished business on contemporary personality development.
Transactional Analysis (TA)	Focus is on games played to avoid intimacy in transactions. The personality is made up of Parent, Adult, and Child. Clients are taught how to recognize which ego state they are functioning in with given transactions. Games, rackets, early decisions, scripting, and injunctions are key concepts.
Behavior Therapy	Focus is on overt behavior, precision in specifying goals of treatment, development of specific treatment plans, and objective evaluation of therapy outcomes. Therapy is based on the principles of learning theory. Normal behavior is learned through reinforcement and imitation. Abnormal behavior is the result of faulty learning. It stresses present behavior and has little concern for past history and origins of disorders.

188

Table 11-2   Key Concepts *(continued)*

Rational-Emotive Therapy (RET)	Neurosis is irrational thinking and behaving. Emotional disturbances are rooted in childhood but are perpetuated through reindoctrination in the now. A person's belief system is the cause of emotional problems. Thus clients are challenged to examine the validity of certain beliefs. The scientific method is applied to everyday living.
Reality Therapy	This approach rejects the medical model and concept of mental illness. Focus is on what can be done now, and rejection of the past is a crucial variable. Value judgments and moral responsibility are stressed. Mental health is equated with acceptance of responsibility.

careful of expectancy. If, for example, I am strictly Adlerian, I expect my client to struggle with power and superiority. Chances are that my vision will be distorted. I will look for certain behavior, expect certain behavior, and may even twist what I experience from my client to fit my preconceived model. My client, out of a desire to please, might unconsciously (or very deliberately, with awareness) fit into my expectations by accommodating me. The word of caution, then, is beware of subscribing exclusively to any one central or universal view of humanity; remain open and selectively incorporate a framework for counseling or therapy that is consistent with your own personality.

Goals in Counseling and Psychotherapy

In surveying the goals of counseling and psychotherapy, one finds a diverse group of objectives, including personality restructuring, finding meaning in life, curing an emotional disturbance, adjusting to society, attaining happiness and satisfaction, attaining self-actualization, reducing anxiety, and unlearning maladaptive behavior and learning adaptive patterns. Is there a common denominator in this range of goals? Can there be any integration of the various theoretical viewpoints on the issue of goals?

The problem of the diversity of goals can be simplified by viewing the issue in terms of the degree of generality or specificity of goals. Goals can be seen as existing on a continuum from general, global, and long-term objectives to specific, concrete, and short-term objectives. The humanistic, or relationship-oriented, therapies tend to stress the former; behavior-oriented therapies stress the latter goals. The goals at opposite ends of the continuum are not necessarily contradictory; it is just a matter of how specifically the goals are defined. Several writers have noted that an integration of the goals of behavior therapy and those of the humanistic approaches is possible and desirable. Truax and Carkhuff (1967) contended that behavior therapy need not be antagonistic, and may even be complementary, to humanistic approaches. They cited evidence that suggests its applicability to psychotherapy in general and to client-centered therapy in particular. Patterson (1973) wrote that "there is thus no basic or necessary contradiction between behavior therapy and relationship therapy. One emphasizes the shaping or changing of specific aspects of behavior by specific rewards or reinforcers. The other emphasizes more general behavioral changes . . . achieved by the use of generalized reinforcers" (p. 534). He mentioned that both approaches are based on learning principles: behavior therapy utilizes a more narrow approach stressing conditioning, and relationship therapy is more broadly based on a social-learning approach. Patterson pointed out that both approaches seem to be coming to the same conclusions, one from experiential and laboratory research with conditioning and the other from clinical experience and therapy research. Wrenn (1966) considered it possible for the "two psychological worlds" to become integrated for the practicing counselor. He raised the question Must the practitioner accept one approach and reject the other? In his view the relationship-oriented therapies can contribute to determining meaningful goals in counseling, and the behavioral approach can contribute the methodologies for producing desired behavior and attitude changes. Thus a convergence is possible between the "two psychological worlds."

Let me examine in more detail the goals of counseling from both the humanistic and the behavioral orientations. As I mentioned earlier, the humanistic and relationship-oriented approaches tend to stress broader, or ultimate, long-term goals, which are frequently difficult to measure objectively. Those goals might include finding autonomy and freedom, becoming more fully functioning or becoming a self-actualizing person, discovering an internal locus of evaluation, becoming more self-integrated, and so on. Some other global objectives could include the following:

1. that the client become more self-aware, move toward fuller awareness of his or her own inner being, and deny and distort less;
2. that the client come to accept more responsibility for who he or she is, accept his or her own feelings, avoid blaming his or her environment or others for his or her condition, and come to recognize that he or she is now responsible for what he or she is doing;
3. that the client come more to grips with his or her inner strengths and personal power, avoid playing the helpless role, and come to accept the power he or she possesses for altering his or her life;
4. that the client clarify his or her own values, get a clearer perspective on his or her problems, and find within himself or herself the resolutions to his or her conflicts;
5. that the client become more integrated and face, recognize, accept, and work through fragmented and disowned aspects of self and that he or she integrate into his or her total being all his or her feelings and experiences;
6. that the client learn to take risks that will open new doors for new ways of being and that he or she appreciate living with some uncertainty, which is necessary for breaking ground for growth;
7. that the client come to trust himself or herself more fully and be willing to extend himself or herself in doing what he or she has chosen to do; and

8. that the client become more conscious of possible alternatives and be more willing to make choices for himself or herself and accept the consequences of choosing.

Behavioral approaches specify therapeutic objectives that are, in contrast to the broad goals just listed, concrete, short-term, observable, and measurable. This does not mean that the behavioral counselor is opposed to global humanistic goals but that the broad goals should be defined through subgoals that can be evaluated. Krumboltz (1966) admitted that he is not opposed to goals of self-actualization, better understanding of self, or promoting adaptive behavior, but he did say that "all of these ways of stating goals suffer from being so global and general that they provide no guidelines for what is to be accomplished. . . . In order to make such generalities useful they must be translated into specific kinds of behavior appropriate to each client's problem so that everyone concerned with the counseling relationship knows exactly what is to be accomplished" (pp. 9–10). Some examples of specific therapeutic goals are to stop smoking, to reduce or eliminate a specific fear, to be more assertive with co-workers, to decide on a vocation, to get a successful divorce, to cure migraine headaches, to learn how to make friends, to cure impotence or frigidity, to cure stuttering, to lessen test anxiety, to develop better study habits, and to cure a specific behavior disorder.

A central question is Who should establish the goals of counseling? Almost all theories are in accord with the principle that it is the client's responsibility to decide the objectives of his or her own counseling, but they also recognize that the therapist also has some basic, general goals. I believe that goal definition is a joint and evolutionary process—that is, something that is done by both the client and the therapist on an ongoing basis as therapy proceeds. The therapist has general goals, and each client has his or her goals. I believe that therapy ought to begin with an exploration of the goals expected from the therapeutic relationship. Perhaps at the beginning clients have very vague and confused ideas of what they expect from therapy. They may simply want answers to their "problems," they may want to stop hurting, or they may ask for ways in which they can be different so that some other significant persons in their lives will accept them more fully. In some cases, clients may have no goals; they are in the therapist's office simply because they were sent there by their parents, probation officers, or teachers and all they want is to be left alone. So, where can a counselor begin? My belief is that the intake session can be used most productively by focusing on the issue of the client's goals or lack of them. The therapist might begin by asking such questions as "What do you expect from counseling?" "What do you want?" "What do you hope to leave with?" "What about yourself or your life situation would you most want to change?"

A therapist will most likely experience frustration when he or she hears the client utter "I'd just like to understand myself more, and I'd like to be happy!" The therapist, however, can bring that global and diffuse wish into sharper focus by asking "What is keeping you from feeling happy?" "What *do* you understand about yourself *now*?" "What would you like to understand about yourself that you don't now understand?" The main point

Table 11-3   Goals of Therapy

Psychoanalytic Therapy	To make the unconscious conscious. To reconstruct the basic personality. To assist the client in reliving earlier past experiences and working through repressed conflicts. Intellectual awareness.
Existential-Humanistic Therapy	To provide conditions for maximizing self-awareness and growth. Removal of blocks to fulfillment of personal potential. To help the client discover and use freedom of choice by expanding self-awareness. To enable one to be free and responsible for the direction of one's own life.
Client-Centered Therapy	To provide a safe climate conducive to client self-exploration, so that the client can recognize blocks to growth and experience aspects of self that were formerly denied or distorted. To enable the client to move toward openness to experience, greater trust in self, willingness to be a process, and increased spontaneity and aliveness.
Gestalt Therapy	To assist the client in gaining awareness of moment-to-moment experiencing. To challenge the client to accept responsibility of taking internal support as opposed to external support.
Transactional Analysis (TA)	To assist the client in becoming a script-free, game-free, autonomous person who is capable of choosing how he or she wants to be. To assist the client in examining early decisions and making new decisions based on awareness.
Behavior Therapy	To eliminate the client's maladaptive behavior patterns and assist the client in learning constructive patterns. Behavior change. Specific goals are selected by the client. Broad goals are broken down into precise subgoals.
Rational-Emotive Therapy (RET)	To eliminate the client's self-defeating outlook on life and assist the client in acquiring a more tolerant and rational view of life.
Reality Therapy	To guide the client toward learning realistic and responsible behavior and developing a "success identity." To assist the client in making value judgments about behavior and in deciding on a plan of action for change.

that I wish to make is that setting goals seems unavoidable, and, if there is to be any productive direction, both the client and therapist need to explore what they both hope to obtain from the counseling relationship. The two need to decide at the outset whether they can work with each other and whether their goals are compatible.

One point needs to be highlighted. I observe in many counselor interns the tendency to embrace some goals only superficially. In my view, goals are vitally related to the values and personhood of the therapist, and the only way to know if one really accepts goals is to examine critically one's activity as a therapist and a person. What seems imperative is that therapists look at what they do in practice, not merely at what they say they believe.

It would also do well here to review some questionable or objectionable therapeutic goals. One common misconception is that therapy should "straighten out" a client by teaching the client "right" and "appropriate" values. Many novice therapists have an urge to impose their own goals on a client and engage in a process of indoctrination of their own beliefs. In their need to make "proper" decisions for the client, they freely dispense advice. As Corlis and Rabe (1969) indicated, "There is no therapy as long as the patient only asks advice. There is no therapy when the therapist decides for the patient what he ought to do" (p. 16).

Another questionable goal is client contentment and happiness. I have heard many counselor interns say that this is their objective and that they want to eliminate suffering, pain, and uncertainty from their clients' experiences. I feel strongly that, if we settle for contentment as an end in counseling or therapy, we are cheating the clients. If therapy is geared toward growth, then some degree of discontent, confusion, anxiety, and pain seems inevitable. In regard to this issue, I think that the therapist's job is to encourage clients to take risks that might well lead to an increase of discontentment for a time but that, hopefully, will result in longer-term satisfaction.

Still another questionable therapeutic aim is social adjustment. Many counseling agencies, and practitioners in schools and mental-health clinics, do not focus their efforts on significant client change in accordance with the client's needs but instead aim at fostering adjustment to the social environment. Whereas an exploration of the demands of society are surely in order in the therapeutic process, I do not think that adjusting a client so that he or she "fits" well should be the primary concern. In his collection of essays *The Radical Therapist,* Jerome Agel (1971) made the point that therapy as it is now practiced has failed. His view is that the only persons helped are the therapists, whose lives are already fairly comfortable. Agel's essays are all geared to one thesis: "Therapy is change, not adjustment. This *means* change—social, personal and political" (p. xi). The point is argued that therapy aimed at adjustment is more than useless; it is destructive. To remedy the situation, drastic changes need to be made in de-mystifying the therapeutic process. For significant personal change to occur, the alienating and oppressing social forces must be changed. As the thesis implies political and social change, one might raise the questions What good does it actually do merely to work with the individual alone? Is any long-lasting change effected, particularly when the client returns to an undesirable social environment? Should therapists get outside their offices and broaden their goals to include changing certain social situations that produce human misery?

Before concluding this section on goals, I wish to raise the issue of the effectiveness of counseling and psychotherapy in achieving the goals of constructive personality and behavioral change. Does therapy make a significant difference? Is a person substantially better with psychotherapy than he or she is without it? Can therapy actually be more harmful than helpful? A thorough discussion of this topic is beyond the scope of this book, but the essence of the Truax and Carkhuff (1967) study is relevant here. They stated that "The evidence now available suggests that, on the average, psychotherapy may be harmful as often as helpful, with an average effect comparable to receiving no help" (pp. 20–21). After an extensive evaluation of the research evidence, Truax and Carkhuff concluded that

1. the therapeutic endeavor is, on the average, ineffective;
2. therapy itself is a non-unitary phenomenon;
3. some counselors and therapists are significantly helpful while others are significantly harmful, with the resulting *average* helpfulness not demonstrably better than the effect of having no professional treatment; and
4. through research it is possible to identify the major ingredient of helpful and harmful therapy, and thus markedly increase the average effectiveness of counseling and psychotherapy [p. 2].*

On the surface, those conclusions drawn from research evidence might seem discouraging in that they seem to suggest that counseling and psychotherapy do not make a significant difference in helping people to achieve the goals of improved behavioral functioning. Yet, there is some hope. Note that the fourth conclusion is that research has identified the specific variables that account for constructive changes. Truax and Carkhuff (1967) stated that "research seems consistently to find empathy, warmth and genuineness characteristic of human encounters that change people—for the better" (p. 141). They found that, conversely, therapists who offer low levels of these "therapeutic conditions" produce either deterioration or no change in clients.

A significant implication here is that counselor-education programs can be designed to include teaching interpersonal skills as well as teaching theoretical content and techniques. In my estimation, counselor education should focus on the personal development of the counselor by including ongoing group therapy designed for personal growth and awareness. It can be integrated into supervision practices and practicum experiences whereby the trainee gets actual experience in applying his or her knowledge and skills to real situations. In addition to paying attention to "problems" of clients, the program can also focus on the dynamics of the counselor intern's behavior. I believe further that a concern for the trainee's personhood should be the core of the program. The conclusions of Truax and Carkhuff appear to support my bias if the concern is to produce therapists who can affect clients for better instead of for worse. I will explore this important issue with more detail in the final chapter, on the personhood of the counselor.

*Reprinted from Charles B. Truax and Robert R. Carkhuff, *Toward Effective Counseling and Psychotherapy* (Chicago: Aldine Publishing Company, 1967); copyright © 1967 by Charles B. Truax and Robert R. Carkhuff. This and all other quotations from this source are reprinted by permission of the authors and Aldine Publishing Company.

The Function and Role of the Therapist

A basic issue that every therapist must face concerns appropriate and inappropriate functions and the definition of the therapist's role. Is the therapist a friend? an expert? an advice-giver? a helper? a clarifier? an information-giver? a confronter? a provider of alternatives? a guru? Is the therapist all of these at various times, and, if so, what is the therapist's basic role in the helping process?

The fact that a range of proper roles exists often confuses beginning therapists. How do therapists determine their roles? What influences do the settings in which therapists practice have on their roles? What do counselors do when they are in conflict with the agency's view of what they should be doing? There is no simple and universal answer to the question of the therapist's proper role; such factors as the type of counseling, personal characteristics, level of training, the clientele to be served, and the therapeutic setting all need to be considered in determining the therapist's role.

One problem that counselors might have to struggle with is what to do when their view of their role is in basic conflict with the requirements of their job position. For example, I worked with school counselors who perceived their role as doing psychological counseling. Their interests were in "real counseling," both individually and in groups, and they resisted adopting what they saw as "inappropriate functions," or roles that were inconsistent with being an effective counselor. However, the school administrators perceived the counselors' roles differently, for they expected counselors to perform the following tasks: policing the bathrooms to detect smokers, supervising the halls during lunchtime, supervising football games, acting as disciplinarians by suspending and expelling students, administering group tests, and working with students primarily as schedule changers and academic programmers. If the counselors were to accept all those noncounseling functions, little time would be left for doing their main work of counseling. In real situations like that, I believe that it is part of the professional responsibility of counselors to define their roles and to educate their administrators. Admittedly, that is not always feasible; thus persons who feel that they are being asked to perform functions that are inconsistent with their views of counseling or their levels of training must decide whether they can in good conscience remain with a particular agency if they cannot bring about certain essential changes.

I encourage each counselor to make a critical evaluation concerning appropriate counseling functions. Counselors could also benefit from deciding in advance certain functions they feel are inconsistent with real counseling. I believe that the central function of counseling is to help clients recognize their own strengths, discover what is preventing them from using their strengths, and clarify what kinds of persons they want to be. I do not believe that problem solving is the primary function of counseling; rather, I believe that counseling is a process by which clients are invited to look honestly at their behavior and life-styles and make certain decisions about the ways in which they want to modify the quality of their lives. My view is that the counselor's job is multifold: he or she needs to provide support and warmth yet care enough to challenge and confront.

Thus an essential function of the counselor is to give honest and direct feedback to the client. How does one perceive the client? What feelings does one have toward the client? How does one experience the client during the counseling sessions? Effective counseling entails a personal commitment and investment of self on the counselor's behalf. I strongly believe counselors must do more than administer techniques and that they must be willing to reveal themselves in the relationship with the client. Clients can then sift and sort the feedback they receive from the counselors, try it on for size to see what fits, and make decisions based on the feedback.

An issue related to the therapist's function and role is the degree to which the therapist exercises control of client behavior both during and outside the session. What is the therapist's job in structuring the therapeutic process? All the various approaches are in basic agreement that the therapist does bring structure to the counseling experience, although they disagree with the nature and degree of this structuring. For example, the rational-emotive therapists operate within a highly directive, didactic, persuasive, and confrontive structure. They frequently prescribe "homework assignments" that are designed to get clients to practice new behavior outside therapy sessions. By contrast, client-centered therapists operate in a much looser and undefined structure, but they do provide a general structure. Even an extremely nondirective practitioner works within some framework; the client defines the direction of the course of therapy by deciding what to talk about while the therapist follows the lead of the client and stays within the client's frame of reference.

Therapists need to realize the importance of the influence of their behavior on their clients. The issue of the therapist's influence is closely related to the issue of the therapist's authenticity as a person. In my opinion, it is a mistake for therapists to restrict themselves primarily to a behavior mode such as teaching responsibility, reflecting feelings, or the like. Instead, I advocate a wide range of behavior that becomes incorporated into the therapist's own style of being. Thus I encourage potential counselors to study various counseling schools and to integrate useful methods from diverse approaches. At times, reflection of feeling and simply listening to a client's verbal and nonverbal messages is what is called for, but to restrict oneself to this mode is to unduly hamper one's effectiveness.

There will be times when it will be appropriate to confront clients with their evasions of reality or their illogical thinking. Again, for therapists to focus primarily on this behavior is to restrict themselves unnecessarily. At times they will need to be interpretive, while at other times they will invite their clients to interpret for themselves the meanings of their behavior. Sometimes it may be appropriate to be very directive and structured, while at other times it may be appropriate to flow without a clear structure. So much depends on the purpose of therapy, the setting, the personality and style of the therapist, and the uniqueness of a particular client. To be prescriptive and to establish a formula are not helpful. This is where the art of therapy reveals itself. Although therapists can learn attitudes and skills and acquire certain knowledge about personality dynamics and the therapeutic process, so much of effective therapy is the product of the art of therapy. I often wonder whether this creativity, this capacity to be an artful and re-sourceful therapist, can be taught. My main point is that I think that it is misleading to dupe student counselors into the idea that counseling is a science that is separate and distinct from the behavior and personality of the counselor.

Thus a significant issue is the degree to which a counselor should be his or her real self during a session. What limitations are appropriate? I believe that as a therapist one ought constantly to ask oneself What am I doing? Whose needs are being met—my client's or my own? What is the effect of my behavior on my client?

Another basic issue regarding structuring is that of division of respon-sibility. This issue must be clarified at the intake session. In my view, it is the therapist's responsibility early in the counseling context to discuss specific matters such as length and overall durations of the sessions, confidentiality, general goals, and methods used to achieve goals. I strongly believe that both the therapist and the client need to assume responsibility for the direc-tion of therapy. If therapists primarily make decisions of what to discuss and are overdirective, they perpetuate the clients' dependency. Clients should be encouraged to assume as much responsibility as possible in the early stages of therapy. Here is where I find contracts and assignments most useful. In both my individual practice and my group work, I typically suggest "homework assignments" that the client might try before the next session. I'll make the suggestion when I intuitively feel that the client might be re-sisting doing something for himself or herself out of fear or passivity. I also invite persons I work with to choose something specific that they would like to experiment with outside the session. The assignments can be very small beginnings, or they can be rather demanding tasks.

Much of this methodology depends on the motivation of the client to change. For example, a client might reveal that he often feels "put down" by his wife and that, when he does, he typically feels hostility, which he swal-lows. My suggestion might be "Next time you feel even slightly put down by your wife, why not take the risk of letting her know how you feel *at that moment?* Why not experiment for one week with expressing your anger in-stead of swallowing it, just to see what happens?" Another client might hurtfully disclose that she feels a real distance from her father and that she would really like to have some closeness with him before it's too late. I might suggest that she write a long letter to her father, telling him exactly what she feels and what she would like with him—and then I might suggest that she *not* send the letter to her father. It is strategy to invite her to come into closer touch with her hurt and with what she intends to do with the hurt. At the next session, she and I could explore the outcome of her as-signment, and she could make her own decision of what she would like to do: to pursue the issue with her father, to write more on her own and keep it private, or simply to forget the issue.

I believe that it is centrally important for the therapist to be alert to the client's efforts to manipulate the therapist into assuming responsibility that the client is capable of assuming. Many clients will push for the "magic answer" from the therapist as a way of escaping the anxiety of making their own resolutions. Client-initiated contracts and specific assignments are extremely helpful in keeping the focus of responsibility on the client. Contracts can be changed, and new contracts can be developed or modified. Formulating contracts can be an ongoing process during the entire counseling relationship. As a therapist each of us must ask ourselves Are my clients doing now what will move them toward greater autonomy and toward a place where they can increasingly find their answers within? If we allow clients to find their directions primarily from us, we foster their dependence and further reinforce their lack of potency. If we care enough, we will be demanding. We can still be tender and compassionate, but it seems to me that caring involves strongly inviting clients to become what they are capable of being, and when they consistently choose to remain less than they could be, we must care enough to demand more. In brief, perhaps the best measure of our general effectiveness as therapists is the degree to which clients are able to say to us "I appreciate what you've been to me, and, because of your faith in me, I feel I can now go it alone." Eventually, if we are good enough, we'll be out of business!

The Client's Experience in Therapy

What are clients like? Who should be a client? What are the expectations clients have as they approach therapy? What are their responsibilities in the process? Is therapy only for the "disturbed"? Can the relatively healthy person benefit from therapy? Are there any commonalities among the diverse types of clients?

Generally, clients have in common some degree of suffering, pain, or at least discontent. There is a discrepancy between how they would like to be and how they see themselves presently functioning. Some initiate therapy because of their awareness of wanting to cure a specific symptom or set of symptoms: they want to get rid of migraine headaches, they want to free themselves of chronic anxiety attacks, they want to lose weight, or they seek relief from depression. Many seek some resolution to conflicts with a marital partner in the hope that they can enjoy their marriage. Increasingly, people are entering therapy with existential problems; their complaints are less defined but relate to the experiences of emptiness, meaninglessness in life, boredom, dead personal relationships, a lack of intense feelings, and a loss of the sense of self.

The initial expectations of many clients are expert help and a fast change. They often have great hope for major changes in their lives, and they expect to alter their lives with the help of the therapist. All too often they have the unrealistic notion that if they merely reveal their "problem" to the therapist, the therapist will draw on his or her magic to "cure" them. As therapy progresses, they discover that they must be active in the process, for they must select their own goals, do much of the "work" in the therapy sessions, and be willing to extend the work beyond the sessions into their outside lives. Hence some clients discover the value of "homework assignments," experiments with new behavior outside the session, and contracts—all of which are geared toward getting clients to put their new learning into action. Other clients quit or find therapy too much work.

I believe that people are increasingly seeing the value of psychotherapeutic help for developmental purposes as well as for remedial goals. With the impetus created by humanistic psychology, people began to be educated to the idea of therapy for the well; they began to accept the idea that one need not be "sick" to benefit from some form of therapy.

Whether clients seek therapy to cure a disorder or to enhance the quality of their personal lives, what are the characteristics of "successful" clients? Truax and Carkhuff (1967) described the type of client that is most likely to benefit from counseling and psychotherapy in the following way: the person has a high degree of inner disturbance but a low degree of behavioral disturbance. This definition is consistent with Rogers' idea that a basic requisite for therapy is that the client perceive that he or she has a problem, which supplies the motivation to change. Also, the successful client exhibits a high degree of readiness for change and has a positive expectancy for personal improvement. Finally, the successful client engages in deep and extensive exploration of self.

The Relationship between Therapist and Client

Most approaches share common ground in accepting the importance of the therapeutic relationship. The existential-humanistic and client-centered views are based on the personal relationship as the crucial determinant of the outcomes of the therapeutic process. It is clear that some other approaches such as rational-emotive therapy and behavior therapy do not ignore the relationship factor, even though they do not give it a place of central importance.

The therapeutic relationship involves characteristics of both the therapist and the client. The therapist's degree of caring, his or her interest and ability in helping the client, and his or her genuineness are factors that influence the relationship. The client also determines the relationship with variables such as his or her motivation, cooperation, interest, concern, attitudes, perceptions, expectations, behavior, and reactions to the therapist. Counseling or psychotherapy is a personal matter that involves a personal relationship, and evidence indicates that honesty, sincerity, acceptance, warmth, understanding, and spontaneity are basic ingredients of successful outcomes.

Patterson (1973) stressed the importance of the therapeutic relationship, maintaining that research indicates that the effective element in therapy is that relationship. He made the point that the therapist serves as a reinforcer, for the therapist's respect and concern for the client become pow-

Table 11-4   The Therapeutic Relationship

Psychoanalytic Therapy	The therapist, or analyst, remains anonymous, and the client develops projections toward the analyst. Focus is on the resistances that develop by working with transference and on establishing more rational control. The client experiences intensive, long-term analysis and engages in free association to uncover conflicts. The client gains insight by talking. The analyst makes interpretations to teach the client the meaning of current behavior as related to the client's past.
Existential- Humanistic Therapy	The therapist's main tasks are to grasp accurately the client's being-in-the-world and to establish a personal and authentic encounter with the client. The client discovers his or her own uniqueness in the relationship with the therapist. The human-to-human encounter, the presence of the client-therapist relationship, and the authenticity of the here-and-now encounter are stressed. Both the client and the therapist can be changed by the encounter.
Client-Centered Therapy	The relationship is of primary importance. The qualities of the therapist, including genuineness, warmth, accurate empathy, respect, and permissiveness, and the communication of these attitudes to the client are stressed. The client uses this real relationship with the therapist for translating self-learnings to other relationships.
Gestalt Therapy	The therapist does not interpret for the client but assists the client in developing the means to make his or her own interpretations. The client is expected to identify and work on unfinished business from the past that interferes with current functioning. The client does so by reexperiencing past traumatic situations as though they were occurring in the present.
Transactional Analysis (TA)	An equal relationship exists, with deemphasis on the status of the therapist. The client contracts with the therapist for the specific changes desired; when the contract is completed therapy is terminated. Transference and dependence on the therapist are deemphasized.
Behavior Therapy	The therapist is active and directive and functions as a teacher or trainer in helping the client learn more effective behavior. The client must be active in the process and experiment with new behaviors. Whereas a personal relationship between the client and the therapist is not highlighted, a good working relationship is the groundwork for implementing behavioral procedures.
Rational-Emotive Therapy (RET)	The therapist functions as a teacher, and the client as a student. A personal relationship between the client and therapist is not essential. The client gains insight into his or her problem and then must practice actively in changing self-defeating behavior.

200

Table 11-4	The Therapeutic Relationship *(continued)*
Reality Therapy	The therapist's main task is to get involved with the client and encourage the client to face reality and make a value judgment regarding present behavior. After the client decides on specific changes desired, plans are formulated, a commitment to follow through is established, and results are evaluated. Insight and attitude change are not deemed crucial.

erful influences on the client's behavior. The therapist also provides a model of a good personal relationship that the client can use for his or her own growth. Patterson made it clear that therapy cannot be mechanical and that the process cannot be reduced to technique alone, for the personhood of the therapist is crucial. He also stated that "the evidence seems to point to the establishment of a particular kind of relationship as the crucial element in counseling or psychotherapy. It is a relationship characterized not so much by what techniques the therapist uses as by what he is, not so much by what he does as by the way he does it" (pp. 535–536). Truax and Carkhuff (1967) support Patterson's contention: "the central ingredients of empathy, warmth, and genuineness do not merely represent 'techniques' of psychotherapy or counseling, but are interpersonal skills that the counselor or therapist employs in *applying* his 'techniques' or 'expert knowledge' " (p. 31).

What are the basic characteristics of a therapist that lead to constructive personality and behavior change in the client? Truax and Carkhuff (1967, p. 25) found three sets of characteristics that appear to thread through almost every major therapeutic approach: accurate empathy, nonpossessive warmth, and genuineness. In summary, most therapeutic approaches emphasize the importance of the therapist's ability to be an integrated, mature, honest, sincere, authentic, and congruent person in his or her therapeutic encounters; to provide a safe, nonthreatening, and trusting climate by demonstrating nonpossessive warmth for the client, which allows the client to engage in deep and significant self-exploration; and to be able to grasp the internal frame of reference of the client's experience and deeply understand the client's meanings.

Issues Related to Techniques and Procedures

Diagnosis

Some practitioners view psychological diagnosis as an essential part of the therapeutic process, and others view it as a detriment to therapeutic counseling. Psychological diagnosis generally means an analysis of the client's problems, the causal factors, and the nature and development of patterns of maladjustment. Diagnosis also implies specifying certain types of therapeutic interventions and predicting the outcomes in terms of future client behavior. It frequently has a broader meaning than merely classifying and labeling a client, for diagnosis has come to be associated with a complete description of the client and his or her present functioning.

The purpose of diagnosis in counseling and psychotherapy is to gain sufficient knowledge of the client's present behavior so that a differential treatment plan can be tailored to that client. Practitioners who are behavior-therapy oriented stress a diagnostic approach with their emphasis on a clear specification of treatment goals. Here an objective appraisal of specific functioning and definite symptoms is in order, for, after an evaluation has been made of what the disturbing behaviors are, then a treatment plan can be developed, and eventually some evaluation can be made of the effects of the treatment.

There are many who are critical of diagnosis in therapy. Rogers (1951) maintained that diagnosis is detrimental to psychological counseling because it is an external way of understanding a client. It tends to pull the client away from his or her internal and subjective experience and foster an external, objective, intellectualized conception *about* the client. According to Rogers, the client is the one who knows the dynamics of his or her behavior, and for change to occur the client must experience a perceptual change, not simply receive data about himself or herself. Since diagnostic knowledge is a knowledge about the client and since it is evaluative in nature, those who accept a client-centered viewpoint generally do not favor a diagnostic approach.

As a proponent of the existential-humanistic view of therapy, Arbuckle (1975) sees diagnosis as inappropriate in counseling because of the "fact that diagnosis misses entirely the reality of the inner person. It is the measure of me from the outside in, it is a measure of me by others, and it ignores my subjective being" (p. 255). Instead of an external diagnostic picture of the client, Arbuckle contended, counselors should attempt to grasp the internal world of the client.

Carkhuff and Berenson (1967) opposed traditional diagnostic categories and saw them as "not only intellectually repugnant but usually meaningless for purposes of differential treatment" (p. 234). But it seems clear that they are not against diagnosis that is an ongoing part of the therapeutic relationship. According to them, "a meaningful diagnostic process flows out of an ongoing interactional process between therapist and client. There is no separate and distinct diagnostic process" (p. 235).

Is there a way to bridge the gap between the extreme view that diagnosis is the essential core of therapy and that diagnosis is a detrimental factor? In my opinion, a broad view of diagnosis is a basic part of the therapy process. I conceive of diagnosis as an ongoing process that focuses on understanding the client. Both the therapist and the client are engaged in the search and discovery process from the initial session to the terminating session. Even though a practitioner might avoid the formal diagnostic procedures and terminology, it seems important that he or she raise certain questions such as What is going on in the client's life now, and what does the client want from therapy? What are the client's strengths and limitations? How far should therapy go? What are some of the basic dynamics involved in the client's life at this time? In dealing with these questions, the therapist is formulating some conception about what a particular client wants and how the client might best attain his or her goals in the therapy situation. Thus diagnosis becomes a form of making tentative hypotheses, and these hunches can be formed with the client and shared with the client throughout the process.

I do have serious reservations about pinning on clients shorthand labels such as "paranoid," "schizophrenic," or "psychopathic." Frequently these labels categorize and stereotype a client, and an entire staff might react to the label and treat the "schizophrenic patient" the way they expect that type of "case" to behave. Instead of seeing the person's uniqueness and individuality, one can easily ignore his or her personhood. Also, the client may soon begin to live up to expectations—that is, to behave in a manner based on the way he or she is viewed and treated.

A point that needs to be stressed is that, just because some diagnostic procedures are carried out in a technical-mechanical or objective-detached style that characterizes diagnosis as something done externally *by* an expert *to* a passive client, this does not mean that all diagnosis needs to be done in such a manner. Diagnosis, if it is seen in a broader context, can be a dimension of the therapeutic process as practiced by a behavior therapist or an existentially oriented therapist. I am in agreement with the view of Brammer and Shostrom (1968): "We find it difficult to escape the fact that the therapeutic psychologist must make some decisions, do some therapeutic planning, be alert for pathology to avoid serious mistakes, and be in the position to make some prognoses or predictions" (p. 153).

Testing

As is that of diagnosis, the place of testing in counseling and therapy is a controversial issue. Models that emphasize the objective view of counseling are inclined to use testing procedures to get information about a client or to provide the client with information so that more realistic decisions can be made. Those of the client-centered and existential orientations view testing much as they do diagnosis—as an external form of understanding that has little to do with effective counseling. Arbuckle (1975) took a skeptical view of testing and diagnosis when he wrote the following:

> Thus if one sees the other person, in the traditional scientific pattern, as being what one is measured to be by outside and external criteria, then testing—and diagnosis—should be an integral part of the counseling process. If, on the other hand, one sees the basic reality of the human being from within, then testing and diagnosis will tend to remove the person even further from the reality of who he is [p. 261].

I do not share Arbuckle's view that testing and diagnosis "will tend to remove the person even further from the reality of who he is." A wide

Table 11-5 Therapy Techniques

Psychoanalytic Therapy	The key techniques are interpretation, dream analysis, free association, analysis of resistance, and analysis of transference. All are designed to help the client gain access to the unconscious conflicts, which leads to insight and eventual assimilation of new material by the ego. Diagnosis and testing are often used. Questions are used to develop a case history.
Existential-Humanistic Therapy	Few techniques flow from this approach, since it stresses understanding first and technique second. The therapist can borrow techniques from other approaches and incorporate them into an existential framework. Diagnosis, testing, and external measurements are not deemed important. The approach can be very confrontive.
Client-Centered Therapy	This approach uses few techniques but stresses the attitudes of the therapist. Basic techniques include active listening and hearing, reflection of feelings, clarification, and "being there" for the client. Support and reassurance are often used when they are appropriate. This model does not include diagnostic testing, interpretation, taking a case history, and questioning or probing for information.
Gestalt Therapy	A wide range of techniques are designed to intensify experiencing and to integrate conflicting feelings. Techniques include confrontation, dialogue with polarities, role-playing, staying with feelings, reaching an impasse, and reliving and reexperiencing unfinished business in the forms of resentment and guilt. Gestalt dreamwork is very useful. Formal diagnosis and testing are not done. Interpretation is done by the client instead of by the therapist. Confrontation is often used to call attention to discrepancies. "How" and "what" questions are used.
Transactional Analysis (TA)	A script-analysis checklist, or questionnaire, is useful in recognizing early injunctions. Many techniques of TA and Gestalt can be fruitfully combined. Some type of diagnosis may be useful to assess the nature of a problem. The client participates actively in diagnosis and interpretations and is taught to make his or her own interpretations and value judgments. Confrontation is often used, and contracts are essential. Questioning is a basic part of TA.
Behavior Therapy	The main techniques are systematic desensitization, implosive therapy, assertive training, aversion therapy, and operant conditioning. All are based on principles of learning, and all are geared toward behavior change. Diagnosis, data gathering, "what," "how," and "when," (but not "why") questions, and testing procedures are frequently used.

Table 11-5 Therapy Techniques *(continued)*

Rational-Emotive Therapy (RET)	The approach uses many diverse procedures such as teaching, reading, "homework assignments," and applying logical scientific method for problem solving. Techniques are designed to engage the client in a critical evaluation of a particular philosophy of life. A specific diagnosis is made. The therapist interprets, questions, probes, challenges, and confronts the client.
Reality Therapy	This approach is basically an active, directive, didactic therapy. It often uses a contract, and, when the contract is fulfilled, therapy is terminated. It does not follow a medical model of diagnosis and evaluation. It aims at having the client make his or her own interpretations and value judgments. This approach can be supportive and confrontational.

variety of tests can be used for counseling purposes, including measures of interest, aptitude, achievement, attitudes and values, and personal characteristics and traits. In my view, tests can be used as an adjunct to counseling; valuable information, which can add to a client's capacity to make decisions, can be gleaned from them. From my experiences in working in a university counseling center, I have formulated some cautions and guidelines regarding the use of tests in counseling:

1. Clients should be involved in the test-selection process. They should decide which general types of tests, if any, they wish to take.
2. A client needs to be aware that tests are only tools, and imperfect ones at that. As means to an end, tests do not provide "the answer" but at best provide additional information about the client that can be useful in exploring in counseling and in coming to certain decisions.
3. That the counselor needs to clarify the purposes of the tests and point out their limitations implies that a counselor has a good grasp of what the test is about and that he or she has taken it.
4. The client's reasons for wanting tests, as well as his or her past experience with tests, should be explored.
5. The test results, not simply scores, should be given to the client, and the meanings that the results have for the client should be explored. In interpreting the results, the counselor's attitude should be one of tentativeness and neutrality. It should be remembered that testing is only one avenue to gain information and that the information derived from tests needs to be validated by other measures. In presenting the results, the counselor needs to refrain from judgment as much as possible and allow the client to formulate his or her own meanings and conclusions regarding the test results.
6. Clients need to be involved in test interpretation as well as in test selection. The counselor needs to determine a client's readiness for receiving test information and for integrating it into his or her self-concept.

I have found that many students seek tests in the hopes of finding "answers." Thus I believe that it is important to explore why a person wants to take a battery of tests and to teach the person the values and limitations of tests. If that is done, I see less chance that tests will be undertaken in mechanical fashion and less chance that unwarranted importance will be attributed to the results. I have also found that a discussion with a student about tests and testing can open the possibilities of counseling to him or her. Instead of seeking shortcut methods, he or she might be willing to invest in counseling as a way to clarify his or her thinking and to aid his or her decision making. In short, my view is that testing itself is not destructive; rather, the way that tests are used or perceived by some counselors is the source of the problem. Tests are simply tools that can be used properly or misused.

Questioning and Probing for Information

The issue of questioning and its value in therapy needs to be discussed. Unfortunately, there are therapists whose main technique is to ask a barrage of questions. They interrogate the client. The therapy session is a question-and-answer period rather than an exploration session. The client frequently leaves feeling thoroughly interrogated but not understood. Used excessively, questioning can distract from the intensity of therapy and can provide the therapist with a safe but ineffectual mode.

In Gestalt therapy, "why" questions are not asked because searching for reasons for behavior typically takes one on an intellectualized and unproductive expedition. Instead, the Gestaltist asks a different set of questions such as "What are you doing?" "How are you behaving now?" "What is going on with you now?" These "what" and "how" questions are designed to get the client to focus on here-and-now experiencing, not to produce an explanation of the cause of the client's behavior. Nor does the reality therapist ask "why" questions. The reality therapist sees knowing the reasons for behavior as unessential.

Questioning is a main procedure in rational-emotive therapy. The hope is that, as a result of the therapist's challenging and questioning of the client's irrational beliefs and behavior, the client will begin to look critically at his or her own thinking and beliefs that he or she has in the past accepted wholesale. The Transactional-Analytic therapist also uses questions to get the client to discover some early decisions and to make new decisions.

As is true of the other procedures, there is a place for questioning in counseling, but therapists need to be aware that excessive use of questions becomes distracting and leads to ineffective therapy. A cross-examination is not helpful. I have often recommended to counselor interns that they tape-record some of their sessions (with the client's permission) and that, in listening to the tape later, they pay attention to the function of their questioning. I sometimes ask "What would happen if you could neither ask nor answer any questions during a session?" The answer is that one could only make definite statements.

One kind of question that I find useful is an open-ended, rhetorical question designed to generate some thought. I might ask "What do you expect that you'll be like in five years if you continue as you are now?" "What is the worst thing that can happen to you if you take a risk and fail?" "How would you like to be different from the way you are now?" and "What or who is preventing you from being a different person?" Questions that lead the client to search within himself or herself for honest answers are different from those that probe for information.

Support and Reassurance

Reassurance and active support are a part of every theory of counseling surveyed in this book. All practitioners agree that some kind of support is an essential ingredient for an effective therapeutic relationship. Client-centered therapy emphasizes the value of creating a supportive atmosphere where the client will feel the freedom to explore threatening aspects of himself or herself. This therapeutic climate is created by a therapist's actively attending and listening to the client's subtle messages, accepting the client as a worthwhile person, understanding the internal world of the client and communicating this understanding, expressing a genuine faith and hope in the client's capacity to change, granting permission to explore any and all feelings, and caring for the client. All these are ways a counselor can provide the support that will allow the client to explore feelings and thoughts and that will encourage action. By the therapist's "being there" as fully as possible for the client as he or she struggles with uncertainty, the client is moved to do and become what he or she might previously have considered impossible. The reassurance of the therapist gives the client a sense of confidence to continue taking risks even though he or she might make mistakes and experience setbacks.

There are some dangers in and limitations to the use of reassurance methods. A major misuse is the "Band-Aid" approach, whereby the therapist rushes in to "aid" and "comfort" a client who is experiencing anxiety and pain. This approach, which short-circuits the client's struggle, is not at all therapeutic. I am convinced that for personal growth to occur, a certain degree of pain and uncertainty is necessary. Instead of giving a Pollyanna response like "I'm sure everything will be okay," the therapist can share in the client's moments of anxiety and be supportive as the client goes ahead and does what he or she fears. Another limitation of reassurance is that, if it is used excessively, it fosters a sense of dependence on the therapist for approval and sanction; the client might look mainly to the therapist for affirmation instead of ultimately attaining his or her own approval and confirmation.

Confrontation

Support is related to confrontation, for a therapist who would limit his or her style to being predominantly reassuring and comforting would not encourage the client to become much more than he or she presently is.

When a climate of trust is created by genuine support, the relationship can endure challenge. Egan (1973) put it well: "Confrontation without support is disastrous; support without confrontation is anemic" (p. 132).

Therapists often misunderstand the nature of confrontation. It is sometimes perceived—and implemented—as a ruthless attack, a dumping of hostile feelings, and a tearing down of the defenses of a vulnerable client. In my view, a brutal approach is not responsible confrontation. Authentic confrontation is basically an invitation to the client to consider some dimension of self that is preventing positive behavioral or attitudinal change. The therapist might do a number of things to challenge the client: call attention to possible forms of self-deception; confront discrepancies between what the client says and what he or she does; point out the client's games and manipulations; point out resistances and evasions; note the ways a client is not recognizing his or her potentials or resources; and confront the client with the way he or she engages in self-deprecation.

Confrontation is aimed at more than the client's untapped resources. It is essential that confrontation be an act of caring and that the therapist demonstrate caring by investing himself or herself in the act of confrontation. Instead of merely confronting the client with what the client is doing or not doing, the therapist can share his or her personal reactions with the client when he or she experiences the client playing certain games, for example. The involvement, as well as the timing and appropriateness, of confrontation is crucial if it is to have a therapeutic effect. The purpose of a confrontational style is, in the hope that this process will lead to increased awareness and constructive action, to encourage the client to nondefensively consider certain aspects of himself or herself that he or she is missing. Therefore, the manner in which the therapist confronts and the way a client receives the confrontation become critical.

Confrontation is very much a part of some of the theoretical approaches discussed in this book. The Gestalt approach is highly confrontational in that the clients are continually made aware of how they are at the moment and what they are doing. Clients are challenged on discrepancies between their verbalizations and their body language. The Gestaltist confronts clients on the ways they resist internal support and seek as a substitute external support. Rational-emotive therapy stresses confrontation of an irrational belief system. The therapist challenges clients to critically examine definite irrational beliefs that they have incorporated and that they continue to keep alive with self-indoctrination. Reality therapy is basically a confrontational approach, for it continually urges clients to determine whether their behavior is realistic and responsible and to see whether their needs are being fulfilled by irresponsible behavior. The Transactional-Analytic therapist confronts clients on the games that they use to avoid intimacy and challenges clients to reevaluate early important decisions that still affect their lives. The clients are encouraged to decide for themselves how they want to change and what new decisions they want to make. The contractual approach keeps clients focusing on the therapeutic goals. The existential-humanistic view confronts clients with their unused capabilities and challenges clients to make use of their freedom in deciding whether to actualize their potentials. The existential therapist's encounter with clients is largely a confrontational process that encourages clients to become aware of their being-in-the-world and to make choices of how they want to be. The client-centered approach deemphasizes confrontation and, in my judgment, overemphasizes support. Listening, hearing, and understanding are limited. In my opinion, they are essential but insufficient qualities in a therapeutic relationship. Krumboltz (1966) contended that counselor understanding and empathy are necessary but not sufficient for therapy to progress. As he put it, "After the client's problem is clarified and the feelings about it are understood by both client and counselor, the client must still learn how to resolve his difficulty. Understanding alone is not enough. It provides only the beginning step upon which appropriate learning experiences can be arranged" (p. 8). In my view, confrontation that is done in a caring and responsible way can be a major tool in helping the client acquire the new learning necessary for constructive behavior change.

Interpretation and Reflection

Recall the detailed discussion in the chapter on client-centered therapy of the technique of reflection and that in the psychoanalytic chapter of the technique of interpretation. I'll not repeat those discussions here; rather, I will examine how the techniques of reflection and interpretation relate to the various models and explore the values and limitations of the techniques.

Reflection of feeling is a primary technique in client-centered therapy. The therapist focuses on the subjective elements of what the client says in order to assist the client to clarify his or her feelings and experience them with more intensity or to think about some of the things that he or she is saying on a deeper level. It is important that more than the surface meaning of what the client is saying be reflected; if it isn't, no movement toward increased awareness occurs. The therapist does not reflect content but the subtle messages underlying the content. On the other hand, the client-centered view assumes that interpretation fosters resistance because it is an external view of understanding, and, therefore, the client creates his or her own meanings. The client-centered therapist does not interpret for the client because to do so would take the therapeutic responsibility away from the client.

On the other end of the continuum is the psychoanalytic approach, which gives a place of central importance to interpretive techniques. Transference, resistances, dreams, free associations—all are interpreted. The analyst assumes a teaching function and indicates to the client the meanings of his or her underlying psychodynamics.

In my view, the therapist can interpret in a tentative way by presenting hypotheses or hunches. In this way, the client can consider the meanings of certain behaviors and begin to examine the relationship between earlier behavior and present behavior. Instead of pontificating, the therapist can share

Table 11-6   Applications and Contributions

Psychoanalytic Therapy	This approach provides a conceptual basis for understanding unconscious dynamics, the importance of early development as related to present difficulties, anxiety and ego defenses as a way of coping, and the nature of transference and countertransference.
Existential-Humanistic Therapy	This model provides an approach for individual and group counseling and therapy and for work with children and adolescents and can be usefully integrated into classroom practices. The major contribution is the recognition of the need for a subjective approach based on a complete view of what it means to be human. It calls attention to the need for a philosophical statement on what it means to be a person.
Client-Centered Therapy	This approach has wide applicability to individual and group counseling and therapy for student-centered teaching. This approach's unique contribution is having the client take an active stance and assume responsibility to direct the course of his or her own therapy. This approach challenged the role of the traditional therapist who commonly used techniques of diagnosis, probing, and interpretation and challenged the view of the therapist as expert.
Gestalt Therapy	These techniques are well suited for individual and group counseling and therapy. It is applicable to teaching/learning situations in classrooms. Its main contribution is the emphasis on doing and experiencing rather than on merely talking about feelings.
Transactional Analysis (TA)	This approach can be applied to parent-child relations, to the classroom, to group and individual counseling and therapy, and to marriage counseling. A key contribution is its attention to transactions related to the functioning of ego states.
Behavior Therapy	This approach has wide applicability to individual and group therapy, institutions, the schools, and to other learning situations. It is a pragmatic approach based on experimental validation of results. Progress (or lack of it) can be continually assessed and new techniques developed.
Rational-Emotive Therapy (RET)	This approach calls attention to the importance of thinking as a basis for personal disturbances. Its main contribution is that it points out the necessity of practice and doing to actually change problem behavior.
Reality Therapy	This approach was originally designed for working with youth in detention facilities. It is now widely used by educators in elementary and secondary schools. It is also applicable to individual therapy, groups, and marriage counseling.

hypotheses with the client in words such as "I wonder if . . ." "As a hunch . . ." and "Why not try . . . on for size to see how it fits?"

There is a danger in making interpretations, particularly for the inexperienced therapist. The obvious danger is that the therapist might be wrong in his or her interpretation. Even if the therapist is accurate, he or she might inappropriately make an interpretation by springing it on the client too soon—that is, before the client is able to recognize and integrate the interpretation—or by giving an interpretation that is too deep for the client's present readiness. Another problem with making excessive interpretations is that the client may depend on the therapist to sort out meanings instead of searching for his or her own meanings.

The Gestalt approach to interpretation is relevant here, for it suggests that learning is acquired through personal discovery and experiencing. In its focus on the what and how of the client's immediate experiencing, the Gestalt approach is geared toward assisting the client to make his or her own interpretations instead of engaging in abstract intellectualizing. As an example, the Gestalt approach to dream work demands that the client reenact all the parts of his or her dream to discover for himself or herself the meanings of the dream. By contrast, the psychoanalytic approach relies heavily on the insightfulness of the therapist in interpreting the meaning of the client's dream to the client.

In summary, reflection and interpretation that are done appropriately and nonmechanically can add significantly to the client's self-exploration and self-understanding. The degree to which these techniques are used depends on the therapist's skill and training, the client's readiness, and the nature of the therapist's theoretical orientation.

References and Suggested Readings

Agel, J. (Ed.). *The radical therapist*. New York: Ballantine, 1971.

Arbuckle, D. *Counseling and psychotherapy: An existential-humanistic view* (3rd ed.). Boston: Allyn & Bacon, 1975.

Brammer, L. *The helping relationship: Process and skills*. Englewood Cliffs, N.J.: Prentice-Hall, 1973.

*Brammer, L., & Shostrom, E. *Therapeutic psychology: Fundamentals of actualization counseling and psychotherapy* (2nd ed.). Englewood Cliffs, N.J.: Prentice-Hall, 1968.

Burton, A. *Interpersonal psychotherapy*. Englewood Cliffs, N.J.: Prentice-Hall, 1972.

*Carkhuff, R., & Berenson, B. *Beyond counseling and therapy*. New York: Holt, Rinehart and Winston, 1967.

Corlis, R., & Rabe, P. *Psychotherapy from the center: A humanistic view of change and of growth*. Scranton, Pa.: International Textbook, 1969.

Dugger, J. *The new professional: Introduction for the human services/mental health worker*. Monterey, Cal.: Brooks/Cole, 1975.

Egan, G. *Face to face*. Monterey, Cal.: Brooks/Cole, 1973.

Egan, G. *The skilled helper*. Monterey, Cal.: Brooks/Cole, 1975.

*Gottman, J., & Leiblum, S. *How to do psychotherapy and how to evaluate it*. New York: Holt, Rinehart and Winston, 1974.

Huber, J., & Millman, H. (Eds.). *Goals and behavior in psychotherapy and counseling.* Columbus, Ohio: Merrill, 1972.

Jourard, S. *The transparent self* (2nd ed.), New York: Van Nostrand Reinhold, 1971.

Kell, B., & Mueller, W. *Impact and change: A study of counseling relationships.* New York: Appleton-Century-Crofts, 1966.

Kemp, C. G. *Intangibles in counseling.* Boston: Houghton Mifflin, 1967.

Kopp, S. *Guru: Metaphors from a therapist.* Palo Alto, Cal.: Science and Behavior Books, 1971.

Krumboltz, J. Promoting adaptive behavior: New answers to familiar questions. In J. Krumboltz (Ed.), *Revolution in counseling.* Boston: Houghton Mifflin, 1966.

Meyer, J., & Meyer, J. *Counseling psychology: Theories and case studies.* Boston: Allyn & Bacon, 1975.

Patterson, C. H. *Theories of counseling and psychotherapy* (2nd ed.). New York: Harper & Row, 1973.

Rogers, C. *Client-centered therapy.* Boston: Houghton Mifflin, 1951.

*Schultz, D. *Theories of personality.* Monterey, Cal.: Brooks/Cole, 1976.

*Truax, C., & Carkhuff, R. *Toward effective counseling and psychotherapy.* Chicago: Aldine, 1967.

Van Kaam, A. Counseling and psychotherapy from the viewpoint of existential psychology. In D. Arbuckle (Ed.), *Counseling and psychotherapy: An overview.* New York: McGraw-Hill, 1967.

Wrenn, G. Two psychological worlds: An attempted rapprochement. In J. Krumboltz (Ed.), *Revolution in counseling.* Boston: Houghton Mifflin, 1966.

Wrenn, G. *The world of the contemporary counselor.* Boston: Houghton Mifflin, 1973.

CHAPTER TWELVE

ETHICAL

ISSUES IN

COUNSELING AND

PSYCHOTHERAPY

Introduction

Each profession has a code and system of ethics. Every professional person is expected to use sound judgment when ethical problems arise in his or her work. The American Psychological Association (APA) has developed a set of guidelines and ethical standards in psychology. All counselors-in-training should study the APA publication *Ethical Standards of Psychologists*.

The APA has developed a list of 19 specific principles that can apply to counselors and psychotherapists. These principles deal with the following areas: (1) responsibility; (2) competence; (3) moral and legal standards; (4) misrepresentation; (5) public statements; (6) confidentiality; (7) client welfare; (8) the client-therapist relationship; (9) impersonal services; (10) announcement of services; (11) interprofessional relations; (12) remuneration; (13) test security; (14) test interpretation; (15) test publication; (16) research precautions; (17) publication credit; (18) responsibility toward organization; and (19) promotional activities. In general, the therapist's primary responsibility is to the client, but the therapist has other responsibilities—to the relatives of the client, to a referring agency, to the profession, to society, and to himself or herself.

Counselor-education programs ought to involve seminars in ethical principles and practices. Real issues dealing with ethical concerns should be topics for exploration in the seminars. Students should, as a beginning, thoroughly familiarize themselves with the ethical standards developed by the APA. They should be sensitive to any ethical problems that arise in their practicum experiences and then discuss the problems in a seminar session or consult their supervisors for consideration of the aspects of the problems. Part of a counselor's education is developing a sense of sound judgment, and basic ethical issues should receive top priority in a person's training.

The American Personnel and Guidance Association has also developed guidelines for ethical practices in counseling. In the past decade there has been increased interest in developing ethical standards to guide practitioners and increased awareness of the role and responsibility of counselors and psychologists in alleviating human suffering. No longer can the practitioner be safely tucked away in the office; the trend is toward urging social action by professionals in cases of social injustice. Associations such as the APA, the Association of Humanistic Psychology, and the American Academy of Psychotherapists emphasize the ethical responsibility of professionals to society by exerting their influence collectively in social issues related to the oppression of and discrimination against women and minority groups, the continuation of racism in society, the neglect of the aged, and certain inhumane practices with children. Seminars and workshops are conducted to awaken the dull consciences of many professionals and to expand the awareness of the personal responsibility of individual members of the helping professions. The trend is toward encouraging professionals to actively apply their knowledge and skills to the underlying causes of social injustice. It behooves the counselor or therapist to be acquainted with pressing social and political issues that have a direct bearing on human rights, and it is important to determine what definite steps to take in effecting necessary changes within the system. In short, psychological counselors are discovering that, to effect significant individual change, they cannot remain blind and deaf to the major social ills that often create and foster individual sickness; they must become active agents of constructive social change.

The Therapist's Responsibilities

The therapist has a responsibility primarily to the client, but, since the client does not live in a vacuum and is affected by other relationships, the therapist has a responsibility also to the family members of the client, to the therapist's own agency, to a referring agency, to society, and to the profession.

Because the best interests of the client are of supreme importance in the counseling or therapeutic relationship, the client's needs and welfare, not the satisfaction of the therapist's needs, become central. The general principle of the primary value of the client's welfare may seem clear, but the issue can easily be clouded when we consider that the therapist also has responsibilities to others besides the client. There are times when there is a conflict of responsibilities or when there are certain clashes between the client's perception of his or her best welfare and the therapist's perception.

The APA (1967) states that "The psychologist attempts to terminate a clinical or consulting relationship when it is reasonably clear to the psychologist that the client is not benefiting from it" (p. 67). But what does the therapist do when he or she believes that the client is "getting nowhere" but the client resists termination? Consider the following.

The client generally shows up for his weekly session, but he typically reports that he has nothing really to discuss. He doesn't seem willing to do much for himself either during or outside the sessions. The therapist has confronted him a number of times on his unwillingness to invest much of himself in counseling and has shared with him that the sessions seem not to be of benefit. The client agrees, yet continues to return. Finally, the therapist becomes more forceful and judges that it is best to terminate this relationship. John raises objections and says that he does not want to end the counseling sessions. What should the therapist do? How long should the therapist continue to see John if he agrees to continue? What should the therapist do if John states that he really doesn't want a therapist but just a friend to visit?

In a similar situation, what should a therapist do when he or she judges that a client should be referred, either because the therapist feels unqualified to continue working with the client or because the therapist believes that the type or duration of treatment at hand is too limited for what the client should receive? For example, Sue has been seeing her high school counselor, Mr. Smith, weekly for two months, and she feels that the sessions are extremely helpful to her. The counselor agrees that she is making progress but is also aware of some other realities: his time is limited since he has 450 counselees; the school has a policy that long-term counseling should not be provided but that, when indicated, a referral should be made; and Sue's emotional problems are deep enough to indicate intensive psychotherapy. Because of these realities, he suggests a referral to Sue and gives her the reasons for the referral. Assume that Sue responds in one of these two ways: One, she might agree to accept the referral and see a private therapist. In this case, when does the counselor's responsibility to Sue end? The guideline is that the responsibility for the client's welfare would continue until she could begin seeing the other therapist. Even after that, some form of consultation with the other therapist might be in order. Two, Sue might refuse to be referred and state that she doesn't want to see anyone else but her own counselor at school. Should the counselor terminate the relationship? Should he continue but still encourage Sue to accept an eventual referral? What if the counselor feels that he is getting "in over his head" with Sue? The guideline from the APA (1967) is that "the psychologist carefully weighs the possible harm to the client, to himself, and to the profession that might ensue from continuing the relationship" (p. 67) when the client refuses a referral. As can be seen, there is frequently a fine line that exists between operating on behalf of the client's best interests and dealing with the realities and limitations of a counselor's capacities in providing this help.

Another major ethical issue relating to client welfare is the use of drugs in mental-health and community clinics, in rehabilitation agencies, in psychiatric hospitals, and in the schools. As a general guideline, the use of accepted drugs is for therapeutic purposes for the client's best interests and not for making the client more tolerable to the staff. When drugs are used, a collaborating physician should provide appropriate safeguards for the client. Unfortunately, drugs are commonly used to sedate or repress problematic behavior in the client for the benefit of others rather than to effect a change in the client. The counselor should be aware of the misuses of drugs and the need to take a position on the issue.

Therapist Competence

As a basic ethical principle, therapists are expected to recognize the boundaries of their competence and their own personal and professional limitations. Ethical therapists do not employ diagnostic or treatment procedures that are beyond the scope of their training, nor do they accept clients whose personal functioning is seriously impaired, unless they are qualified to work with those clients. A therapist who becomes aware of his or her lack of competence in a particular case has the responsibility to seek consultation with colleagues or with a supervisor, or to make a referral.

What constitutes "qualified"? Is the possession of an advanced degree or of a credential or license sufficient to specify "competence"? The standards of what constitutes competence vary markedly from state to state. A further problem is that many practitioners "qualified" on paper are in actual fact unqualified to enter into therapeutic practice. Conversely, there are those who are "unqualified" according to state licensing boards but who in practice are far more effective than those licensed by the state boards. The issue is not clear.

Competent practitioners must continually assess their competence as related to particular clients to judge whether they should enter into relationships with them. There will be times that most experienced counselors or therapists will need to consult colleagues or a specialist in a related field. It is possible that a therapist who has worked with one client over a long period of time might lose his or her perspective with that client. At times, it is wise for therapists to confer with colleagues to share their perceptions of what is occurring with their clients, within themselves, and between them and their clients. If a client continually complains of physical symptoms (such as headaches), it would seem essential that any organicity be ruled out by a physician before the assumption is made that the client's problem is psychologically caused. What if the client were actually to have a brain tumor and the psychological counselor failed to refer him to a physician for a physical examination?

If experienced practitioners need occasional consultation, it goes without saying that beginning therapists need supervision and ongoing consultation. In my work with counselors-in-training, I have found most of them eager for direction and supervision. They often ask for extra time and are quite willing to discuss openly their reactions, blockages, frustrations, and confusions in practicum meetings. Realizing that they need skills in working effectively with the problems that clients bring, they tend to want a chance to discuss their fieldwork. It thus becomes an ethical and practical concern that appropriate supervision be given to the intern, for the sake of the client's welfare and the intern's professional growth. A problem can arise when the counselor intern is placed in a community agency and the on-the-job supervisor is so steeped in his or her duties in the agency that he or she has little time left over for supervising interns. I have encouraged the counselor interns to actively and aggressively seek supervision and, at times, demand that they be given an hour a week to explore their case load. If the supervisor doesn't initiate close supervision, then the trainee will have to learn to continue to ask for what he or she needs if he or she is to get close supervision.

Related to the issue of competence are the questions What kind of education, training, and supervision are necessary for insuring competent practice? and What kinds of experiences are necessary for prospective counselors? There are two rather opposed points of view regarding preparation necessary for the practice of counseling. On the one hand is the position that clinical work of any form, even under supervision, should not be undertaken until late in a candidate's doctoral program or even until the post-doctoral period. This view regards as dangerous untrained and unseasoned "amateurs" who have not acquired the Ph.D. and considers it unwise (perhaps unethical) to allow a person to practice counseling below a doctoral level. On the other hand are those who favor training in counseling and various practicum experiences at an early stage in the student's program. This viewpoint endorses the initiation of supervised practical experience as early in the course of preparation as the maturity and responsibility of the individual student allow. I subscribe to the latter viewpoint. My view is that a counseling program ought to incorporate both the academic and the experiential phases and that counselors can be effectively trained at the subdoctoral level.

As an example, let me describe the essential features of the human-services program at California State University at Fullerton. Work toward the Bachelor of Science degree in human services has at its core supervised practicum experiences and academic course work in the behavioral sciences. The course work includes "Theories and Techniques of Counseling," "Research Analysis," "Assessment Seminar," "Developmental Psychology," "Psychology of Personality," "Abnormal Psychology," "Behavior Modification," "Social Deviancy," "Case Intervention Techniques," "Program Analysis," "Cross-Cultural Studies," a group-oriented course in personal growth, and five electives customed to the interests of each student. Students experience four semesters of practicum—two semesters of on-campus, supervised fieldwork and two semesters of off-campus, supervised work with various community agencies. The students engage in counseling, group work, child care, community change, and a wide variety of mental-health activities in various human-services agencies. Students involved in the two-year practicum are given direct supervision and meet weekly in small seminar groups to discuss their field placements, to explore cases, and to learn techniques of counseling and casework. Students also have on-the-job supervisors who meet with them in the setting in which they are doing their fieldwork.

What are the results of such a program? Since the program is only in its fourth year of operation, it is difficult to evaluate the results. Students are extremely enthusiastic about their involvement in the program. They exhibit a great deal of investment and, from some initial research, seem far more committed to their education than do majors in other fields. They particularly appreciate the combination of the experiential and practical aspects with academic course work. The experiential features seem to give more meaning to related courses in psychology, sociology, counseling, research, and so forth. The course work becomes far more meaningful as the student can see real applications in his or her practicum experiences.

Community feedback has been highly favorable. From those who pursue higher degrees, we frequently hear comments that their total experience at the undergraduate level seems more sophisticated and meaningful than much of their course work in the Master of Arts degree program in counseling.

In summary, I believe that it is possible to produce effective counselors at the bachelor's level. My belief is based on the assumption that these people are initially screened carefully for the program and that rigorous screening continues during the practica. Evaluation of students in this program gives a good picture of the prospective counselor's capabilities, as the actual performance of a student can be assessed in accordance with the criterion of the implementation of knowledge and skills in real situations.

The Client-Therapist Relationship

The APA (1967) specifies that: "The psychologist informs his prospective client of the important aspects of the potential relationship that might affect the client's decision to enter the relationship" (p. 67). Several factors are likely to affect the client's decision to enter the relationship. For example, the recording of an interview, by audio-video tape, or by tape recorder, might affect the client. Others besides the client and the therapist may listen to or view the tapes. Also, some agencies use observation through one-way glass, so that supervisors or trainees can monitor the sessions. Some school districts have a policy that, if clients reveal that they use drugs, the counselor is obliged to report the names of those persons to the principal; or that, if a girl reveals to a counselor that she is pregnant, or wants information about contraceptives or abortion, the counselor must report the girl to the school nurse, who must then inform the parents. Often persons are required by others to seek counseling or psychiatric help; they do not voluntarily initiate a therapeutic relationship but are subjects of "mandatory counseling." It is clear that in each of these instances certain policies or conditions can affect the client's decision to enter a therapeutic relationship. Thus it is ethical practice for the therapist to make known to the potential client the limitations of the relationship. Let's examine the issues underlying practices that may affect the therapeutic relationship.

First, there are the ethics of taping an interview or of using one-way glass for observational purposes. A clear guideline in using either of those procedures is to secure the client's permission in advance; it is considered unethical to make use of the procedures without the client's awareness and consent. Tape-recording for supervision purposes is a common procedure in counselor education. This can be important for the client as well as for the therapist. A client may wish to listen to some earlier sessions as his or her therapy progresses. A client's anxiety can be diminished by letting him or her know that observers wish to focus on the therapist's movement in the session. Whereas the client's anxiety may lessen, however, the therapist's anxiety may remain.

I typically find that therapists (beginning or experienced) are hesitant to tape-record their interviews. Many times a therapist will build a case for not recording the interview based, supposedly, on the client's mistrust or discomfort. I question where the mistrust and anxiety are—with the client or with the therapist? My hope is that supervisors can create a climate where the student counselor, even though he or she may be anxious, will be able voluntarily to bring in tapes for consultation. The supervisor's attitude is important. If supervisors adopt a harsh, critical, domineering style, then the intern is apt to conceal any element of uncertainty. Instead, if the counselor-in-training and the supervisor take the approach that one can learn by experience and that the trainee is not expected to be a polished therapist, then the chances of exposing oneself to opportunities for learning will be maximized.

A second issue, as mentioned earlier, that might affect the client's decision to enter into a counseling relationship is that, unfortunately, some school districts have policies that are geared more toward the legal protection of the district than toward helping students in crisis. For example, some school counselors are prohibited from exploring a pregnant girl's alternatives unless the parents are notified and brought into the conference. This practice may have merit at times, but what becomes of the terrified girl who feels that she either cannot or, for her own reasons, does not want to tell her parents she is pregnant? Must the counselor refuse even to see her or to have a session where she can at least express her feelings of panic? In a related issue, I have been told by continuation-high-school counselors in some of my counselor-in-service training workshops that they must report the names of any students who admit to using drugs. This puts a severe strain on a potential counseling relationship when we consider the reality that most of their clients are regular-high-school drop-outs and drug users as well. If these counselors follow school policy, how much "real counseling" will occur? A point of ethics is that at the very least the counselor is obligated to inform the potential client of the limitations of confidentiality. Then the client is able to decide how much he or she wants to disclose or whether he or she even wants to begin a counseling relationship.

A third issue to be explored here is whether therapy can occur under mandatory conditions. Is "mandatory counseling" a contradiction in terms? What can a counselor do when the population he or she serves consists of those who are required to come for counseling but are generally unwilling to get involved? The issue is the ethics of forcing counseling upon a person, even if he or she is clearly opposed to any form of therapeutic intervention. As a counselor, consider your position in the following four instances:

1. The client is sent to your private practice by the probation department as a condition of probation. He's not much interested in counseling, but he is interested in being "out."
2. You work in a youth rehabilitation center, and you must see many resistant clients who are in your office only because they have been ordered to report to you.
3. The parents send their adolescent daughter to see you in the local counseling clinic, and she comes unwillingly.
4. A student with failing grades reports to your office for "counseling" because the school has a policy that any student who has an "F" must report for counseling. He really doesn't want to be in your office.

In my opinion, therapy can be effective only if the client is willing to cooperate with the therapist in working toward mutually acceptable goals. The clients mentioned above may not be willing to be cooperative. One avenue open to counselors in situations with a resistant client is to present the client with some of the possibilities that counseling might offer. For example, the counselor may agree to see the adolescent girl for three sessions simply to explore the possibilities of that relationship and then to terminate therapy if the girl still does not want to continue. The school counselor can see the student once and explain what he or she has to offer and then leave it to the student to decide whether he wants to seek counseling.

Confidentiality

Every therapist must come to grips with the thorny issue of the limits and guidelines of confidentiality of information. Surely no genuine therapy can occur unless clients trust the privacy of their revelations to their therapists. It is the therapist's responsibility to define the parameters of confidentiality, which includes determining the degree of confidentiality that can be promised. In making their determinations, therapists must consider the requirements of the institution in which they work and the clientele they serve. While most therapists agree on the essential value of confidentiality, they realize that it cannot be considered an absolute; there are times when privileged communication must be divulged, and there are many instances where whether to keep or to break confidentiality becomes a cloudy issue.

The APA (1967) recognizes a general principle: "Information received in confidence is revealed only after most careful deliberation and when there is clear and imminent danger to an individual or to society, and then only to appropriate professional workers or public authorities" (p. 66). Therapists have responsibilities to society and to others besides the client. If it becomes apparent that the client will inflict harm on others, then the counselor must make the possible danger known to those concerned and to the appropriate authorities. It is, however, still the therapist's responsibility to inform the client of the limits of confidentiality. Even though information may be used against the client and even though its divulgence may negatively affect the counseling relationship, the client should be warned.

With these general principles in mind, what would your position be if you were the counselor in the following four cases:

1. You have been seeing an adolescent girl in a community mental-health clinic for three months. Lately she has complained of severe depression and says that life seems hopeless. She is threatening suicide and even wants details from you concerning how she can successfully carry through with it. Are you obliged to disclose this information to her guardians since she is under legal age? What would you tell your client? What kind of consultation would you seek, if any?

2. Your client reveals to you that he has stolen some expensive laboratory equipment from the college where you are counselor. A week later the dean calls you into her office to talk with you about this particular client. What do you tell the dean? And what do you not tell her?

3. In the course of a counseling session, a youth tells you that he is planning to do serious physical harm to a fellow student. What would you tell your client? Would you report this plan to anyone and, if so, to whom?

4. Your client is a 15-year-old girl sent to you by her parents. One day her parents request a session to discuss their daughter's progress and to see what they can do to help. What kind of information can you share with the parents, and what can you not disclose? What might you discuss with the girl before you see her parents? What would you do if she made it clear that she didn't want you to see her parents or tell them anything?

It is generally accepted that therapists will have no professional contact with the family or friends of a client without first securing the client's permission. It is accepted in addition that information obtained from therapeutic relationships should be discussed with others for professional purposes only and with persons who are clearly related to the case. In my opinion, it is good practice to inform the client early in the relationship that you may be discussing certain details of the relationship with a supervisor or a colleague. This practice can also apply to the use of a tape recording. There are times when a therapist may want to share a tape recording of a particular session with a colleague simply because the therapist wants to confirm his or her perspective by obtaining another viewpoint of the dynamics of the therapeutic relationship. The possibility of consultation should be discussed with the client so that the client knows that it may occur.

The use of tape recordings and video tapings is also a part of the issue of safeguarding the confidentiality of client information. If these methods are part of the therapist's practice, he or she must secure the client's permission before making tapes. It is good practice to discuss with the client the purposes and possible uses for such tapes, and, of course, they should be shared only with professional persons who are related to the case or who are consulting with the therapist or supervising his or her work.

One very important area of confidentiality is that which applies to group practice. In therapy groups or in group-counseling settings, the therapist, or group leader, has the responsibility of pointing out the importance of confidentiality. Confidentiality is a topic that should be introduced and discussed as a group is initially formed, but it should also be discussed as the process continues. Clearly, group members share in the responsibility of retaining the privacy of members' disclosures. If confidentiality is not secured, the group soon tends to disintegrate, for people are not willing to reveal private material that they suspect will become public knowledge. I have found that betrayed confidence in group work is generally not due to malicious gossip but more often to the carelessness of members. A person may reveal certain facts or events, and, as gossip is passed from person to person, distortions occur. Hence it is crucial that the group leader make every effort to caution the group members to keep the nature of the sessions private.

The Therapist's Values and Philosophy of Life

Therapists are sometimes taught that they should remain "value neutral," that they should avoid passing value judgments on to their clients, and that they should keep their own value systems and philosophies of life separate from the therapeutic relationship. I maintain that we cannot exclude our values and beliefs from the relationships we establish with clients, unless we do routine and mechanical "counseling." It is sensible to me that we make our values known to our clients and that we be willing to discuss openly the issue of values in counseling. To do so implies at times that the counselor reveal his or her own biases, philosophy, and central values. I believe that, whereas we have an obligation to expose our values, we have an ethical obligation to refrain from imposing our values on clients.

I do not view therapy as a form of indoctrination whereby the therapist lectures to or manipulates the client to act or feel in the "right way." Unfortunately, there are many well-intentioned therapists who are overzealous in "helping" to "straighten people out." The implication is that, by virtue of the therapist's greater wisdom, he or she will provide answers for the troubled client. But therapy is not synonymous with preaching or teaching. This is not to say that therapists should maintain an indifferent, neutral, or passive role by simply silently listening to and accepting everything the client reports. Instead, I propose that therapists challenge the values of their clients, and, if they care, when they sense that certain behavior is destructive, they will confront their clients and invite them to examine the pay-offs and the consequences of their actions.

A core issue in therapy is the degree to which the therapist's values should enter into a therapeutic relationship. A therapist cannot have goals for clients and yet be devoid of value judgments, for goals are based on our values. Let me pose a series of questions designed to help you search yourself for your own tentative answers with respect to the role of values in therapy:

1. Is it desirable that therapists not pass on to their clients value judgments with respect to their clients' behavior and choices? Is it possible for therapists to make value judgments only about events that affect their own personal lives and pass no value judgments on to clients?
2. What kind of person is the therapist who insists that he or she does not make value judgments with respect to certain actions of his or her clients? Does a therapist have to deny much of himself or herself to remain "neutral"?
3. How can therapists retain their own senses of values and remain true to themselves, yet at the same time allow their clients the freedom to select their own values and behavior that differ sharply from those of the therapists.
4. What's the essential difference between therapists who honestly expose their core values when appropriate and therapists who in subtle ways "guide" their clients to accept the therapists' own values or the values that they deem would be good for their clients?
5. In what way is the issue of values at the core of all therapy? Is it possible to separate the role of values from therapy?
6. What would you do if your client had a value system sharply contradictory to yours? What if you honestly felt that your client's values were destructive to himself or herself or to others?

The question of the influence of the therapist's values on the client has ethical implications when we consider that the goals and therapeutic methods of the therapist are expressions of his or her philosophy of life. Even though the therapist does not directly teach the client or impose specific values on the client, the therapist does implement a philosophy of therapy, which is, in effect, a philosophy of life. The ethically sensitive therapist is one who becomes aware of his or her own values and who encourages his or her clients to develop their own values. His or her job is to confront and challenge the values of the client and to help the client decide whether he or she is truly living by his or her own values or merely incorporating parental and societal values totally without evaluating them. The therapist needs to be alert to the possibility of his or her manipulating the client to accept the therapist's values wholesale, for to do so would mean that the therapist would simply become another parent substitute.

As an example of the influence that the therapist's philosophy of life can have on a client and of possible clashes over values between the client and the therapist, consider this case: The client is a married woman in her late thirties, with three children who are approaching their teen years. She has been in weekly individual therapy for six months. She is now struggling to decide whether or not she wishes to remain married to her husband, whom she perceives as boring, uninvolved with her and the children, complacent, and overly involved in his work. Although she has urged him to join her in marriage counseling or some form of therapy for himself, he has consistently refused. He maintains that he is okay and that she is the one with the problems. She tells the therapist that she would divorce him right now "if it were not for the kids" and that when the children finish high school she will surely leave him. She is, however, presently ambivalent; she can't decide whether she wants to accept the security that she now has (along with the deadness of her relationship with her husband) or whether she is willing to leave this security and risk making a better life for herself (as well as risk being stuck with even less than she has now). She has been contemplating having an affair so that someone other than her husband can meet her physical and emotional needs. She is also exploring the possibility of getting a job so that she will be less dependent on her husband. By getting a job she could find outside opportunities for personal satisfaction and still remain in her present marriage by deciding to accept what she has with him.

Several value orientations emerge here, and it seems imperative that the therapist examine his or her own views and the effects they might have on the client's decisions. In this light, consider the following questions and decide what value judgments can be made:

1. One of her reasons for staying married is for the "sake of the children." What if you, as her therapist, were to accept this value and believe that she should not challenge her marriage because children need both parents and you feel that a divorce is damaging? Assume that you believe that she is burdening her children with a "good reason" to stay a victim. What if your judgment would be that she is better off by divorcing now? What do your beliefs about divorce, marriage, and children have to do with her possible decisions?
2. She is talking about an affair as a possibility. What are your values concerning monogamy and extramarital sex? Do you believe that having an affair would be helpful or destructive for your client? What influence might your views have on her?
3. There is the value question of security versus possible growth. If you are conservative and place primary value on security, what effects might your view have on your client? What are some of your own life experiences that might have some bearing on her decisions?

I think that we engage in self-deception when we attempt to convince ourselves that our own life experiences and our systems of values and beliefs do not enter into our therapeutic relationships and that they do not have an influence on a client's decision making and behavior. It behooves us to clarify our positions related to such controversial issues as the following:

1. *Religion.* If a therapist calls himself or herself a "Christian counselor" and has definite beliefs about the "good life," salvation, sin, and the person's relationship with Christ and if he or she sees these beliefs as a central part of the therapeutic process, how does his or her view influence clients who are nonreligious? or nonChristian? or who are Christian but do not accept the therapist's religious beliefs? What potential impact does an atheistic therapist have on a client with a definite religious persuasion? Can the atheistic therapist allow his or her client to hold onto religious values, or will the therapist confront these values as forms of "immature defenses"?

2. *Abortion.* When a client who is unmarried and pregnant and wants to explore alternatives enters counseling, how might you work if you fully believed that she should have an abortion? if you were firmly and morally opposed to abortion on the grounds that it is murder? How would your values affect the range of the client's exploring for herself possible alternatives?

3. *Sex.* In working with clients who are homosexual, with married people who are engaging in extramarital sex, and with unmarried people who are living together, what role do your values play? If you see homosexuality as immoral or as a form of psychopathology, would you be genuinely able to allow your client to retain his or her homosexual behavior and values? What does your viewpoint on marriage have to do with a client's freedom to explore alternatives ranging from a "traditional" marriage to an "open" marriage?

4. *Drugs.* Many of your clients may use various drugs. What are your values relating to taking drugs and how might they influence your capacity in working with drug users? Assume that your client is a habitual drug user and, whereas your perception is that he is escaping through drugs, your client disagrees and sees no harm in "getting loaded" or going on "acid trips." What might you do when there is a clash of values and perceptions in a case like this?

The Influence of the Therapist's Personality and Needs

Just as therapists cannot exclude their values from the therapeutic relationship, neither can they hope to keep their needs and personality separate, for these attributes have a bearing on the client. I strongly believe that ethically sensitive counselors are those who recognize the supreme importance of becoming aware of their own needs, areas of unfinished business, potential personal conflicts, and defenses and vulnerability and of how these realities might prevent the client from freely and fully exploring certain dimensions of himself or herself. I am convinced that, unless a practitioner develops this self-awareness, he or she will obstruct the client's change or in various ways will use the client for satisfying his or her own needs. Therapy then shifts from a matter of client satisfaction to one of therapist satisfaction.

What kind of awareness is crucial? We all have certain "blind spots" and distortions of reality. I see it as the therapists' responsibility to themselves and to their clients to work actively toward expanding their own self-awareness and to learn to recognize their own areas of distortion, biases and prejudices, and vulnerability. Therapists need at least to become increasingly aware of the nature of their unfinished business that may become operant in their relationships with clients. Therapists must develop a sensitivity to their unmet needs so that they don't use the therapeutic relationship as a main avenue of satisfying those needs. By recognizing and working through their own personality problems, there is less chance that they will project them onto the clients. If certain areas of struggle are surfaced and old conflicts become reactivated, then therapists have, in my opinion, the ethical obligation to seek their own therapy so that they will be able to help clients explore in themselves these same struggles.

The APA offers guidelines on this issue of therapist self-awareness. Therapists recognize that their effectiveness depends on their abilities to maintain sound personal relationships and that their own personal problems may interfere with creating these relationships. It would surely seem that the mental health and level of self-integration and self-awareness of the practitioner are vitally related to his or her ability to establish and maintain a therapeutic relationship, as opposed to a toxic one. The APA (1967) guideline is that "he refrains from undertaking any activity in which his personal problems are likely to result in inferior professional services or harm to the client, or, if he is already engaged in such an activity when he becomes aware of his personal problems, he seeks competent professional assistance to determine whether he should continue or terminate his services to his client" (p. 65).

There are other aspects of his or her personality that the therapist must examine if he or she hopes to be instrumental in using himself or herself to create therapeutic relationships. These other aspects include the need for control and power; the need to be nurturing and helpful; the need to change others in the direction of his or her own values; the need to teach and preach and to persuade and suggest as well; the need for feeling adequate, particularly when it becomes overly important that the client confirm the therapist's competence; and the need to be respected and appreciated. I am not asserting that these needs are neurotic or necessarily destructive; on the contrary, I believe that it is essential that the therapist's needs be met if he or she is to be involved with helping others to find satisfaction in their lives. Nor do I think that there is anything amiss in a helping person's deriving deep personal satisfaction from his or her work. And surely many of one's needs for feeling worthwhile, important, respected, and adequate may be a function of the quality of one's work with others.

The questions are Does the therapist depend primarily on his or her clients to give this confirmation? Does the therapist use the therapeutic relationship to enhance his or her own glory and promote his or her own cause of self-interest? Is the therapist able to place the client's welfare in a primary position? This is no simple matter; self-deception is a very real danger. It is the main reason that I urge that all people who offer counseling and psychotherapy for others have the courage and ethical sensibility to have experienced their own therapy so that they will be better able to differentiate between fulfilling oneself in direct and healthy ways and attempting to compensate for one's own frustrations by vicariously living through another's experience. One of my strong biases is that it is the ethical responsibility of any person who works with others in an intimate way to obtain counseling or therapy before attempting to intervene in the lives of others. How can a therapist help a client to face and work through fears of death if the therapist is escaping from his or her own fears of death? Can a therapist who is unaware of his or her own sexual needs or who has not examined his or her sexual motivations and dynamics possibly help a client develop sexual maturity? If the therapist flees from intimacy and is afraid of experiencing the depth of his or her own feelings of depression, anxiety, guilt, uncertainty, hopelessness, or helplessness, then can he or she honestly expect to be able to "be there" with others as they come close to experiencing those same feelings within themselves? Or will the unaware therapist actively disrupt clients in their own processes of struggle out of his or her feelings of uneasiness? If therapists refuse to look at these dimensions in their own life, I cannot see how they can encourage the clients to plunge into unknown territory that may be anxiety-arousing for them as well as for the client. I make the broad assumption that ethical practitioners will recognize the value of taking for themselves what they offer as valuable to their clients and that, through some form of personal-growth experience, they will be better able to avoid inflicting harm on their clients.

Now let's examine briefly some of the specific areas of the therapist's personality that may have a bearing on clients. First is the issue of the power of therapists and their use of control. In my estimation, power is a quality that every effective helping person possesses. Power is a vital component of good therapy, and I believe that many clients improve as a result of their sharing in the power of their therapists. It has been suggested that therapists be models, and one aspect of modeling is for therapists to be potent persons—that is, have in their life what they want or be in a position to know how to obtain the kind of life they desire. Persons who genuinely feel powerful do not dominate the lives of others and do not encourage others to remain in a dwarfed state so that they can feel superior. They do not enjoy power over others in a dictatorial and controlling fashion but are able to appreciate other people's potency and their own at the same time. The client's accomplishments, strengths, and newly discovered potencies are a source of joy to the potent therapist, not a source of threat as they are to the impotent therapist who uses clients in his or her own attempt to achieve potency.

Clearly, the fact that power can be used against the client is an ethical concern. For example, consider the therapist's use of control as a way of reducing personal threat and anxiety. If the therapist fears losing control because of his or her need to maintain control of the client and the relationship, then he or she may resort to all sorts of strategies (both consciously and unconsciously). Thus, if a female client is behaving seductively and the male counselor is unsure of his own sexuality, he might deal with her by distancing her with abstract, intellectual interpretations or by assuming an aloof "professional" stance. If she desires to become a sexually mature woman and he feels uncomfortable in the presence of powerful women (particularly sexually attractive and mature women), he may subvert her attempts to become a woman and encourage her to remain in a dependent, little-girl-like condition because then he is not so threatened and he can control the relationship.

Another issue is the counselor's need to nurture. In my observation, many are attracted to the "helping professions" because of their need to "help others," to "teach people how to live the good life," to "straighten people out," and to "solve others' problems." There is also the motivation of people who at one point recognized that they were miserable or at least that they wanted to make basic changes in their life and who then did make a decision, with positive outcome, to embark on a self-exploration journey. Now these people may deeply desire to be instrumental in assisting others in finding their own way, and, in so doing, provide for themselves a sense of meaningfulness and personal significance. One aspect of a therapist's need to nurture frequently is his or her own need for succorance—that is, the need for others to nurture him or her through their respect, admiration, approval, appreciation, affection, and caring. The helping person quickly learns that the rewards are abundant for being nurturing to others.

Again, I see nothing amiss in the therapist's need for being nurtured, nor even in the rewards that he or she receives from his or her acts of giving to clients. The ethical questions are What are the dangers to the client's well-being when the therapist has an exaggerated need for being nurtured by the client? Can therapists distinguish between therapy for the client's benefit and that for their own gains? Are therapists sufficiently aware of their needs for approval and appreciation? Do they base their perceptions of their adequacies strictly on feedback from clients? What are the dangers that exist when therapists depend too heavily on client confirmation of their adequacies, worth, and values as both therapists and persons?

In summary, I believe that many are motivated to become "helpers" because of their needs for power, for feeling useful and significant, and for bolstering their feelings of adequacy. I see it as crucial that the therapist enter the therapeutic relationship as a person who is relatively integrated and fulfilled. If the helping person must have others continually feed his or her ego and reinforce his or her personal adequacy, then it is apparent that the helper must keep others in a dependent position. Thus, the helper must be in control of the relationship with the client. Because of his or her own emotional hunger and his or her own need to be psychologically fed and nurtured, he or she is unable to genuinely focus attention on the client's deprivations and concerns. At the extreme, the relationship becomes one in which the "helper" is in greater need of the "helpee" than the other way around. For these reasons, ethical practice demands that the helping person recognize the central importance of engaging in an ongoing self-exploratory process to determine in which direction—for betterment or for stagnation—his or her personality might influence clients.

References and Suggested Readings

American Psychological Association. *Ethical standards of psychologists*. Washington, D.C.: Author, 1967.

American Psychological Association. *Ethical principles in the conduct of research with human participants*. Washington, D.C.: Author, 1973.

Arbuckle, D. *Counseling and psychotherapy: An existential-humanistic view* (3rd ed.). Boston: Allyn & Bacon, 1975.

Corey, G. *Teachers can make a difference.* Columbus, Ohio: Merrill, 1973.

Dugger, J. *The new professional: Introduction for the human services/mental health worker.* Monterey, Cal.: Brooks/Cole, 1975.

Patterson, C. H. *Counseling and psychotherapy: Theory and practice.* New York: Harper & Row, 1959.

Peterson, J. *Counseling and values.* Scranton, Pa.: International Textbook, 1970.

Wrenn, G. *The world of the contemporary counselor.* Boston: Houghton Mifflin, 1973.

CHAPTER THIRTEEN

THE

THERAPIST

AS A PERSON

Introduction

Therapists can acquire a knowledge of the theories of personality and psychotherapy, and they can learn diagnostic skills, interviewing skills, and a wide range of techniques. I believe that ultimately what therapists bring to their therapeutic work is themselves as persons. They bring their life experiences into the relationships with their clients. I believe that persons can be well versed in the theories and techniques of therapy but still be inadequate therapists unless they are therapeutic persons. If they are able to be therapeutic with others, they are able first to be therapeutic to themselves. Being therapeutic persons implies a willingness to openly explore facets of their own lives, to work toward becoming the persons they are capable of becoming, and to do for themselves what they encourage their clients to do for themselves. This does not mean that they have nothing but themselves to offer, for their knowledge of the dynamics of behavior and specific therapeutic skills are essential. Knowledge and skills are not enough, however. Persons who are interested in understanding their own needs and motivations and who are committed to their personal growth can always acquire the technical skills that are necessary.

This chapter is based on my bias and contention that the therapist's personhood is both the greatest asset and the greatest obstacle to his or her efforts to induce change in clients. The therapist needs to be aware of the dimensions of his or her own being, as expressed in relationship to his or her clients' capacity to change. My bias is a result of my work during the past nine years in teacher education and counselor education. My association with elementary and secondary teachers as well as with teacher candidates has taught me that the key to any significant change in education rests with the teacher, not merely with his or her methods, nor with the curriculum, nor with the school system. In my book *Teachers Can Make a Difference* I explored the foundation of humanistic education as related to the teacher's willingness to use his or her personhood in teaching and relating with students. Later, my work with counselors-in-training led me to a similar conclusion: a counselor's most important facet is that he or she brings to the counseling relationship his or her ability to be genuine. In my book *The Struggle toward Realness* I describe the areas that, in my estimation, are critical for counselors and therapists to explore in their own lives.

This chapter, then, makes certain assumptions related to the therapist's personhood that are derived from my observations and experiences in the professional education of counselors. An important part of the chapter includes a discussion of personal issues that face the beginning therapist. Probably there is no other time when the therapist realizes more acutely that his or her own development as a person is so vitally related to effectiveness in helping clients as when he or she begins to see and work with "real clients."

The Therapist's Personhood and Behavior

The Authenticity of the Therapist

Therapy, because it is a deeply intimate kind of learning, demands a practitioner who is willing to take the risks of shedding stereotyped roles and of being a real person in a relationship. It is precisely within the context of the person-to-person relationship that the client experiences growth. If the therapist adopts a role, plays the expected role, does what a therapist is "supposed" to do, and mechanically implements technique, we can expect not only less than a little client growth but also that the client's growth might be even further arrested. The source of the client's personal learning is found in an authentic relationship with a therapist who is a person, who has feelings and beliefs, and who is willing to share his or her reactions with the client as they are appropriate within the relationship. If the therapist is a mere reflector of feeling, is simply a detached observer who makes objective interpretations and evaluations, or is a mechanical person hiding behind the safety of the prescribed role, then how can he or she expect the client to move toward increased authenticity?

The burden—although I prefer to think of it as a challenging and exciting responsibility—is on the potential therapist: if the therapist expects to attempt to assist others in getting more in touch with their real beings, then it behooves the therapist to be in touch with his or her real being. He or she must be willing to be that real person in the self-to-self transactions with the client. In my view, therapists serve as models. If the therapist models incongruent behavior, low-risk activity, and deceit by remaining hidden and vague, then he or she can expect the client also to stay closed and untrusting. If the therapist models authenticity by being for the moment what he or she is, by being open, and by engaging in appropriate and facilitative self-disclosure, then he or she can anticipate that the client will integrate more of the same characteristics into himself or herself. To be sure, therapy can be for better or for worse. Clients can become more actualized, or they can become less healthy. In my judgment, the degree of self-actualization of the therapist is the crucial variable that determines the outcome.

This discussion brings up a number of questions relating to therapists as models, authenticity as a model, and the role of therapist self-disclosure that I suggest you ask yourself:

1. Should a therapist suggest that he or she is a model whom the client should imitate?
2. Is it wise to tell prospective clients in advance that they will be expected to imitate the therapist? What behavior should be imitated? What should not?
3. What is the responsibility of the therapist who purports to serve as a model? What does he or she need to do to become a viable model? Does the modeling concept imply therapist perfection, or does it imply the therapist's willingness to show himself or herself as a struggling and unfinished person?
4. To what extent should the therapist be himself or herself with clients? What is the meaning of "being real"? Is it a means or an end? Should a therapist be real with the client in the same way that he or she is real with others in his or her personal life?
5. Should the goal be to be completely open and real and tell the client of every passing mood and feeling?
6. What is the distinction between appropriate, relevant, and facilitative disclosure and disclosure that is used as a gimmick or as a manipulative device or disclosure (although real) that may be an outgrowth of the therapist's need? What are some guidelines to help us determine when and to what degree disclosure is facilitative?
7. Does the degree of realness, humanness, and honest disclosure on the therapist's part lead to an increase of the same type of behavior on the client's part?
8. What are some games that therapists play that keep them inauthentic and stuck in a role? What ways can therapists hide behind a professional facade as a way of staying safe and remaining personally uninvolved with a client? Can the role that a therapist performs block out his or her personhood?
9. As therapists can accept that they do have functions to perform, can they not also develop capacities to be persons instead of fixed roles? What happens when a therapist refuses to play a role that is inconsistent with his or her own style of being? Do clients sometimes react with suspicion as therapists attempt to be what they are?

Self-Disclosure

In my work as a counseling psychologist I have wrestled with the issue of self-disclosure and have asked myself how I can determine its appropriateness and relevance as a catalyst for growth of individual clients or of members in a group. I have found the following characteristics useful guidelines in determining when self-disclosure is facilitative. First, disclosing my persistent feelings that are directly related to the present transaction can be useful. If I am consistently bored or irritated in a session, then it becomes essential to reveal my feeling. On the other hand, I think it is unwise to share every fleeting fantasy or feeling that I experience. Timing is important. I recall sharing my feelings of being "grouped out" at an initial session of a personal-growth group. This admission burdened the group with doubt about their willingness to place additional stress on me. If I had continued to feel distant and uninvolved, it would have been appropriate to reveal that I did, but to do so with my opening statement had the effect of creating defenses within the group. Second, I find it helpful to distinguish between disclosure that is history-telling and disclosure that is an unrehearsed expression of my present experiencing. For me to mechanically report events of my past might be pseudodisclosure. If it is easy to relate or if it sounds rehearsed and mechanical to me, I have a clue that I am trying too hard to be authentic. However, if my disclosure is an outgrowth of something I am feeling in the moment and if, as I share this feeling, it has some freshness of expression, I can be more sure that my self-disclosure is facilitative. Third, I often ask myself why I am revealing myself and to what degree it is appropriate. To use my group to explore my own feelings, I believe, is to burden the group. Perhaps one may need outside therapy, but I do not see it as appropriate that one should consistently use the group of which one is a leader for working through one's own problems. I ask myself frequently "Am I attempting to prove my own humanness?" "Am I disclosing this or that so I'll be seen as an open therapist?" and "Am I using a gimmick?" Fourth, I consider the effect of my disclosure on the client or members of the group. One needs to recognize that self-disclosure does not mean that one is not a private person; the therapist does have the right to privacy. Here is where the issue of deciding what to share and when to share is crucial. In other words, self-disclosure itself is not the end, but disclosure of self when appropriate and genuine seems to me to be the significant issue.

Therapists as Therapeutic Persons

Tied to the issue of the therapist's personhood and behavior are the central questions How can counselors *be* therapeutic persons? How can they be instruments, catalysts, and agents of the awareness and growth of their clients? I have examined, sometimes painfully, the issue of therapeutic personhood to determine for myself how I can be either a therapeutic or a toxic therapist—that is, how I can have an effect that is either for better or for worse with my clients. When I think of counselors who are therapeutic persons, I come up with a lengthy list of personal qualities and characteristics. Let me emphasize before I share this list that I do not expect any therapist to be fully all these things, and I do not propose a perfection model. Rather, I suggest that these dimensions of a therapist's being are those that he or she is struggling to attain. For me the willingness not to become a finished product but to remain open to the struggle to become a more therapeutic person is precisely the quality that is most crucial for counseling experience. My list is incomplete and still evolving; I propose it, not as a dogmatic list of the "right" ways to be a therapist, but as a stimulus for you to examine your own concept of what it means to be a therapeutic counselor. My view of therapeutic persons includes the following characteristics:

1. They have found their own ways. They are in process of developing styles that are uniquely theirs, and their counseling styles are expressions of their philosophies of life and their own personal styles of living. Although they might freely borrow ideas and techniques from many other therapists, they do not mechanically imitate another's style.

2. They possess self-respect and self-appreciation. They can give out of their own senses of self-worth and strength rather than out of a need to receive false feelings of strength. They are also able to ask, to be needed, and to receive from others, and they do not isolate themselves from others as a demonstration of pseudostrength.

3. They are able to be powerful, and they recognize and accept their own power. They are able to feel okay with others and allow others to feel powerful with them. They do not diminish others, nor do they encourage others to maintain a powerless stance so that they might feel a sense of power out of others' senses of helplessness or dependence. They use their power and model for clients their healthy uses of power, but they attempt to avoid abusing their power.

4. They are open to change, generally in touch with themselves, and willing to risk for more. Rather than settling for less, they extend themselves to become more. They are aware that becoming more demands taking risks, and they exhibit willingness and courage to leave the security of the known and to plunge into the unknown, where they might tap many of their untapped potentials.

5. They are engaged in processes of expanding their awarenesses of self and others. They realize that with limited awareness comes only limited freedom and that awareness increases the possibilities for choosing a richer life as it permeates several levels: feelings, values, beliefs, personal motivations, basic life attitudes, bodily reactions, sensory capacities, and so on. Instead of investing energy in defensive behavior designed to block out experiences, they direct energy toward allowing for a maximum of experiences and an expansion of awareness.

6. They are willing and able to tolerate ambiguity. Most of us have low thresholds for tolerating or coping with a lack of clarity. Since growth depends on leaving the familiar and entering into unknown territory, therapeutic persons seek out a degree of ambiguity in life. Instead of per-

ceiving ambiguity as a threat to their existence, they are attracted to it. As they build their ego strengths, they develop more self-trust, more trust in their intuitive processes, more willingness to experiment with novel behavior, and more trust in both their feelings and their judgments, and they come to realize that they are trustworthy. Although their behavior may not be predictable at all times, they are usually reliable.

7. They have identities. They know who they are, what they are capable of becoming, what they want out of life, and what's essential. They question life, and they are willing to reexamine their values. They are not mere reflections of what others expect or want them to be but strive to get in touch with their inner cores and live from their own centers. Essentially, their standards are internalized, and they have the courage to act in a way in which they believe, even though they might not be rewarded by others for their beliefs or actions.

8. They are capable of nonpossessive empathy. They can experience and know the world of the other. They are aware of their own struggles and pain, and they have frames of reference for identifying with others while at the same time not losing their own identities by overidentification with others.

9. They are alive! Their choices are life-oriented. They feel intensely, can participate in life, and like to live. They can feel their feelings and get their rewards directly rather than by secondary gains. They are committed to living life rather than settling for mere existence.

10. They are authentic, real, congruent, sincere, and honest. They don't live by pretenses but attempt to be what they think and feel. They are willing to appropriately disclose of themselves to selected others, and, by making themselves known to others, they come to know themselves more fully. They do not hide behind masks, defenses, sterile roles, and facades; instead, they prefer to be genuine.

11. They are able to give and to receive love. They are able to give out of their fullness and from their souls, not out of their deprivations and inner emptiness. They are vulnerable to those they love, and they have capacities to care for others.

12. They live in the present. They don't badger themselves with what they should have done or could have done in the past, nor do they fixate in the future. They are able to experience the now, live in the now, and be present with others in the now.

13. They make mistakes and are willing to admit to their mistakes. Although they are not overburdened with guilt over how they could, should, or ought to have been, they learn from their mistakes. They don't dismiss their errors lightly, yet they do not choose to dwell on misery.

14. They are able to become deeply involved in their work and their creative projects; they derive rich meanings in life through their projects. They can accept the rewards flowing from their work, and they can honestly admit to the ego needs that are gratified in their work. Yet they are not slaves to their work, and they do not depend exclusively on their work to live full lives. They have other dimensions in life that provide them with senses of purpose and fulfillment.

15. They are able to reinvent themselves and to revitalize and recreate significant relationships in their lives. They make decisions about how they would like to change, and they work toward becoming the persons they would like to become. They are not bound by their past ways of being; they are capable of changing.

This picture of the characteristics of the therapeutic person might appear monumental and unrealistic. Who could ever be all those things? Again, I emphasize that, although none of us is fully actualized, the point is our striving to become more of our potential selves. I have presented the picture with the hope that you will examine it and develop your own concept of what personality traits you deem essential to work toward if you are to be able to facilitate personal growth. Researchers have identified many other traits of the effective therapist, some of which are a deep interest in people, sensitivity to the attitudes and reactions of others, emotional stability and objectivity, a capacity for being trusted by others, a sense of humor, broadmindedness toward and tolerance of divergent beliefs and life-styles, intelligence and perceptivity, respect for people, knowledge of human behavior, and the interest in continuing to learn, just to mention a few. Today the trend is toward the psychological aspects of the therapist as a human being. Much of the literature on counselor education emphasizes the therapist's ability to look at, understand, and accept his or her self as well as the self of the other person.

Personal Counseling/Psychotherapy for Therapists

Discussion of the therapist as a person raises another debated issue in counselor education: whether therapists should experience their own counseling or therapy before they become practitioners. My view is that therapists should have the experience of being a client at some time. It might be prior to their training or during their training, but I strongly endorse some form of personal-growth experience, either individual or group, or both, as a prerequisite to counseling others.

I do not assume that potential therapists are "sick" and need to be "cured," but I do believe that we all have our blind spots, that we all have forms of our own unfinished business that may interfere with our effectiveness as therapists, and that we can all become more. I do feel that therapy should be viewed not as an end in itself but as a means to help a potential therapist become more of a therapeutic person who will have a greater chance of having a significant and positive influence on clients.

I want to emphasize the value of ongoing individual or group counseling for us as we begin to counsel. In my experience I found that, when I began counseling others, old wounds were opened and feelings that I had not explored in depth came to the surface. I found myself unable to encounter a client's depression because I had failed to come to terms with the way I escaped my own depression. Being a therapist forces us to confront our unexplored blocks related to loneliness, power, death, sexuality, our parents, and so on. Also, as we begin our work as counselors, we often feel a sense of professional impotence, and we frequently feel like quitting. I encourage student counselors to feel their helplessness and despair but to decide not to quit too soon, at least not without giving themselves a chance to test their potentials. Here is where I find personal counseling a natural adjunct for beginning therapists' work. As therapists, they cannot expect to use the client's time or the group's time to resolve their own problems, but, by surfacing their awareness, they can commit themselves to working on areas in their own life that need to be explored in greater depth. Learning to become a counselor can then be something more than merely acquiring skills for the therapeutic intervention in others' lives; it can be a force in promoting the personal growth of the therapist as well.

Ideally, I would like to see some individual counseling and group-oriented growth experiences combined. My preference is for personal-growth groups, for here counselor candidates can benefit from the feedback of many. The focus of the group experience should be on helping the person to become more aware of why he or she wants to become a counselor. Some questions for exploration are Why do I want to pursue a career in the helping professions? What are my own needs and motivations? What kinds of rewards do I receive from being a counselor? How can I differentiate between satisfaction of client needs and satisfaction of my own needs? Some other questions that might profitably be asked in some kind of personal-growth experience include What are some of my problems, and what am I doing to resolve them? How might my own problems get in the way of effectively working as a counselor? What are my values, where did they originate, and how will they affect my counseling style? How in touch am I with my own feelings? How courageous and risk-taking am I? Am I willing to experience and do what I would like to encourage my clients to do? What are some ways that I avoid using my own strengths? And how can I more fully utilize my potential power? What keeps me from being as open, honest, and real as I might be? Who are the people I am particularly attracted to, and who are those whom I take a dislike to? How do others experience me? What impact do I have on others? How sensitive am I to the reactions of others and to how they respond to me and I to them?

Those questions reflect but a few of the possible areas of focus in a personal-growth experience. The aim of the experience is to provide a situation where counselors can come to greater self-understanding. I never cease to be surprised by the amount of resistance I encounter from the ranks of professionals on this issue. I hear the argument "Requiring the therapist to be a client in personal counseling is based on a medical model of sickness. It's like saying that a surgeon cannot perform an operation that he or she has not also undergone." I simply cannot accept the analogy. I am left with the strong conviction that no therapist can hope to open doors for clients that he or she has not opened for himself or herself. If I am fearful of acknowledging my own demons and fears, how can I help others accept their demons and fears? If I have limited vision, how can I help my clients expand their visions of what they might become? However, although I deem a therapeutic experience necessary for prospective counselors, I do not believe it to be a sufficient and complete experience in and of itself. I believe that it is but one way in which a therapist can actively do something about becoming more therapeutic in his or her relationships with people.

Issues Faced by Beginning Therapists

This section is based on my observation and work with counselors-in-training and on my own struggles when I began practicing counseling psychology. My attempt is to identify some of the major issues that most of us typically face particularly during the beginning stages of learning how to be therapists. I have become aware of a recurring pattern of questions, conflicts, and issues that provide the substance of seminars and practicum experiences in counseling. I believe that these issues are vitally related to the counselor as a person. When counselor interns complete their formal course work and begin facing clients, they are put to the test of being able to integrate and apply what they have learned. They soon realize that all they really have to work with is themselves—their own life experiences, values, and humanity. At that point arise some real concerns regarding their adequacies as counselors and as persons and about what they can bring of themselves to the counseling relationship. In what follows I share my viewpoints based on my training and supervision with counselors, and I attempt to formulate some useful guidelines for beginning counselors.

Our Anxiety Is Not Necessarily Neurotic

Most novice therapists, regardless of their degree of academic and experiential backgrounds, generally anticipate with ambivalent feelings meeting their initial clients. As beginners, if we have enough sense, we are probably anxiety-ridden and ask ourselves such questions as What will I say? How will I say it? Will I be able to help? What if I make mistakes? and Will my client return, and, if he does, what will I do next? In my view, a certain level of anxiety demonstrates that we are aware of the uncertainties of the future with our client and of our abilities to really be there and stay with our client. Since therapy is serious business and what we do can have an impact on the other, we can accept our anxieties as normal. Whereas too much anxiety can torpedo any confidence we might have and cause us to be frozen, we have every right to experience some anxiety. Consider for a moment the novice counselor. Why should he or she feel confident? He or she has read the books on counseling theory and technique and has had course work and fieldwork but has not yet really been tested. It seems only natural that he or she would experience a range of self-doubts. What are some of the anxieties that the beginning counselor typically experiences? Perhaps they are expressed in his or her questions such as Will I be effective? Suppose I discover that I'm not really suited to be a counselor? Will my supervisor like the way I work? Will my client think that I know what I'm doing? Now that I've been through all the theory, can I apply it to real clients? What if I make terrible mistakes? Can I ruin my client by my blundering? What will I feel like if most of the feedback I get indicates that my clients don't improve? Will I be able to be myself, or will I get lost in a role that I feel is expected of me? Will I know what to do? When it is appropriate to act on my intuitions? Can I feel empathy yet not get so involved that I cannot sleep from worrying about my clients? Will I be confrontive enough? What if I'm too confrontive?

We Need Not Be Perfect

One thing I attempt to teach counselor interns is that they don't need to burden themselves with thinking that they must be perfect. To be sure, we will make mistakes, whether we are novices or seasoned therapists. I do not believe that our clients are fragile and that they will be destroyed for life because of our mistakes. If our energies are aimed at presenting the image of perfection, then where will we get the energy to pay attention to our client—or to our reactions to the client?

I find that many counselors-in-training are afraid of revealing their mistakes to their supervisors. Whereas I don't wish to discount this fear, I would urge students to have the courage to share their mistakes or what they perceive as errors. Only if we are willing to reveal our uncertainties with fellow students and supervisors can we hope to profit from our errors. Also, we might need consultation with others because we are too close to a situation to acquire a perspective; our myopia prevents clear vision. If we can discuss with others our feelings of frustration or of not handling a case as we would like, then consultation can help us through an impasse.

On this point I'd like to share a personal experience. A while back I reached an impasse with a person whom I had been counseling for two years. The client began seriously examining the possibility of committing suicide, saying that suicide was preferable to living. This situation caused me to examine seriously what I had been doing in our relationship. At that time I felt both hopeless and helpless and not at all sure how to proceed. I decided to bring the case up for consideration in a colleague's seminar. At the seminar were ten students (many of them my own) and two fellow faculty members. After I gave some descriptive background on the case and spoke of my feelings of fear and uncertainty in proceeding with my client, we did some role-playing. I received feedback from most of those present. What I became aware of was how mechanical I had become with my client and how I really felt hopeless. Of course, the client sensed my hopelessness, and part of the motivation for suicide was a test to see if I cared about the client at all. I became aware not only of my own inauthenticity but also of my need to become more demanding. As a result of this experience, I found myself demanding more of both myself and of the clients I was then seeing. To this day, I do not have any fear that my students lost confidence or respect in me because of my disclosure of my mistakes with my client.

Silence: A Threatening Experience

Those silent moments during a therapeutic session may seem like silent hours to a beginning therapist. It is not uncommon to be threatened by silences to the point that we frequently do something counterproductive to break the silence and thus relieve our anxiety. I recall when I was a counselor intern and was tape-recording an individual session with a highly verbal high school girl. Toward the end of the session she became silent for a moment, and my anxiety level rose to the degree that I felt compelled to rush in and give several interpretations to what she had been saying earlier. When my supervisor heard the tape he exclaimed, "Hell, your talk really got in her way. You didn't hear what she was saying! I'll bet she doesn't come back for her session next week." Well, she came back, but by that time I was determined not to intervene and talk my anxiety away. So, rather than take the initiative of beginning the session, I waited for her to begin. We waited for about half an hour. We played a game of "you first." Each of us sat and stared at the other. Finally, we began exploring what this silence felt like for each of us.

Silence can have many meanings, and I believe that it is essential to learn how to effectively understand the meanings of silence. Some of the possible meanings of silence, either during an individual session or a group session are the following: the client might be quietly thinking about some things that were discussed earlier or evaluating some insight just acquired; the client might be waiting for the therapist to take the lead and decide what to say next, or the therapist might be waiting for the client to do this; either the client or the therapist might be bored, distracted, preoccupied, or just not have anything to say for the moment; the client might be feeling hostile toward the therapist and thus playing the game of "I'll just sit here like a stone and see if he (she) can get to me"; the client and the therapist might be communicating without words, the silence may be refreshing, or the silence might say much more than words; and perhaps the interaction has been on a surface level, and both persons sense that it has yet have some fear or hesitancy about getting to a deeper level.

I suggest that you explore alternative meanings of silences and that, when silences occur, you explore with your client what a particular silence means. You could first acknowledge the silence and your feelings about it and then, rather than pretend it doesn't exist and make noisy talk simply to make each other comfortable, pursue the meaning of the silence.

Dealing with Demanding Clients

A major issue that puzzles many beginning therapists is how to deal with the overdemanding client. Typically, because therapists feel that they should extend themselves in being helpful, they often burden themselves with the unrealistic standard that they should give unselfishly, regardless of how great the demands on them are. The demands might manifest themselves in a variety of ways, a few of which are that a client calls you frequently at your home and expects you to talk at length over the telephone; demands that he or she see you more often or for a longer period of time than you can provide; wants to see you socially; wants you to adopt or in some other way take care of him or her and assume his or her responsibilities; expects you to manipulate another person (spouse, child, parent) to see and accept his or her point of view; demands that you not leave him or her and that you continually demonstrate how much you care; or demands that you tell him or her what to do and how to solve a problem.

It might be useful for you to review some of your encounters with clients to assess the ways you feel that you have been the victim of excessive demands of clients. What are some demands that were placed on you? How did you handle those situations? Can you say "no" to clients when you want to? Are you able to value yourself enough that you can make demands for yourself? Do you confront the demanding client, or do you allow him or her to manipulate you in the same way that he or she has manipulated others? If you let the client manipulate you, do you do him or her a favor?

I suspect that one problem that inexperienced therapists must work through is their need to be needed. The demanding client can feed the ego of a hungry therapist, just as there are pay-offs in the relationship between a spoiled child and an overprotective parent. At least the parent feels needed! We can delude ourselves into an exaggerated sense of importance by thinking that we must always be available or by believing that we are essential to the very lives of our clients. What would they do without us? I think that there are two imperatives in dealing with the demanding client: first, we need to be aware of the nature of the demands and our reactions to them; second, we must have the courage to confront the client with our perceptions of his or her behavior and of our own demands.

Dealing with Noncommitted Clients

Related to the problem of the demanding client is that of the client who really has very little investment in his or her own counseling. The client's lack of motivation might be evidenced by his or her frequent "forgetting" or cancelling of appointments, stated indifference, or unwillingness to assume any of his or her own responsibility in the counseling process.

A mistake that I see many novice therapists perpetuating is allowing themselves to be drawn into the game with their clients. Thus the therapist finds himself or herself waiting and wondering where the client is, reminding the client of appointments, or trying too hard to be understanding and accepting. I believe that it is crucial that we value ourselves enough that we are discriminating about our commitments. If we care for ourselves we will also expect a degree of commitment from our clients. To do any less is to play into the manipulative traps set for us, perhaps by a client who has an investment in failing and in proving that nobody can help him or her.

Social Relationships with Clients

Frequently, a beginning therapist must struggle with the issue of blending a social relationship with a therapeutic relationship. In an attempt to be democratic and equal, and well liked as well, a therapist might find himself or herself lured into a social relationship or a developing friendship with a client. I think friendships can be therapeutic, but I find it extremely difficult to be concerned primarily with the therapeutic relationship and at the same time maintain with the person an intense friendship or an outside social relationship. Questions relevant to this issue are Isn't a therapeutic relationship by its very nature unequal? Would I be as confrontive as I might be if there were no friendship? Will my own needs for keeping the friendship interfere with my therapeutic activities and defeat the purpose of therapy? One of the reasons most therapists cannot counsel members of their own family is that they are too close to them, and their own needs interlock with the problems experienced by their loved ones. This same dynamic, as I see it, operates in a friendship. Thus perhaps it is better to decide which kind of relationship you want most—a social one or a therapeutic one. This does not mean, of course, that one must exclude developing more fully a friendship after the therapeutic relationship has terminated.

Expecting Instant Results

Don't expect instant results. You won't "cure" clients in a few sessions. So many beginning therapists experience the anxiety of not seeing the fruits of their labor. They ask themselves "Am I really doing my client any good?" "Is the client perhaps getting worse?" "Is anything really occurring as a result of our sessions, or am I just deceiving myself into believing we are making progress?" I hope that you will learn to tolerate the ambiguity of not knowing for sure whether your client is improving, at least during the initial sessions. Understand that clients might apparently "get worse" before they show therapeutic gains. After a person has decided to work toward self-honesty and drops his or her defenses and facades, he or she can be expected to experience an increase of personal pain and disorganization, which might result in depression or a panic reaction. Many a client has uttered, "My God, I was better off before I started therapy. Now I feel more vulnerable than before! Maybe I was better off when I was ignorant!" Also, realize that the fruitful effects of the joint efforts of the therapist and the client might not be manifest for months (or even years) after the conclusion of therapy.

The year that I began doing full-time individual and group counseling in a college counseling center was, professionally, the most trying year for me. Up until that time, I was teaching a variety of psychology courses, and I could sense relatively immediate results or the lack of them. I found teaching gratifying, reinforcing, and many times exciting; by contrast, counseling seemed like a laborious and thankless task. The students who came to the counseling center did not evidence any miraculous cures, and some would come each week with the same complaints. They saw little progress, sought answers, wanted some formula for feeling better, or wanted a shot of motivation. I was plagued with self-doubts and skepticism. My needs for reinforcement were so great that I was antitherapeutic for some. I needed them to need me, to tell me that I was effective, to assure me that they were noticing positive changes, and so on. I became aware that I attempted to refer the depressed male students to other counselors while I put effort into encouraging a bright, attractive, young female to continue in counseling. Learning the dynamics of my motivation did not come easily, and I appreciated the confrontation that several of my colleagues provided in helping me become more honest about whose needs were really being met. Eventually I discovered that growth and change did occur in a number of my clients as a result of our joint efforts. They were willing to assume their responsibilities for taking risks and I became more willing to stay with them, even though I was not at all sure of the results.

My beginning experiences taught me that I need to be able to tolerate not knowing for sure whether a client is progressing or whether I am instrumental in that person's growth or change. I learned that the only way to acquire self-trust as a therapist was to allow myself to feel my helplessness, self-doubts, feelings of impotence, uncertainty as to my effectiveness, and ambivalence about whether I wanted to continue as a counseling psychologist. As I became less anxious over my performance, I was able to pay increasing attention both to the other and to myself in the therapeutic relationship. Gradually, I found that clients did make changes in a direction that they liked and that they influenced others in their lives to become involved in personal counseling. Over the past nine years that I have been in therapeutic practice, I have grown to trust myself more fully in my therapeutic skills; feedback from former clients has confirmed my self-trust. But when each of us begins, we do not have the benefit of feedback, and we may expect to flounder for a time as we wonder whether we will see any results.

We Won't Succeed with Everyone

We can't realistically expect to succeed with every client. Even experienced therapists at times become glum and begin to doubt their value when they are forced to admit that there are clients whom they are not able to touch, much less reach in a significant way. Be honest enough with yourself and with your client to admit that you cannot work successfully with everyone. You may need to refer to other therapists, and you may often have to tell clients that you cannot work with them. I believe that we do a prospective client a disservice if we accept him or her when we deeply feel that we don't want to work with him or her. The image of an altruistic, selfless, and nondiscriminating therapist is one that needs to be smashed. Eventually, unwanted clients will sense that we really don't want to (or can't) counsel them, and they may develop generalized resentments toward all therapy and therapists based on their encounters with our dishonesty in not being straight with them. I'm not, however, suggesting that we send away all clients that we might have negative or mixed feelings toward, for we can in some cases profit from facing some of our internal dynamics that lead us to believe that we can't work with a particular client.

Being Ourselves

Because we are typically self-conscious and anxious when we begin counseling, we tend to be overconcerned with what the books say and with the mechanics of how we should proceed. In my work as a supervisor, I've noted that too often inexperienced therapists fail to appreciate the values inherent in simply being themselves. I have suggested to many of my students that they attempt to put their theories and academic learning into the background and that they follow their intuitions, even though they do not fully trust their hunches. One hopes that course work, readings, fieldwork, and other training experiences have been integrated into the person of the therapist and that he or she can call on his or her acquired knowledge and skill as it is appropriate. I frequently encourage counselors-in-training to follow through with some of their hunches and later to confirm their intuitive directions with a fellow student, the client, a supervisor, or with their own internal reactions.

A common tendency is for therapists to become passive. They listen. They reflect. They have insights and hunches but mull over them so long that, even if they decide to act on a hunch, the appropriate time for action has already passed. So, they sit back, passively wondering whether internal reactions are correct. Thus I tend to encourage an active stance for the student counselor because I believe that it is generally better to risk being inappropriate (which is a risk with an active counselor) rather than almost to insure bland results by adopting passive, nondirective stances.

Let me push further with the issue of being oneself. I don't believe that we should be either of two extremes: one is the therapist who loses himself or herself in his or her fixed role as therapist and who hides behind a professional facade; the other is the therapist who strives too hard to prove that he or she, too, is human. If we are at either of these poles, we are not being ourselves. Take the first extreme. Here the role functions of the therapist hide his or her humanity; he or she is so bound up in maintaining stereotyped role expectations that little of him or her as a person shows through. Although we do have role functions, it is still possible for us to responsibly perform our functions without blurring our identities and becoming lost in our roles. I believe that the more insecure, frightened, and uncertain we are in our professional work, the more we will cling to the defense afforded by a role. Also, I believe that the unrealistic expectation that to be therapists we must be superhuman leads to becoming ossified in fixed roles. Consider some unrealistic expectations that a beginning counselor often becomes ensnared with: I should always care; I need always to demonstrate warmth (whether I feel it or not); I should like and enjoy all my clients; I must be all-understanding and fully empathetic; I should know what is going on at all times; I can't be acceptable as a counselor unless I'm fully put together myself, and any indication of personal problems rules against my effectiveness; I am expected to have answers for clients, answers that they say they cannot find within themselves; and so on. If we accept these unrealistic notions, then we can fall victim to presenting roles to clients instead of presenting ourselves. By accepting these lofty standards, we deceive ourselves into being that which we are really not, because we indoctrinate ourselves with the idea that we should be a certain way. The roles we play are not always congruent with the ways we deeply feel. Thus, finding ourselves bored, we deny our boredom and force attention; or, discovering negative feelings toward clients, we deny our feelings by stressing the positive qualities we see in clients; or, becoming aware that we are uncaring in a particular moment, we trick ourselves into caring instead of letting the feeling stand.

At the other extreme, the therapist actively works at demonstrating his or her humanness. Instead of getting lost in a professionally aloof and nondisclosing role, such therapists overreact to their differences as a therapist in their relationship with the client. They blur any distinction between helper and one who is helped. They would rather be seen as a buddy with similar hang-ups than as a therapist. Their approach is one of sharing their own problems, past and present, and of using the relationship to work on their own needs. A pseudorealness develops out of their need to be seen as human, and, in a desperate attempt to be themselves, they fail. This kind of therapist has not learned appropriate self-disclosure, for facilitative disclosure on the therapist's part generally entails revealing his or her reactions that stem from the relationship with the client, not disclosing some unrelated experience out of the therapist's past. To be sure, facilitative disclosure enhances the therapeutic process, for it admits the client into the therapist's private world when to do so is relevant and timely within the context of the therapeutic relationship. Appropriate disclosure of self is not contrived, and it is one way of being oneself and revealing oneself to the other without working to prove one's humanity to the point of phoniness.

Being Honest with Clients

One fear that most of us have is in facing our limitations as therapists. We fear losing the client's respect if we say "I really feel that I can't help you on this point" or "I just don't have the kind of information or skill to help you with this problem." From client feedback, the evidence is overwhelming in favor of direct honesty as opposed to the attempt to fake competence. Not only will the therapist perhaps not lose his or her client's respect, but he or she may gain the client's respect by frankly admitting his or her limitations. An illustration comes to mind. A counselor-in-training had intake duty in a college counseling center. Her first client came in wanting to discuss the possibilities of an abortion for his girl friend. Many questions raced through her mind: "Should I admit to him my lack of awareness and skill in dealing with his problem, or should I somehow bluff my way through to avoid looking like a neophyte? Should I know how to help him? Will he get a negative impression of the counseling center if I tell him I don't have the skill for this case? What about the girl in this situation? Is it really enough to work only with him? Is all that he really needs at this point simply information? Will information resolve the issue?" Fortunately, the counselor-in-training let the client know directly that the matter was too complicated for her to tackle, and she got another counselor on duty to help him. A point of this illustration is that we sometimes burden ourselves with the expectation that we should be all-knowing and skillful even without experience. The counselor-in-training's willingness to be realistic helped her avoid the pitfalls of trying to look good for the client and of presenting a false image.

Self-Deception in Therapy

No discussion of guidelines for beginning therapists could be complete without mentioning the phenomenon of self-deception as it occurs in the counseling process—on the parts both of the therapist and of the client. Self-deception is not necessarily conscious lying, for it can be subtle and unconscious. For both the client and the therapist, the motivation for deception may be based on the need to make the relationship worthwhile and productive; both are invested in seeing positive results. Our needs to witness personal changes may blur reality and cause us to be less skeptical than we should be. Let's examine client self-deception first.

Clients are invested in their growth generally. They want to be cured, and they want to be persuaded that their pains and struggles have been worth the effort. I have developed a healthy suspicion of some of the occurrences, for example, in group settings. There have been times when my co-leaders and I have suspected that participants do not want to be considered nonconforming, unproductive group members. During the course of a week-long session they might conduct a desperate search to uncover some traumatic event that would lend itself to dramatic catharsis and receive group approval. If most participants in the group have an intensive confrontation psychologically with their parents, some members will in a subtle way deceive themselves into pseudofeelings of anger, hurt, or whatever. In such cases, I believe that the underlying dynamic is their need for group approval and approval of self, so that they can say: "I really got a lot from the group. I am working, and changing, and doing a lot for myself." Such self-deception is particularly a danger for a person who has been only marginally involved in the group and, as he or she realizes that the time is short, might increase his or her efforts to dig up some problem that he or she feels will be acceptable—to himself or herself and to others. Another manifestation of self-deception consists of the client's eagerness to blindly accept an interpretation, diagnosis, or appraisal from a therapist, a group leader, or another group member. Instead of critically evaluating feedback, the client might contribute to his or her shaky judgment of self by incorporating everything another tells him or her. Again, the need for approval by others is so strong that he or she elevates another's judgment over his or her own. And what happens if the client was correct about himself or herself and the other person was wrong?

Therapist self-deception needs to be explored as well. Just as the client has investment in seeing a pay-off for his or her pain, so is a therapist invested in seeing clients get well. What would happen if most clients complained that they did not get better, or if most groups were a flop? I have asked myself this question often. Our needs to feel that we are instrumental in assisting another to enjoy life more fully and our needs to feel a sense that we do make significant differences do at times lead to self-deception. We look for evidence of progress, and we rationalize away elements of failure. Or we give ourselves credit for our clients' growth when it may be due largely to another variable, perhaps to something unrelated to the therapeutic relationship. My point is that being aware of a tendency toward self-deception in a counseling relationship can lead to an exploration of the phenomenon and thus lessen the chances of its occurring.

The Danger of Losing Ourselves in Our Clients

A common mistake for beginners is to worry too much about clients. There is a danger of incorporating clients' neuroses into our own personalities. We lose sleep wondering what decisions they are making. We sometimes identify so closely with clients that we lose our own senses of identity and assume their identities. Empathy becomes distorted and militates against a therapeutic intervention. We need to learn how to "let clients go" and not carry around their problems until we see them again. The most therapeutic thing to do is to be as fully present as we are able to be (feeling with our clients and experiencing their struggles with them) but learn to let the other assume the responsibility of his or her living and choosing outside of the session. If we become lost in clients' struggles and confusion, we cease being effective agents in helping them find their ways out of the darkness. If we take upon ourselves the responsibility our clients need to learn to direct their lives, then we are blocking rather than fostering the growth of others.

Developing a Sense of Humor

Whereas therapy is a responsible matter, it need not be deadly serious. Both clients and therapists can enrich a relationship by laughing. I've found that humor and tragedy are closely linked and that, after allowing ourselves to feel some experiences that are painfully tragic, we can also genuinely laugh at how seriously we have taken our situations. We secretly delude ourselves into believing that we are unique in that we are alone in our pain and we alone have experienced the tragic. What a welcome relief when we can admit that pain is not our exclusive domain. The important point is that therapists recognize that laughter or humor does not mean that work is not being accomplished. And there are times, of course, when laughter is used to cover up anxiety or to escape from the experience of facing threatening material. The therapist needs to distinguish between humor that distracts and humor that enhances the situation.

Establishing Realistic Goals

Realistic goals are essential for a potential relationship with a client. Let's assume that your client is truly in need of a major overhaul. He presents himself as a man who is intensely dissatisfied with life, rarely accomplishes what he begins, and feels inadequate and helpless. Now for the reality of the situation. He comes into a community crisis-counseling clinic where you work. Your agency has a policy of limiting a person to a series of six counseling sessions. There are long lines, waiting lists, and many persons in need of crisis counseling. The man comes to you because of his personal inability to function; his wife has just abandoned him. Even though both of you might agree that he needs more than a minor tune-up, the limitations of the services at hand prevent exploring his problems in depth. Both counselor and client need to decide on realistic goals. This does not mean that the two need to settle on patch-up or Band-Aid work. One possibility could be to explore the underlying dynamics of the presenting problem, with attention to what alternatives are open beyond the six sessions. If our aims are realistic, we may be sad that we could not accomplish more, but at least we won't be steeped in frustration for not accomplishing miracles.

On Giving Advice

A mistaken notion of those who are unsophisticated about the nature of therapy is to equate advice-giving with the therapy process. Quite often clients who are suffering come to a therapy session seeking and even demanding advice. They want more than direction; they want a wise counselor to make a decision or resolve a problem for them. Therapy should not be confused with the dispensing of information or advice. As I view it, a therapist's tasks are to help the client discover his or her own solutions and to help the client recognize his or her own freedom of action, not to deprive the client of his or her opportunity to risk exercising his or her freedom. It seems to me that a common escape by many clients is that they don't trust themselves to find solutions, or to use their freedom, or to discover their own directions. Even if we, as counselors or therapists, were able to effectively resolve their struggles for them, we would be fostering their dependence on us. They would continually need to seek our counsel for every new twist in their difficulties. Our job is to help them independently make choices and have the courage to accept the consequences of their choices. Giving advice (as a style) does not work toward this end.

I am not ruling out occasional use, however, of the technique of giving advice. There are appropriate times for direct advice, particularly when the client is clearly in danger of harming himself or herself or others, or when for the time being he or she is unable to make choices. Also, information can be used legitimately in therapy as a basis for helping the client make his or her own choices. Essential to decision making is having pertinent information.

My caution is to avoid the tendency to overuse the technique of giving information and advice and to consider doing so as therapy. Far too many inexperienced therapists fall into the trap of believing that they are not doing their jobs unless they are being prescriptive and meeting the apparent demands for advice from clients. I recommend that, instead of merely being advice givers, we ask our clients questions such as "What alternatives are open to you?" "What possibilities do you see?" "If I were able to solve this particular problem, how would this help you with future problems?" "Are you asking me to assume your responsibility for you?" "How have you avoided accepting the responsibility for directing your own life in the past?" and "Can part of your present problem stem from listening to the advice of others earlier?"

Suggestion and Persuasion in Therapy

Closely related to the issue of giving advice is the role of suggestion and persuasion in therapy. First, let me begin by admitting that most of us do suggest and persuade as we counsel. I can't see how we can avoid doing so unless we assume extremely passive stances of keeping ourselves out of the relationships with clients, stances from which we operate chiefly as mirrors reflecting to others our observations. Whereas suggestion is related to giving advice, I do not link the two inseparably, for we can make suggestions and stimulate clients to see other avenues. Let me give some examples of instances when I use suggestion and persuasion.

A person hesitates to apply for college because he feels that he'll never succeed. I might urge him to take some beginning steps to test out his suspicion of failure, perhaps only by enrolling in an evening class. (But I would explore his feelings of being doomed to failure, the realism of his view, and how he perpetuates a fatalistic view.)

A person experiences ambivalence over whether or not she should attend a weekend marathon group. She states her fears that she will be overwhelmed, that she is too fragile, that she is not yet ready for such a "heavy" experience, and on and on. If I feel that she is ready for such an experience, I may strongly persuade her to attend the group. Many members have told me that my enthusiastic salesmanship of the benefits of a group was the determining factor that tilted the scale in favor of their risking attending a group. (But first I would explore my client's presenting fear, not merely rely on my convincing manner to persuade her to do something against her will.)

Suggestion can be a supportive device if used appropriately and if not overdone. In essence, we are saying "I have confidence in you even though you may not yet feel that confidence in yourself. Trust my confidence in you and perhaps you'll discover this confidence in yourself." I recall a letter that I received from a client who was certain that not even a junior college would accept him. He allowed his poor record during high school to determine his decision whether to enter college. As a result of my persuasion, he enrolled in a junior college and took on a light load. In his letter a year later, he indicated that he was on the dean's list and was carrying a full load.

Whereas suggestion and persuasion might produce results, I want to caution against the abuses of these techniques in therapy. Clients might strive to follow our suggestions out of their need to receive our approval. If they sense that we have certain expectations for them, they may incorporate our expectations for them into their own expectations for themselves. Instead of working for self-approval, they perpetuate their need to be liked, to be thought well of, and to be respected by the therapist. Pleasing the counselor is counterproductive to therapeutic growth when it becomes more important a goal than pleasing oneself.

Some Realistic Cautions

I have developed the policy of encouraging beginning therapists to proceed with caution when taking risks. I feel that being a bit more conservative at the beginning stages is safer for both the client and the therapist. A cautious approach is specifically applicable to lessening the tendency of the beginning therapist to provoke the expression of anger in a client. Sometimes an unsuspecting counselor or group leader will tease a client, even to the point of becoming physically aggressive, to get the client's hostility out into the open. Although an explosive person needs to have a safe outlet to explore this repressed rage, there are times when the therapist will attempt prematurely to lift the lid off this dynamo and then be very unprepared for what follows. It is relatively easy for a therapist to encourage a client to stomp and pound and have a grand catharsis, but my question is usually "So the catharsis is over, now what?" I don't wish to encourage the development of an impotent therapist who is afraid of taking risks and who becomes hesitant to the point that he fails to be active, but I want to underscore the value of developing a healthy respect for possible hazards.

Developing Our Own Counseling Styles

Counselors-in-training need to be cautioned about the tendency to mimic the styles of their supervisors, therapists, or some other models. It is important that we accept that there is no "right" way of therapy and that wide variations in approach can be effective. I believe that we inhibit our potential effectiveness in reaching others when we attempt to imitate another therapist's style or when we fit most of our behavior during the session into the Procrustean mold of some expert's theory. Although I am fully aware that one's style as a therapist will be influenced by teachers, therapists, and supervisors, I caution against blurring one's own potential uniqueness by trying to imitate them. At best one becomes a carbon copy, a poor imitation of the other. I don't have any formula for the way to develop a unique therapeutic style, but I do think that the awareness of our tendency to copy our teachers is critical in freeing ourselves and finding a direction that is compatible with our personalities. I advocate borrowing from others but, at the same time, finding a way that is distinctive to oneself.

Suggested Readings

Corey, G. *Teachers can make a difference*. Columbus, Ohio: Merrill, 1973.

Corey, G. *The struggle toward realness: A manual for therapeutic groups*. Dubuque, Iowa: Kendall/Hunt, 1974.

INDEX